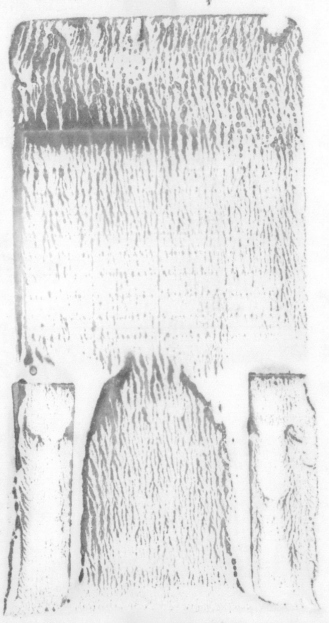

CONTAINING THE ARMS RACE
Some Specific Proposals

Jeremy J. Stone

THE M.I.T. PRESS
Massachusetts Institute of Technology
Cambridge, Massachusetts, and London, England

To
I. F. STONE

FOREWORD

WE ARE COMPLETING twenty years of the greatest arms race the world has ever witnessed; a period in which both American and Russian technologists have worked intensively to develop new weapons that might provide a military advantage. Concurrently, to this same end, military intellectuals on both sides have formulated strategies for the use of the new weapons and influenced plans for their purchase. This process has been a confusing and frightening one for the average citizen to watch. Lacking classified information, available only to government officials, about either the characteristics of our weapons or about Soviet activities, the spectator citizen has generally concluded that it is impossible for him to form any responsible judgment concerning the major policy battles of which he has caught glimpses in newspaper "leaks," in speeches by military leaders, or in parts of Congressional testimony that are made public. Told that it is vital for him to understand and express himself on these issues and those of disarmament he has often asked, "How can we get enough facts and a good enough understanding of the choices to have a conscientious position?"

There was a time when the answer to that question had to be, "You can't," but that is hardly the case today, and this book is one of several available to which the serious spectator, intent upon understanding contemporary military and arms control debates, can turn.

In the 1950's new military technology was being introduced so rapidly that existing strategic concepts were obsolete. Not even the experts understood adequately the implications of the revolutionary increases in fire power and speed of delivery that thermonuclear bombs, ballistic missiles, and electronic computers — employed together — had made possible. Nor did they possess sufficient information about Soviet military achievements to reach a consensus on the potential threat that U.S. weapons had to counter. Furthermore, during that period of very rapid technological change, great military advantage accrued to a policy of secrecy that withheld new developments from the competitor, and hence from the American public, for as long as possible.

However, the situation is very different today. For the moment, weapons technology and strategic thinking have reached a plateau. New weapons developments of the past several years have been primarily refinements leading to greater reliability, greater fire power, higher efficiency, and greater economy; they have hardly been of a sort to make either side fear that any one development would disrupt, even partially, the established nuclear stalemate. At the same time the increased openness of the Soviet society and our improved ability to obtain information by other means have provided a much more realistic assessment of Soviet capabilities than existed in the 1950's. With these developments has come a sufficient diminution of fears on both sides to permit a serious search for means to halt the arms race. This, in turn, has focused professional interest on alternatives to the present "quiet arms race" with its inherent costs and dangers.

A major consequence of the new conditions has been a willingness, almost an anxiety, on the part of the Department of Defense officials to explain to the public and to Congress the reasoning by which they have arrived at their weapons decisions. In Congressional testimony and speeches, Mr. McNamara, Dr. Harold Brown, and other Defense Department officials have provided comprehensive discussions of our current military strategy and the weapons plans to support it. The exhaustive hearings in 1962 on the Nuclear Test Ban Treaty made available a vast amount of information about contemporary military problems, particularly those related to the prospects of achieving an adequate defense against attack by ballistic missiles.

Similarly, one can find much information in the reports of Congressional hearings on strategic bombing and bombers, on civilian defense, on air defense, and on many other military subjects. Although published proceedings of Congressional investigations are often couched in general terms, much technical information can be found in the aerospace journals that vie with one another to be the first to disclose such details.

In this book, Dr. Stone has brought together much of this publicly available information on strategic military systems — bombers, missiles, and antimissile defenses — as well as much information pertinent to the problems of their control. The book examines in considerable depth the arguments for and against two of the most important current arms control proposals — the freeze of strategic delivery systems, and agreements between the United States and the Soviet Union not to deploy missile defense systems. The unique characteristic of this book is that it musters the facts and arguments pertinent to current and emerging public debates; in a real sense, it is a textbook for persons with a genuine desire to understand the contemporary arguments. Though specialists with access to secret information will, I am certain, believe that some technical issues are treated inadequately, and even completely disagree with some of the author's judgments, the book provides nonetheless a thoroughly adequate basis for understanding current strategic problems. With this book available no person need feel that he lacks the information required for a sound judgment on these issues. With it, he can identify the basic assumptions and uncertainties that underlie the debates; he will be able to see why reasonable people using the same basic data can come to very different conclusions concerning proposals for controlling the strategic weapons arms race.

The chapters on the antiballistic missile defenses are particularly timely. Technical developments seem to be forcing the leadership of both the United States and the Soviet Union to face continuously the decision to purchase, or to defer the purchase of, full-scale antiballistic missile systems — a decision that will be both costly and fateful. Many observers believe that an affirmative decision to deploy substantial missile defenses will signal a new round in the arms race, leading almost certainly to a massive civil defense program, and the procurement of many more ballistic missiles by both sides. The cost of these actions will be measured in tens of billions of dollars. Furthermore, the present strained, but real, calm and the prospects for any reduction in armaments are almost certain to be casualties of these actions. These decisions could determine much of the course of U.S.-Soviet relations for the next decade, until a new stable position is achieved. And such is the power of offensive weapons that, when this round is over, it is likely that the ability of each side to inflict damage on the other will have been increased rather than curtailed.

In attempting to evaluate the feasibility and acceptability of arms control proposals, it is necessary to make assumptions regarding the perspective from which an opponent, whose real attitudes and objectives are unknown, will view the measure. Dr. Stone's analysis of real Soviet interests and their possible reactions to U.S. moves seems generally sound; in fact, his attempt to be a neutral observer in judging the reactions of both sides to the various proposals for arms control is an outstanding feature of this book. Even so, he sometimes clearly fails to take into account important aspects of the proposals that will probably make at least one of them unacceptable to Russian leaders. For example, in the discussion of heavy-bomber disarmament, Dr. Stone excludes the new U.S. fighter-bomber, the F-111, from the list of bombers that would be destroyed. Distinguishing heavy bombers from fighter-bombers is consistent with the U.S. draft proposal for a freeze on nuclear delivery systems, but is rather difficult to justify from a military viewpoint. True, the F-111 was planned for use as a tactical and fighter aircraft. But the global nature of U.S. commitments placed a high premium on an aircraft that could be deployed quickly from one point to another. This dictated a large, fast, well-instrumented aircraft, which turns out to be a very satisfactory bomber. In fact, in the short interval since the book was completed, Secretary of Defense McNamara has announced his intention to purchase 250 modified F-111's as future replacements for B-52 bombers.

How should these problems of categorizing weapons systems be handled? If the F-111 is regarded as a strategic aircraft and included in bomber disarmament or a freeze, U.S. tactical forces will be required to use a smaller, less satisfactory, aircraft. If it is excluded, the United States will be permitted to build a bomber force of major proportions (plans have been discussed for the purchase of about 1,500 F-111's by the Air Force and the Navy). On the whole, however, Dr. Stone's discussions are well balanced, and I should guess that Soviet military planners would agree with as much of the author's analysis as would Americans.

Since Soviet acceptance of arms control proposals is no less important than our own, it would be especially useful if this book, and others like it that throw light on the underlying choices in the arms race, were generally available in the Soviet Union, as well as in the West. Maybe the Russians will translate and publish it.

JEROME B. WIESNER

December 16, 1965

ACKNOWLEDGMENTS

THIS BOOK was conceived in January 1964 when I was working at the Hudson Institute. An early version of Chapter One, entitled "Should the Soviet Union build an Antiballistic Missile System?," had been written. It was increasingly apparent that the main arms control problems and opportunities could be discerned by reading the open literature. A book of studies seemed indicated.

After leaving Hudson Institute, I completed Chapter Two.* At this point, thanks to the sponsorship of Thomas C. Schelling, I had the splendid opportunity to complete this volume at the Harvard Center for International Affairs.

Since I knew nothing of strategy or arms control before entering Hudson Institute in March 1962, a certain amount of the blame or credit for this volume attaches to it, and to its director, Herman Kahn. From him, like so many others, I learned a great deal despite my best efforts to avoid it. Some time after my appointment, Donald G. Brennan became Hudson's president; I was thus privileged to work for, and with, this extraordinarily diligent, tenacious, and talented arms controller. For much of my education in this subject I am indebted to him.

At the Harvard Center for International Affairs, I had the pleasure of enjoying the wit and wisdom of Tom Schelling. To Mort Halperin I am especially indebted for a gentle treatment of my residual misconceptions, for encouragement, ad-

---

* It is here reprinted, much as it appeared in *World Politics*, to whose editors I am grateful for the right of republication.

vice, and comradeship. And to Ina Halperin I owe the index to this volume.

At one time or another, the chapters got a fairly wide circulation in Cambridge and Washington; it is difficult to thank all who have commented on them so I shall thank none by name, but I am grateful to all. Finally, this book has benefited from Bob Erwin's cheerful editing; and I am obliged to him for shepherding it through the shoals of publication.

I add, as is customary, that I am solely responsible for the book's contents and form and for the opinions expressed within.

JEREMY J. STONE

January, 1966

CONTENTS

CONTENTS

INTRODUCTION

THE MOST dramatic and fearsome aspect of armaments production in the United States and the Soviet Union has been the procurement of long-range strategic nuclear forces —bombers and missiles. Parallel to the construction of the forces have been the attempts to procure strategic defenses against them: bomber defenses, missile defenses, and defenses against submarines.

This volume considers the important arms control and disarmament issues that involve these U.S. and Soviet strategic weapons. It attempts to consider, from a technical and political point of view, how the United States and the Soviet Union might reach various arms control agreements.

The book is composed of five chapters that are closely related. Two are devoted to bombers, and one each is given to missile defense, to missile reductions, and to a proposal to limit strategic force levels. Every chapter puts forth a policy suggestion and argues for it. For this reason, the chapters are in a sense studies of, or briefs for, particular policy proposals. On the other hand, the existing problems do not present a wide range of quite different policy alternatives. Hence, by revealing the basic political and technical issues that are involved in any proposal concerned with a certain weapon system, the chapters allow the reader to consider for himself what other policy might be followed.

The chapters are closely related in their subject matter even when they refer primarily to different strategic weapons. The question posed by one strategic weapon generally involves others. For example, if we are to build a defense against one strategic weapon, must we build defenses against others lest we leave a weak link in our posture? Must a treaty to halt the procurement of offensive weapons include provisions to halt the procurement of defensive weapons so as to maintain the existing balance? If an agreement called for the dismantlement of heavy bombers, would the missiles targeted on airfields become surplus to the needs of the major powers and hence themselves become ripe for reductions? Has the construction of missiles made bombers of sufficiently little use to permit their destruction by a treaty or by informal agreement?

The book is organized in the following way. Perhaps the most important arms control issue at the present time is whether to encourage or discourage the construction of missile defenses in our own country or in the Soviet Union. The first chapter sets forth the situation and argues that missile defenses should be avoided.

The second chapter discusses heavy-bomber disarmament and argues that the elimination of heavy bombers from the armories of both major powers should be considered. It sets forth the underlying considerations, as of early 1964.

By late 1964 it was becoming possible to see how the problem of dismantling heavy bombers would be handled by the major powers in the absence of a formal treaty. The third chapter describes the situation and suggests that informal bomber disarmament agreements are more likely to be implemented than formal ones.

In Chapters One, Two, and Three, discussion of bomber disarmament and missile defenses can be set forth without a very close analysis of the character of modern missiles. Chapter Four, however, which treats the problem of missile reductions, requires and supplies a good deal more such information. It is suggested here that a Soviet proposal calling for "reductions to strictly limited and agreed numbers" of missiles might be accepted in principle.

Chapter Five discusses the problem of "freezing" numbers and characteristics of strategic weapons, and rests upon the information introduced in Chapter Four. A proposal is made in

Chapter Five that the United States should consider a freeze of strategic weapons: a "pause" that would last for five years and would be renewable.

In short, each of the five chapters supports a specific policy goal. Each treats arms control and disarmament in concrete rather than in general terms. Each assumes that there is *mutual* interest in arms control. None attempts to conceal those one-sided advantages that we may find in disarmament. An agreement based on such deception is neither likely to be achieved nor likely to be maintained.*

In general, we in the United States must endeavor to seek the Soviet interest just as we seek our own. And the Soviets must be persuaded to agree not only to what is good for us but also to what is good for them. Their misunderstanding of their interests is no less an obstacle than our misunderstanding of our own. Persuading the one side is no less important than persuading the other.

While we have a greater right to presume to advise our own government there are questions for which American analysts may find the Soviets a more logical audience. Much of arms control involves considering the impact of the decisions of one side on those of the other. To this extent the Soviets are an important audience for those predictions of U.S. reactions that may forestall miscalculation on their side.

Reasons for believing that there is merit in the actions suggested are set forth in the course of the discussion. These are not restricted to those advantages that seem especially desirable to me; included also are those arguments that appeal to others of a different turn of mind. No nation, no group of men, has a single motivation for action. If some analysts are, by and

---

* Ware Adams put it this way: "There is however a tendency at times to think of international agreements as devices for one party to get an advantage over the other, either by imposition or trickery, or sleight-of-hand or just plain out-smarting him, as a device to compel a nation to undertake something contrary to its own interest. This is foolish. No nation keeps such agreements, not even we. Even if achieved such an agreement would be dangerous not merely for one, but for both parties, because of its inherent instability, resting on false premises." [1]

large, obsessed with irrelevant calculations, I have not hesitated to describe the benefits of my proposals in them. If others ignore strategic computations to a greater extent than would I, I have nonetheless been willing to describe the consistencies between their point of view and these proposals.

This approach produces a set of arguments that will often seem improper, if not inconsistent, to those who argue for arms control and disarmament for any one particular reason. For example, if someone believes that the central purpose of agreements is to reduce destruction if war occurs, what is he to make of the argument that, under a particular agreement, our forces would increase in destructive capacity? Or, if he believes that security is paramount, what is he to make of a great emphasis on the saving of resources?

In fact, these proposals do not stem from any single overriding concern to modify the strategic context in some particular way. They are not discussed from a consistent philosophy or viewpoint. Nor has there been any particular reason to sort out exactly on which grounds these proposals most appeal to me. I have been their lawyer and not their judge.

There is some controversy over the utility of posing "solutions," and of doing so in a spirit of advocacy. But it can be useful in generating interest, in furthering the discussion, and in instructing if not in solving the problems — which it may also do in some cases. And it tends to overcome one of the main obstacles to the study of such low probability events as a comprehensive arms control agreement: the inability of the analyst to do more than conclude that the agreement is, on the whole, unlikely. That analysts are often unable to supply a plausible explanation of how the agreement will be achieved — considering de Gaulle, the rate of fatigue of aircraft, and the statements of Senator Russell — is not very interesting. Many problems will turn out not to matter, and the policies advocated will only take effect after many conditions have changed. These discussions therefore concentrate on the most important technical and political issues.

Such discussions would slight the "other side" of the argument if there were one. But, in fact, there is no "other side," only a variety of different positions, the proponents of which argue different courses of actions for different, often wildly different, reasons. It is not possible to do justice to all of these from a public vantage point. The information available, somewhat surprisingly, permits an interesting and often a cogent case for given policies. It does not provide a comprehensive, certainly not a decisive, case. It can be used to prove that something should be studied but not that it should be done.

Most readers will find disturbing the extent to which computations made in this volume concern destruction of people and cities; and well they may. It is surprising, as well as disturbing, that decisions should be made upon a weapon, or a defense, because it can take or save X million lives if an unimaginable catastrophe descends upon us. Those who accept the necessity to make such decisions may yet be appalled that these are so delicately influenced by cost. And those who appreciate the extent to which we habitually determine by cost our capacity to destroy or protect may be disturbed, in turn, by the impact of these strategic computations on disarmament. If the world becomes safer, future generations will find it hard to believe that the calculations involved in this kind of reasoning could have influenced defense and disarmament policy.

Working from Public Sources

It is surprising how little unofficial work attempts to deal with the policy problems of arms control measures involving specific strategic weapon systems. The problem is difficult, the analysts are often unfriendly to the subject, many are frustrated by the problems of getting the government to take action, and the Soviet attitude is not encouraging. Many who are sympathetic to arms control have tended to discuss other than concrete problems. The difficulties of attaining sufficient public information are inhibiting. The number of articles that present a problem, propose a solution, and make some attempt to discuss its political and strategic implications for both U.S. and Soviet policy are very few.*

For example, it is revealing to note that until the United States proposed a freeze on strategic weapon procurement the very sizable literature on arms control studies had not dealt in a significant way with this alternative to disarmament. To have proposed this possibility, and to have sketched its implications, would have been a contribution both to arms control and to defense thinking. A large part of what follows is meant to "stretch" arms control thinking in much the same way. Thus, the discussions of bomber disarmament are designed in part to anticipate the obsolescence of the B-52's and to stimulate thinking about their disposal. The discussion of a "freeze" presents the idea of a "pause" in procurement. The chapter on antiballistic missile systems argues on arms control grounds against a *defensive* system. These chapters deal with issues that deserve a great deal more public and governmental attention than they are likely to get.

These chapters attempt to predict policies. It is not possible to study arms control without such predictions. If the government is soon to cease funding new missile silos, and one wants this act to be accompanied by a resounding announcement, it is necessary to predict the event in time to advocate the choice. Similarly, if one wants to influence whether bombers are destroyed unilaterally — or bilaterally through an agreement — U.S. plans to phase down the B-52 force must be anticipated. And it is only if one perceives that antiballistic missile systems are unlikely to be highly desired by governments that one can see an opportunity for restraint based on arms control grounds. Part of the problem is to be sufficiently ahead of government thinking to add something new and yet not so far ahead that everyone believes nothing can be done. Of course, being somewhat ahead of the thinking of one agency may mean being a good deal ahead of the thinking of

* The Test Ban has received such treatment in "Policy Considerations of a Nuclear Test Ban," by D. G. Brennan and M. H. Halperin.[2] There are some other examples.

another. Where the government position is when no position has yet been fought out is often very hard to say. For this reason, the exact extent to which these chapters are "unrealistic" is sometimes difficult to estimate.

Nothing is discussed that could not reasonably be considered by a President who felt deeply the need for progress. By the same token, however, many Presidents might see no purpose in seeking any formal restraints whatsoever on missiles or bombers. What is a "workable, acceptable" plan often depends, perhaps most often depends, upon the President himself and his most private assessment of the political forces at work, the chances for success, the risks of trying, and the obligation to take them. As no less an authority than a Presidential Adviser on National Security Affairs, McGeorge Bundy, said:

> It is only the American President who can carry the American Senate and the American people in any agreement on arms control, and it is only with American participation that any such agreement can have meaning for the Soviet Government.
>
> Unless a President uses these powers with energy, arms control agreements are improbable.[3]

The contentions concerning strategy have been documented with relevant quotations. In some cases this may be misleading, even within the restraints of public information. But the elementary details of the strategic situation are for the most part accurately reflected in the public literature; this has been the consensus of many observers. However, the possibility certainly remains that large gaps exist in the literature.

The present Secretary of Defense is one of the most common sources and, of course, one of the most authoritative, for establishing simple facts or for documenting agreed national doctrines or estimates. His testimony has been used for these purposes, as well as for his judgments. This has sometimes given an exaggerated impression of the extent to which the chapters depend upon the Secretary of Defense's preferences among policy alternatives; but that I have a high degree of sympathy with Secretary McNamara's record is undeniable.

7

Mr. McNamara is not the first Secretary of Defense to have emphasized, both by direct comment and by the depth of his disclosures, how important it is that potential adversaries appreciate the extent and nature of our strength. This has provided a good deal of information to the public, but several other sources have also. It is well known to the community of defense analysts, and to the Soviets, that such journals as *Aviation Week and Space Technology* and *Missiles and Rockets,* in combination with Congressional hearings, reveal the broad outlines of the strategic situation. The reports of the Institute for Strategic Studies, and the military commentators of *The New York Times* and the *Washington Star* are also useful sources of information that can hardly be overlooked by interested parties.

Is the U.S. government right to release so much information? Should it be used for estimating the likelihood of arms control agreements and the forms that they might take? I, personally, am sympathetic to the government efforts and believe that they might go somewhat further than they do. The missile gap is an excellent example of the unfortunate consequences of classifying information too highly. Until quite recently, the government never gave even upper estimates on the number of missiles constructed by the Soviets. This maintained a climate in which it was difficult to object to U.S. procurement of (I believe) a disproportionately large number of intercontinental ballistic missiles. An informed electorate might at least have understood the issues, if not encouraged still better explanations, had this information been available.* In any case, the information exists and can be found in sources

---

* My general view is not too dissimilar to that of former Deputy Secretary of Defense, Roswell Gilpatric. For example, under the title "Gilpatric Asks Defense Facts for the Public," *The Christian Science Monitor* quoted the former Deputy Secretary of Defense as saying: "I don't feel we should put as high a barrier on strategic information. . . . In the end, those in positions of authority will have to make the final decisions. . . . But, nevertheless, there should be enough understanding of public affairs in the public sector to provide support for (or condemnation of) basic national policies." [4]

which, according to the testimony of defecting Soviet spies, are carefully examined by Soviet authorities.† There seems no cost to our consideration of it; the question is what we might be able to do with it.

The Strategic Context

The strategic situation changes so rapidly and the action of the major powers in procurement and dismantlement proceeds so steadily that the information is rapidly outdated. Indeed, over a few years the nature of the problems and the best approach to them can change. If we watch closely, we discover that disarmament proposals, like "old soldiers," tend only to fade away. Those most hostile to them tend to ignore them. Those most sympathetic are unlikely to consider their time well spent in destructive criticism. Hence the proposals simply get less and less attention as the technological and political presuppositions become less favorable, until even the most sympathetic arms controller avoids them in his considerations.

The strategic context has been changing especially rapidly over the last few years. For those concerned with arms control, even the plans and hopes of 1961 seem hopelessly outdated. And the speed with which these plans have become implausible is itself an important consideration in assessing the chances for present plans.

Control of strategic weapons is now pursued in an environment in which both powers are incredibly well armed. In the last five years, the United States has deployed approximately 1,000 land-based intercontinental missiles, about 500 sea-based strategic missiles, and innumerable tactical nuclear weapons, many of which are larger than the Hiroshima bomb. We have, in addition, continued to maintain a force of several hundred strategic bombers. There are a variety of ways of describing

† The former Chief of the Central Intelligence Agency, Allen Dulles, gives an interesting discussion of this situation in his widely read book.[5]

the unprecedented power of this force. It is sufficient to say that these weapons are capable, indeed are designed to be capable, of destroying a sizable portion of the world's population. The United States has built these forces at a cost measured in tens of billions of dollars. It has deployed submarine-launched missiles in the Atlantic and the Pacific oceans and in adjoining seas. Intercontinental missiles have been installed on the continental United States. The tactical nuclear weapons are largely in Europe or on ships on the surface of the sea. It is generally believed, but difficult to verify, that the nuclear force is under close control, and that it is not very susceptible to accidental or inadvertent launching or unauthorized behavior.

The Soviet Union has the second largest strategic nuclear force in the world — a force of a few hundred intercontinental missiles and a few hundred intercontinental bombers. It has several hundred shorter-range strategic missiles targeted on Western Europe and many hundreds of bombers capable of following up any attack. It has a small but growing fleet of missile-launching submarines. Like the United States, the Soviet Union has procured a force capable of destroying, and designed to be capable of destroying, a sizable portion of the world's population. While the Soviet force is much smaller, much less sophisticated, and procured at somewhat greater cost to the Soviet economy, it holds hostage much the same number of civilians in the United States and the allied countries as we ourselves hold hostage in the Soviet Union. Except for a number of submarines deployed on the high seas, the Soviet force is based in the Soviet Union. Like the American strategic force, it is believed to be under careful and prudent control; but, as with ours, it is difficult to know precisely what this will mean in practice over the years.

The strategic forces of the two sides have emerged from a race. What kind of race has been involved is not completely clear. In part there has been competition in particular weapons. In part there has been competition for the political power that can be gleaned from nuclear weapons. This race has proceeded with unexpected swiftness. By and large, the perspective of those concerned with arms control has been too short, changes in weapons too rapid, and the general situation too unprecedented and too broad in scope to be grasped completely.

A few years ago there was much discussion on measures that would discourage surprise attack. Since that time both major powers have made such progress toward diminishing the vulnerability of their forces that much of the motivation for these measures has been lost. Moreover, the rapid changes from aircraft to missile have removed many of the technological presuppositions of the discussion. Aircraft, but not missiles, gave hours of warning of attack as they were readied for a mission. And again, aircraft, but not missiles, could be moved to safety in the warning time that might have been provided.

In 1961, we sought to limit stockpiles of bombs. Now we think in terms of cutting off the production of fissionable materials, production which is only tenuously related to the limitation of a destructive capability that has already reached enormous heights. Fissionable material cutoffs have become arms control measures in form and political measures in fact.

We used to speak of "no-first-use" of nuclear weapons policies that would encourage and reflect strengthened conventional NATO forces in Europe. But it is doubtful whether the situation could ever have been brought to that point of conventional adequacy sufficient to induce a no-first-use policy by the United States.

The prospects for substantial reductions in strategic forces have decreased as weapons have been built. The problems of proliferation have changed as France and China have built nuclear weapons. The prospects for halting wars once begun or for restricting attacks to military targets seem to have increased with changes in U.S. doctrine that have responded to this possibility. Virtually every aspect of arms control problems has changed over the last few years.

An Approach to Arms Control

At the present time, there seem to be three related functions for arms control measures pertaining to strategic weapon systems. The first and most general is simply to reach a better understanding with the Soviet Union on a range of arms race problems. The second, and more specific, goal is to achieve a "freeze" in procurement of certain strategic weapon systems either by informal understanding or by agreement. Third, the achievement of a somewhat larger number of arms control agreements of almost any nature between the two powers would seem useful.

The most fundamental and lasting arms control achievement that could be constructed between the Soviets and ourselves would be a suitable understanding of the problems that face us. By suitable is meant an understanding that would diminish rather than exacerbate differences and would encourage the generation of feasible solutions. Such an understanding need not exist. In principle, greater understanding could lead to greater differences, to heightened awareness of inequities, to diminished confidence and increased suspicion. Certainly in particular cases — for example, in discussion of certain very sensitive issues — it is easy to create more misunderstanding than one can immediately resolve. But it is hard to believe that this would be the case in general and for the indefinite future. I hold the view, on strategic matters, that a great increase in the U.S.-Soviet strategic dialogue, if handled with care, would ultimately be to our advantage as well as to that of the Soviets. This dialogue should be accompanied by personal contacts. These, more than any increase in transmitted words, are likely to erode the suspicion that has accumulated.

In any case, in the absence of a carefully conceived dialogue we shall have a continuing less formal conversation. Our Congressional testimony, our action in procuring and deploying weapons, our reaction to Soviet volumes on strategy, and so on, all speak for us. The question may be whether we shall leave discussions with the Soviets to air shows, to tough or friendly talk in speeches, and to trade magazines sympathetic to the procurement of strategic weapons.

In a more concrete vein, our goal should be to control the procurement of strategic weapons. It is much easier, though still difficult, to prevent the procurement of further strategic weapons than to arrange for the reduction of existing systems. Until that reduction has gone a very long way, the capacities for destruction will not be very significantly changed. Nor will reductions have very substantial effects on the likelihood of war. This likelihood is now very small: the reductions are not directly related in strategic terms to the probability of war, and the political effects of reductions can be gained, in large measure, by agreements to halt procurement. More generally, it may be a mistake at present to attempt to link most arms control measures to the probability of war and the destruction that will follow if it occurs. Most of the feasible measures at the present time are not portrayed realistically by rationalizations of this type.

It is true that a significant motivation for arms control remains the desire to prevent nations from achieving a still greater capacity for destruction. There are, presumably, types of very destructive and undesirable weapons that either side could build but that neither has yet built. And the United States has an interest in limiting the growth in numbers of the Soviet force so as to limit its capacity for destruction. (The converse is not true. The U.S. force is now so large that a further increase in numbers would not significantly increase its capacity to destroy Soviet population and industry.) But the desire to forestall any increase in destructive capacity is now simply one reason among others for limiting major-power procurement of strategic weapons. Depending upon the weapon system, motivations of comparable importance can be the waste involved in buying the weapons, the political or strategic instability caused by them, and their tendency to induce further procurement.

13

This last point is especially important: since the procurement of strategic weapons tends to breed further procurement of strategic weapons, it may be well even to halt the procurement of some strategic weapons that would not in themselves be highly undesirable. The case against antiballistic missile defenses is the most important instance of this principle. But, in general, it may be worth while to slow the rate at which procurement proceeds simply because a few developments that are especially undesirable may be forestalled in this fashion. The case against individual procurement of particular weapons is thus part of a general interest in slowing "progress" in weapon development.

Strategic weapons have more than strategic consequences. They also impinge upon the national consciousness in a variety of ways and have political consequences. Programs of procurement with strategic consequences may have almost as much impact upon domestic politics or upon the prospects for a U.S.-Soviet *détente* as a war in Vietnam, a severely divided electorate, or disarray within the Alliance. In this sense, agreement on limiting procurement represents a political opportunity. Since a great many political problems underlie the arms race, the proper short-term goal for arms controllers may be to keep weapon procurement from interfering with better political relations. Most of the time this will mean restraining ourselves and the Soviets either from procuring more strategic weapons or from provoking the procurement of more.

If we increase the dialogue with the Soviets, if we make attempts to halt procurement of strategic weapons, we shall, I think, be doing much that arms control of strategic weapons should now be doing. But, in addition, I think we should try to secure a number of minor or innocuous *formal* arms control agreements of whatever nature. The political impact of minor agreements will, during this period, almost invariably outweigh their strategic impact. To this extent there is likely to be some gain involved in such agreements if the will is there to sign them. Indeed, it is the reflection of this will to sign agreements that gives the agreement its importance as a political signal.

Containing the Arms Race

Considering the speed of weapons development and the predilections of policy makers, it is quite possible, of course, that no single one of the proposals made here can be achieved in the form discussed. Neither reductions of missiles, nor bonfires of heavy bombers, nor even tacit or formal halts in further procurement of offensive or defensive weapons may be possible. It therefore behooves us to consider carefully the course to be followed in the event that the major-power arms race continues to spiral.

Obviously we must stand ready to achieve whatever agreements and understandings seem to us useful. Equally clearly, we must have a philosophy with which to deal with the spiraling process itself. Most of the time treaties and understandings will not be feasible for one reason or another. If arms control can usefully influence the form and nature of the spirals, then obviously considerable effort should be devoted to this goal.

The answer to these problems may be to seek the course that seems most likely to *contain* the competition. We need not pursue this goal because we see in any simple-minded way how a course of containing the arms race will reduce the probability of war or diminish its destructiveness. We should be mature enough to recognize the desirability of discouraging continued strategic weapon expenditures for reasons both more direct and more indirect. On the one hand, there should be motivations arising from such (direct) implications of strategic weapon procurement as we have mentioned, for instance, their cost and potential political implications. On the other hand, there should be motivations arising from a responsible concern for the long-run risks of a continuing arms race.

15

These reasons do not constitute a case for following a course of "containment." Other approaches to the arms race are possible, and there are arguments for them. We could try to "win," to stay ahead, to reshape the competition, or to turn it back, and there are other possibilities as well. This volume makes no attempt to grapple with issues on the level of abstraction that such a comparative discussion would require. But it may be useful to describe in some detail what containing the arms race means.

A policy of containing the arms race is one that strives to slow the rate, and influence the kind, of procurement of strategic weapons in each major power and throughout the world. It is a policy in which we buy or avoid buying weapons in part so as to inhibit later buying.

What does this mean in practice? Consider some examples. If the Soviets discover some novel way of destroying a large number of U.S. land-based (Minuteman) missiles, we shall feel obliged to take some counter action. One choice would be to build more Minuteman missiles; another would be to protect Minuteman missiles; a third might be to buy more Polaris submarines or to replace Minuteman with mobile missiles. Whatever response we chose would have an effect on the Soviet posture, which might, in turn, again require modifications of our own course. A policy of containing the arms race would reflect upon these possibilities quite as much as it would upon the relative cost effectiveness of the initial response by the United States.

Another case would be one in which the Soviets made efforts to build an antiballistic missile system. Should our response to it be one of building offensive weapons that would negate the effectiveness of the Soviet defense? Or should our response be to build a defense of our own? These different responses have very different implications.

On the one hand, we could build a defense. It could lead to the purchase of larger numbers of Soviet ICBM's to improve the Soviet capacity to attack us despite the defenses. But a relatively larger number of Soviet ICBM's might begin to threaten the future of the existing U.S. land-based missiles. This might, in turn, precipitate the rearrangement of our own land-based missiles or the purchase of additional missiles. Both alternatives would be expensive. Each might give rise to further adjustments and to another spiral of activity.

On the other hand, the procurement of additional offensive weapons designed to negate the Soviet defense might add only marginally to our threat against Soviet land-based missiles and might pose no problem for Soviet penetration of our defenses. Hence it might lead to only a few extra Soviet missiles and thus add only marginally to the vulnerability of our land-based missiles. In this case, the impact of the Soviet action in procuring defenses would tend to die out.

In fact, our response to a Soviet defense would probably lie somewhere between these two illustrative reactions, and what would be open to influence might only be nuances. Nevertheless, we can, in principle, achieve some control over the spiraling of arms procurement.

Clearly, even if it were determined that one response led to a new spiral while the other did not, many other considerations would be involved in determining which course to take. The prominent difference between the two responses outlined is that in the first we would have a better active defense, which might (or might not) function sufficiently well to save some people if war occurred. But, if we bought offensive weapons, we might save resources — offenses are likely to cost less — and achieve a more satisfactory retaliatory force.

The question here may be, as it often is, how much we are to emphasize the short-run response and how much the relatively longer-run implications.

Because it is difficult to know all the implications of specific strategic weapon policies and because these decisions involve a host of uncertainties, there is room for argument over the emphasis to be given to future problems and future potential costs. Those who argue for containing the arms race are arguing that these problems should be given greater emphasis and greater consideration. They are also arguing that little of significance is likely to be gained by continuing to engage in spirals of action and response, even if these spirals are slow and quiet.

In any case, in the long run only a sensible procurement policy can contain the arms race, can decelerate, check, curb, confine, and restrain the pressures in both powers to reinstitute an arms spiral.

Such a policy of restraint would have many facets. If we adopted it, we would not telegraph punches that we had no intention of throwing; we would not pointlessly startle or frighten; we would not boast or bluff. Thus we would not exaggerate the likelihood of our buying a missile defense; we would not distort the capability of newer offensive weapons; we could be sober in determining what to do in the future. We *would* telegraph what we intended to do, and we would encourage the adversary to reciprocate; we would seek no short-run advantage in surprise.

A policy of restraint would not tinker with the existing capabilities in an effort to achieve purposeless marginal improvements. Such a policy presents an impression of quiet sufficiency. It suggests that the procurement race is, if not over, at least much less important.

A policy of restraint avoids significant enlargements of the competition. It does not procure, without very good reason, the weapons that will lead arms competition into a new spiral or dimension. It seeks to avoid competition in outer space, in cheaper weapons, or in novel defensive schemes. It neither builds "super" weapons nor makes strenuous efforts to add greatly to the destructive power of present ones. It is not eager to exploit novel weapons effects. Such a policy is conscious of the rapidity with which our new weapons developments reach the hands of adversaries who then arm themselves with them.

A policy of restraint seeks to induce or persuade competitors to refrain from enlarging the arms race; in particular it seeks to deter them from pushing ahead, if this is possible. Such a policy places less emphasis on beating adversaries to the punch than on avoiding an exchange of "blows." Self-restraint becomes a corollary to success in inducing restraint.

A policy of restraint does not emphasize the short-term advantage over the long-run disadvantage. It does not "cross bridges when it comes to them." Instead, it gives full measure in advance to the possibility of adversary actions. It considers the illogical response as well as the logical. And it encourages decision makers to view with some skepticism the possibility that such significant advantages could be maintained indefinitely that they would justify upsetting the *status quo*. It puts relatively little emphasis on spurts of effort that are likely, after a few years, to find the rival steadily closing a gap whose creation has left both sides poorer, in greater danger, or in greater opposition.

A policy of restraint emphasizes, in its doctrine and in the corresponding actions, that economy is sought and that the probability of nuclear war is low. Both attitudes are catching: if one side takes this view, it is far more likely that its opponent will. Each judges the likelihood of war, in part, by assessing the other's fears. Each judges the feasibility of making savings, in part, by the willingness of the other to curb expenses.

A policy of restraint would attempt to justify restraint by emphasizing the finality of the situation, the inevitability of retaliation, the pointlessness of further efforts, and the extent of our break with the past: we have reached a level of weapons development where further preparation for general war is very unlikely to be of any significance.

Finally, a policy of restraint would try to arrange rules and methods for policing and inducing restraint. If weapons must be improved, perhaps their number can remain fixed for such periods as will make this "rule" a tradition that can be depended upon. A policy of restraint would make use of treaties, U.N. resolutions, understandings, or coordinated announcements. It would value token reductions and a variety of other signals that further procurement was being halted.

Finally, a policy of restraint would be careful not to procure systems that are so vulnerable as to encourage an opponent to take advantage of them. The pressures to maintain an advantage are already strong enough. Vulnerable or slow-reacting systems may provide built-in rationalizations that would induce an opponent to prepare to exploit them if war should occur. Each side should strive to get the most "survivability," lest it tempt the other to spend rubles or dollars to neutralize the expenditures. If the longer-term goal is to slow down procurement, each may be more afraid of the other's mistakes than of his sensible efforts. Unfortunate policies can tempt a renewal of the competition that each seeks to avoid.

What does all this mean in practice? It means that the instructions given to the Defense Department should now be quite similar to those that could be given to the Arms Control and Disarmament Agency. Each is now seeking to confine the competition. While in the past the interest in stability and the interest in achieving a secure posture in the arms race may have seemed to conflict, this conflict has now diminished with the virtual completion of our missile force buildup. If, in the past, it was argued that arms control policy was a part of military policy, it may now be argued that strategic weapon policy is an adjunct to arms control efforts. If, in the past, arms control seemed more urgent, it now seems more feasible and, in the long run, no less vital. This is a time for renewed, subtle, and coordinated efforts to keep the competition within bounds.

ANTIBALLISTIC MISSILES AND ARMS CONTROL

Introduction

THIS CHAPTER is devoted to certain problems of anti-ballistic missile (ABM) procurement and their relation to arms control. But these problems immediately raise far more fundamental questions concerning the relationship between active defense and the strategic balance in which we find ourselves. It seems useful to describe some of these fundamental questions because they are of very great importance and also because they have influenced the approach and tone of this chapter.

We live in a world in which active defense seems impotent compared to the powers of the strategic offense. It would be surprising if this peculiar and, in many ways, unprecedented strategic context did not have surprising and unprecedented corollaries for the stability of the strategic balance of forces. One such corollary, in my view, affirms that the development of a very effective defense is likely to be pernicious, destabilizing, and dangerous. Moreover, this corollary suggests that the procurement of less effective defenses may have correspondingly reduced, but still significant, drawbacks of an unusual nature.

We are only now being delivered from some serious instabilities associated with vulnerable weapons as an era unfolds in which an ever more stable "balance of terror" is developing. As Secretary of Defense Robert McNamara put it: "We are approaching an era when it will become increasingly improbable that either side could destroy a sufficiently 'large' portion of the other's strategic nuclear force." [1] This situation has obvious disadvantages, but it seems fairly stable. What could cause this stability to be lost if it continues to be possible to provide weapons with a high order of invulnerability? Speaking in the abstract, the answer is clear: the invention of an effective defense. This has been noted by many analysts, in particular by the famous Soviet physicist, P. Kapitsa, who wrote in 1956:

> In the struggle for the prevention of atomic war, it is essential to take into account the possibility that there will be found a reliable defense against nuclear weapons. If this is achieved by a country with aggressive intentions, then being itself protected against the direct effects of nuclear weapons, it can much more easily decide to launch an atomic war.[2]

Speaking very generally, it seems that if we want the stability associated with defense, we must make the effective use of nuclear weapons impossible. And if we want the stability of deterrence, we must avoid the construction of effective defenses. Between these two extremes, there can only be a continuing contest between offensive and defensive strategic weapons.

What would this contest be like? What would happen if each major power proceeded to buy ballistic missile defenses? If the defenses were ineffective, there would be great waste because defenses against missiles are very expensive even by present standards. What if the defenses became effective? In this case each power would redouble its efforts to procure offensive strategic weapons. In sufficiently extreme cases, there would be political repercussions inside countries as the responsibility for the loss or impairment of the "deterrent" was fixed. In relations between major powers, and in their alliances, there would be repercussions associated with a perceived shift in the major-power balance. In the United States, which is still politically committed to maintain a capacity to destroy the entire Communist bloc in a retaliatory blow, the political impact of even partly successful Soviet defenses would be especially substantial.

It should not be difficult to persuade either the Americans or the Russians of the existence of the phenomenon just described. There is a strong analogy between, on the one hand, a race in which each power attempts, or is thought to be attempting, to maintain a capacity to *strike* the other's forces and, on the other hand, a race in which each attempts or is thought to be attempting to achieve the capacity to *defend against* the other's forces. And, to our dismay, we have already seen the former situation unfold.

In the late fifties, we in the United States believed that the Soviets might be attempting to achieve the capacity to destroy all U.S. forces on the ground. Whether or not there might have been a "delicate balance of terror," the political impact of that possibility cannot be denied. The fear among strategists, the "missile gap" debates of the Kennedy-Nixon campaign, the efforts of the Strategic Air Command to disperse bombers and to develop an airborne alert were all very real. If the Soviets had seemed to be developing a *defense* as effective in neutralizing our retaliatory force as a surprise missile attack, the fears would have been no different.

The Soviets must understand even better than we do what it means to maintain a retaliatory capacity against an adversary who seeks to undermine it. In the early sixties we bought enough missiles to target virtually all Soviet missiles simultaneously. In principle, an effective defense would have been as unsettling.

Thus we can ask about such a race to achieve defenses, as we can about the race to achieve the capacity to disarm adversaries, whether both competitors can achieve their goal while each maintains the capacity to retaliate effectively. In both cases, there is an essential incompatibility from which practical difficulties flow. By contrast, attempts by the two sides to achieve only the ability to retaliate are highly compatible. In these cases, defense departments are not charged with the problem of obstructing each other from achieving the goal. If a race occurs to install a new weapon, each side races only to the completion of the task. In short, two sides can both seek a retaliatory capability without a contest, but they cannot both so easily seek to deter *and* to defend, just as they cannot *both* effectively deter and threaten.

What has this meant in practice? So far it has meant that both have been satisfied primarily to deter. Neither has attempted to procure an expensive defense against missiles with its concomitant need for improvements in civil defense, bomber defense, and antisubmarine defense. This effort has been largely too difficult and too expensive. Nevertheless, in view of the long "lead times" involved in developing offensive weapons and the uncertainties of defensive actions by the adversary, even the prospect of defenses has already encouraged offensive weapon procurement.

What would happen if the race got started now? Some analysts in the United States think we could have our cake and eat it too. We would construct a fairly effective defense at considerable cost, and by constructing suitable offensive weapons would neutralize the Soviet defenses. The Soviets would then hold *relatively* few Americans hostage (a few tens of millions), while we would continue to be able to destroy the Soviet Union outright. Western casualties — those involving the allies as well as ourselves — would remain high (many tens of millions). For this reason and because the Soviets seem to have been willing to acquiesce in this situation so far, they might be satisfied with it. And this situation might obtain for some time. This is the most favorable view of the outcome.

But there are other possibilities. Our missile defense might be a tremendous waste (as many believe our bomber defenses have been), either because the Soviet capacity to destroy Americans could not be reduced, when Soviet countermeasures were taken into consideration, or because the likelihood of war was so low. Or, in the long run, the Soviets might develop an especially effective defense.

Hence, the two extreme possibilities for a race involving defenses are, on the one hand, waste and, on the other, political and strategic uneasiness. In between these two extremes, of ineffective defenses and strategic imbalance, lies the possibility of accelerated procurement or of replacement of offensive and defensive strategic weapons.

Therefore if the probability of war is sufficiently low and the cost of defenses sufficiently high, if the value placed on a stable strategic situation is sufficiently high and the need for further improvement in our strategic superiority sufficiently low, it might be well to consider ways of preventing or inhibiting, by treaty or otherwise, the development or procurement of defenses. This is the position adopted in this chapter.

There are three reasons why this point of view receives less recognition than it should. First, present-day defenses are only just beginning to be effective, and, as a result, the potential political and strategic effects of their bilateral deployment and further development are obscured. Second, the historic role of defense and even the general connotation of the word make it difficult to argue against it. Third, and most important, there is little understanding or discussion about the possibility of controlling the development of defense on *both* sides. It will help neither side to control defenses — if it helps at all — unless this control is bilateral. Therefore arms controllers must take up the subject; others may have no immediate interest in it.

Can bilateral control over defenses be achieved? Technically, the problem may be relatively easy. First, defenses are at present expensive, and no one expects them to be very effective. Hence the motivation for their installation is reduced. Second, for the foreseeable future it will be far easier to inspect for defenses than for offensive weapons. For example, with present defenses the very idea of a clandestine defense problem is ludicrous. By contrast, the clandestine weapon problem, at low levels of weapons, looks insoluble. Third, effective defenses will take several years to install. The length of this lead time will be reassuring so long as the procurement decision is likely to be detected.

Indeed, at the present time if we are undecided between the

stability of very effective defense and the stability of mutual deterrence, we would probably be well advised to try for the latter. This effort would act *with* the forces of technology — as they are presently perceived — rather than against them. But even if we were to try to return to a world of defense, through disarmament, we would surely have to control defenses just as carefully as we limited armament — at least until the treaty required each side to have no second-strike capability at all. Hence the decision to control defenses *now* does not require a choice between disarmament and mutual deterrence. Either will find this control necessary.

The control of defense is not as inappropriate as it may seem. If it is true that "we must either live together or die together," then there can be no more fundamentally appropriate agreement than one which, by controlling defenses, emphasizes the fundamental vulnerability of each side to the weapons of the other.

If the speculations of this chapter are borne out, the situation is both hopeful and urgent for the control of defenses. It seems (*a*) that the United States is uncertain about procuring ABM defenses, for doctrinal and economic reasons; (*b*) that Soviet procurement of ABM systems would probably lead to U.S. procurement; (*c*) that bilateral procurement of ABM systems would not serve the real interest of either major power; (*d*) that restraint in procurement of ABM systems can be arranged to entail little risk for either major power; and therefore (*e*) that both powers should give consideration to such restraint. And it may also be that U.S. procurement would give rise to the otherwise avoidable Soviet procurement of ABM systems. Obviously, it is difficult for an American analyst to discuss this question because there is no suitable Soviet source material available. For this reason, the following analysis shows considerable lack of symmetry.

In any case, the chain of reasoning may be wrong, on one or several counts. But it deserves careful study because it is likely to be relevant to future problems involving the procurement of defenses that will plague arms controllers in the coming years. In the present strategic context, it may be the defense, and not the offense, to which the attention of arms controllers should be drawn. For this reason, we must reach a consensus on these issues as soon as possible.

Of course, these general propositions do not decide concrete cases: in particular, the ABM problem has its own special characteristics, which are discussed in this chapter.

Progress in the United States

Antiballistic missile systems are only beginning to show any significant effectiveness. The first substantial U.S. attempt at such a system was the proposed Army Nike-Zeus system designed, essentially, to shoot down only a single incoming missile at a time.[3] In the late fifties, the Army proposed the development of this system but did not receive the support of the other members of the Joint Chiefs of Staff or of the Secretary of Defense.[4] The system would have cost $8 or $9 billion and would have been operational in 1963–1964.[5] However, Secretary McNamara pointed out in 1962 that this money would have been effectively wasted, considering the requirements of 1963–1964. And even General Taylor, a long-time supporter of Nike-Zeus, was in substantial agreement: testifying immediately after the Secretary, he could only argue in defense of its procurement that

> One, we would now be learning by doing. As far as my experience goes with new weapons, that is the only way you can make any great progress. It takes a considerable amount of actual employment of weapons systems to get the best out of them. . . .
> The other point is that we would have had a technological triumph over the Soviets. Some day there will be a great ballyhoo that the Soviets have an antiballistic missile and we do not. The claim may be largely sham and propaganda, but we face that possibility of a cold war defeat.[6]

Over the years the Nike-Zeus technology has improved; nevertheless, in 1963 the Secretary of Defense decided not to procure an operational system of this type or two alternative modifications of it. His reasoning was, in part, that he could deploy a Nike-Zeus type of system (with two improvements) by 1968 but that he was "certain they could introduce into their warheads, if they have not already done so, the capability to penetrate such a system by 1966." [7] Further improvements were indicated, and it was decided to wait, at least until these could be made.

These improvements were to constitute a new system, Nike-X, which would have an enhanced capacity to distinguish decoys from actual missiles. A year later, in January 1964, the Secretary of Defense was more optimistic concerning the effectiveness of the system. He stated:

> The continued testing of the NIKE-ZEUS and preliminary studies of the NIKE-X system's characteristics and effectiveness provide grounds for believing that the technical problems of at least a partial defense against a ballistic missile attack may be solved within the next several years. [8]

The basic philosophy behind Nike-Zeus and Nike-X was to attack incoming missiles at the lowest possible altitudes consistent with safety. In this way, we would buy time and permit the atmosphere to "screen" out decoys, that is, permit atmospheric effects such as "drag" to affect the perceived motions of incoming objects. [9] Partly because of this low-level, terminal-intercept approach, civil defense preparations have become an important complement to ABM systems. Some believe that shelters will be required to protect against the blast effects of the detonating ABM warheads. Thus *Air Force and Space Digest* states: "Department of Defense studies show that persons on the ground in the target area would have to be in shelters to prevent their being injured by the blasts from the nuclear-warhead Sprint missiles." [10] Whether or not this is correct, the fact that larger enemy warheads could be detonated at the intercept height probably indicates a need for blast shelters.

In any case, fallout shelters will be required to prevent an adversary from attacking unprotected rural areas in such a way as to kill urban residents with fallout. The Secretary of Defense maintained in 1963 that he "will never recommend an anti-ICBM program unless a fallout program does accompany it." [11]

The cost of the presently proposed Nike-X ABM system, for deployment alone, around "20-odd metropolitan centers, containing some 35 percent of the population" is projected to be about $14 billion.[12] This would presumably be spent over a period of a few years. Nevertheless the cost is significant. There are some indications, however, that the Defense Department's strategic budget will drop for a time until presently procured missile systems require replacement. For example, Secretary McNamara pointed out in November, 1963:

> The funding for the initial introduction of missiles into our forces is nearing completion. We can anticipate that the annual expenditure on strategic forces will drop substantially, and level off well below the present rate of spending. This is not to rule out the possibility that research now in progress on possible new technological developments, including the possibility of useful ballistic missile defenses, will require major new expenditures.*

And Senator Symington reports being told that our expenditures for strategic forces will drop from around 16 per cent of the budget to 7 per cent (that is, a decline of $4 to $5 billion).[15] About three or four years of such "saving" would provide approximately $15 billion. This would procure the system just discussed. Hence the cost of an ABM system might, in part, be absorbed in the budget.

But the lifetime of the system is uncertain. Most people be-

---

* These remarks were substantiated by pointing out that "The U.S. force now contains more than 500 operational long-range ballistic missiles — ATLAS, TITAN, MINUTEMAN, POLARIS — and is planned to increase to over 1,700 by 1966. There is no doubt in our minds and none in the minds of the Soviets that these missiles can penetrate to their targets. In addition, the U.S. has Strategic Air Command bombers on air alert and over 500 bombers on quick reaction ground alert." [13] The Secretary argued elsewhere in 1963 that "our second strike would exceed the weight of the first strike that was directed against us." [14]

lieve that the offense can install countermeasures more rapidly than the defense can prepare to defeat them. Thus Harold Brown in his capacity as Director of Defense Research and Engineering said

> Major changes in deployed ABM systems will generally take more time than major changes in penetration aid systems. Remembering that wide deployment of an ABM system will take several years, that our intelligence should give us information of its development even before then, that we can carry out very extensive development and deployment of still more advanced penetration aids in only a few years, and that a substantial increase in the numbers of our offensive forces can also be made relatively quickly, it appears that our retaliatory capability can be preserved with a large margin of safety. . . .[16]

And the costs to the offense are likely to be much lower than those of the defense. For example, if the $14-billion system referred to above covered 25 areas, and assuming that strategic missiles could be procured by the Soviet Union at about $4 million apiece — as they are by us — then 140 missiles of the Minuteman type (in their silos) could be purchased by the Soviet Union for *each* defended area at a total cost equal to that of the proposed system. Polaris-type missiles (in submarines) cost somewhat more — $9 to $10 million each — but would permit 56–62 missiles per metropolitan area.[17]

Against salvos or even repeated firings of such numbers of missiles, the ABM system would surely fail to protect the area from substantial destruction. Moreover, improvement of existing missiles to give them penetration advantages against deployed systems is probably much cheaper and somewhat quicker than buying new missiles. Other possibilities might include techniques for destroying defended areas without penetration, for instance, the use of fallout from bombs exploded in rural areas. This does not necessarily indicate that ABM defense is hopeless or even that it is not worth buying. It does indicate that active defense is relatively expensive in an arms race where the offense applies resources to nullify it and strikes with a substantially undamaged force.

The Likelihood of U.S. Procurement

For reasons such as these, it is uncertain, at the moment, whether the presently proposed Nike-X system will or will not be procured. The Secretary of Defense has recognized the reasons for procuring even a limited capability, and has maintained that every effort should be made to design an effective system even if no decision is made to procure and deploy it.[18] He said in 1963: "Would it be wise to deploy the NIKE-X system? I think the question is open." He further affirmed that, although the point had not been reached where a production decision could properly be made, "were we at that point today, I do not know what I would recommend to you, because it would be a very, very difficult decision." [19]

By 1964, the Secretary of Defense was carefully linking a variety of other defensive measures to the decision to procure Nike-X. It was argued that a decision to go ahead with Nike-X would commit us "to continue and perhaps improve" our defense against manned bombers and to build a system of fallout shelters costing "perhaps $3 to $6 billion." Hinting at a need for blast shelters or further protection, he suggested that a decision to procure a ballistic missile defense would require us to "carefully consider what additional civil defense measures might be required for the population." Procurement cost estimates of the type given earlier were made, but it was noted that these "may prove to be low." [20] Maintenance costs were quoted at "maybe a billion and a half a year to operating expenses." [21] Over-all, the Secretary suggested that

> the cost to the Soviets of adding additional missiles to their force or augmenting their missiles with penetration aids would probably be but a fraction of the cost to us of offsetting these additional missiles or increased penetration capability with additional defense measures.[22]

It was widely believed that the time was still not ripe for a final decision while further improvements and tests were pending. Many reports suggested a final decision in January

31

1965, but in that month the President's defense statement to Congress called only for a continuation of research and development. It suggested that "we must always be alert" to the possibilities for limiting destruction, noted that "many proposals have been advanced" to this end, and went on to emphasize the complexity of the decision and the many costs as follows:

> Shifting strategy and advancing technology make the program of building adequate defense against nuclear attack extremely complex.
>
> Decisions with respect to further limitation of damage require complex calculations concerning the effectiveness of many inter-related elements. Any comprehensive program would involve the expenditure of tens of billions of dollars. We must not shrink from any expense that is justified by its effectiveness, but we must not hastily expend vast sums on massive programs that do not meet this test.
>
> It is already clear that without fall-out shelter protection all defense weapons lose much of their effectiveness in saving millions of lives. . . . We will continue our existing programs. . . .
>
> We shall continue the research and development which retains the options to deploy an anti-ballistic missile system, and manned interceptors and surface to air missiles against bombers.[23]

Evidently, the Department of Defense was still not ready to procure a system.*

Among the important considerations that may determine whether currently conceived systems will be procured are

---

* As this book goes to press in December 1965 a high-level citizen's panel report on arms control — associated with the International Co-operation Year activities — has proposed a three-year moratorium on the production of ballistic missile defenses in the United States and the Soviet Union. The resulting stir — already three editorials have appeared in *The New York Times* — brought to light the unanimity of the Joint Chiefs of Staff behind a decision to deploy. However, an article by Jack Raymond suggests that the decision will be put off for another year, with the possible purchase of some long-lead-time items that would not commit the later choice. The common public argument for a defense continues to be the possibility of conflict with a nuclear-armed China; the possibility of on-going Soviet preparations for a defense has figured in a few articles without much public impact on the recent debate.

our perception of Soviet progress in developing or deploying antimissile systems; the extent to which the need for complementary civil defense may dampen enthusiasm for procurement; the ease with which the system can be quickly neutralized; the likelihood that the system will have an Achilles' heel; and, especially, the political climate.

Particularly important is the progress, or apparent progress, of the Soviet Union. Many informed persons in our government seem to think that the United States is at least on a par with, if not slightly in advance of, the Soviet Union in ABM development. For instance, Harold Brown said in 1963: "I think that we are roughly comparable. If I were forced to say one side or the other is ahead on knowledge, I would say that we were, but I don't think that is a very firm statement on my part." [24] However, the Soviet Union was for a time evidently following a course of proclaiming its progress somewhat prematurely.* And, according to several public reports, the Soviet Union has established an ABM battery around Leningrad that can shoot down the Polaris missile, if not the Minuteman missile.[26]

The relative vulnerability of Polaris or, more generally, of IRBM's, as opposed to ICBM's, is due to the angles and speed of re-entry.[27] This claimed progress has caused concern of several kinds. For instance, repeated references to the Leningrad installation have been made in Congressional testimony. Congress has always been very sensitive to the problems of matching the Soviet Union in procurement of individual weapons, whether or not this has been indicated from a purely logical point of view. Thus, a bomber gap in the fifties generated more interest in the rate of bomber production than in

* See, for example, the volume edited by Sokolovskii.[25] A note by the American translators points out that Soviet authors have been more sober in their assessment of the effectiveness of antimissile defense than have public Soviet claims. Public claims have ranged from, "The problem of destroying missiles in flight has been successfully solved," to the assertion that Soviet antimissile missiles could "hit a fly in outer space," and, finally, to the more recent and repeated announcement that the Soviet Union has prepared "complexes of numerous means for the defense of our country against enemy missile attacks."

defense against Soviet bombers. Concern could well arise over a "defense gap" similar to the earlier bomber and missile gaps.* Congress is not the only decision-making element that wishes to maintain at least a parity in each separate area of importance. For example, in discussing the U.S. need to test in response to Soviet tests, allegedly with the aim of *developing* an antimissile defense system, President Kennedy said: "Were we to stand still while the Soviets surpassed us — *or even appeared to surpass us* — the Free World's ability to deter, to survive and to respond to an all-out attack would be seriously weakened." [29] (Italics added.) Certainly the Soviet Union would seem to some to be overtaking us if it *built* a defensive capability while we had none.

Whether or not "matching" plays an important role in determining the likelihood that U.S. ABM systems would be procured, Soviet ABM systems may be a source of more than psychological concern. For instance, Governor Rockefeller, in giving his views on the Test Ban Treaty, stated:

> The possession by the Soviets of large missiles and warheads together with their aggressive development of anti-missile defenses in fact opens up somber prospects about Soviet intentions. The possibility must not be ruled out that large Soviet explosions or use of multiple warheads may jeopardize our hardened Minuteman sites, while the Soviet ballistic missile defense may deal with the counterblow launched from our Polaris submarines.[30]

These fears and speculations would not affect U.S. procurement of ABM directly, if that decision were to be made both on the basis of cost effectiveness and in the absence of a perceived increase in the risk of war. Instead it would lead to

---

* Take, for example the words of Senator Thurmond: " . . . by rejecting the alternative of initial deployment of an anti-missile missile system until after the perfection of the NIKE-X the United States is faced with a period in which there may be a defensive gap which would be more dangerous than a substantial missile gap. . . ." [28] While there is relatively little such talk at present, there is also little evidence, or fear, that the Soviet Union is *procuring* the ABM systems necessary to exploit any such gap visibly. Soviet procurement of many batteries would give rise to considerably more concern.

the procurement of penetration capability and invulnerability. If, however, Governor Rockefeller and others can argue that the Soviet system will lead to increased Soviet risk taking, much less to a surprise attack, then the cost effectiveness of an ABM system will be influenced by a perceived increase in the risk of war. And, in any case, there are political problems associated with failing to procure an ABM system if the Soviets do so, as illustrated by Governor Rockefeller's statement. The Democrats attacked the Eisenhower administration for a missile gap during the 1960 campaign, and they are presumably well aware of the ammunition that any semblance of a "defense gap" would hand to the Republican Presidential candidate in 1968. Here, particularly, Soviet procurement is an important factor in U.S. decision making.

On the other hand, if the Soviet Union does not procure its own system, there may be a reluctance on the part of some within the Johnson administration to procure a system that seems to be the start of another "round" in the arms race. Thus Secretary of State Dean Rusk sees "mounting defense budgets that go beyond anything now contemplated if the qualitative arms race proceeds on the basis of weapons in outer space, antimissile missiles, and missiles to penetrate those. . . ." Rusk argued for the test ban as an act that might "put some . . . lid" on this qualitative race.[31]

U.S. restraint would be further encouraged by certain relatively new strategic doctrines or attitudes that might make it easier to avoid procuring active defenses. First, recent government statements have tended to acquiesce in Soviet second-strike capabilities. Thus the Secretary of Defense said:

> A very large increase in the number of fully hard Soviet ICBM's and nuclear-powered ballistic missile-launching submarines would considerably detract from our ability to destroy completely the Soviet strategic nuclear forces. It would become increasingly difficult, regardless of the form of the attack, to destroy a sufficiently large proportion of the Soviets' strategic nuclear forces to preclude major damage to the United States, regardless of how large or what kind of strategic forces we build. Even if we were to double and triple our forces we would not

be able to destroy quickly all or almost all of the hardened ICBM sites. And even if we could do that, we know no way to destroy the enemy's missile-launching submarines at the same time. We do not anticipate that either the United States or the Soviet Union will acquire that capability in the foreseeable future. Moreover, to minimize damage to the United States, such a force would also have to be accompanied by an extensive missile defense system and a much more elaborate civil defense program than has thus far been contemplated. Even then we could not preclude casualties counted in the tens of millions. *What we are proposing is a capability to strike back after absorbing the first blow.*[32] (Italics added.)

This kind of statement indicates that the nation may be led to accept as unavoidable the absence of a true defense against the effects of nuclear weapons. It is no isolated remark. The Secretary of Defense has spoken mostly of maintaining "a superior strategic nuclear power" or "over-all U.S. superiority." [33] While statements indicating that the absence of a defense may be unavoidable tend to encourage U.S. restraint in response to Soviet restraint, the Secretary's claim to "over-all" superiority, to which these admissions seem to be linked, will encourage U.S. procurement in response to Soviet procurement. Both of these effects increase the potential impact of Soviet decision making on our own decisions.

Next it should be noted that U.S. policy increasingly attempts to resolve the problem of European defense by viewing allied European territory as an extension of our own, to be defended without consideration of outcome. President Kennedy, in a speech in Bonn, on June 23, 1963, stated: "So long as our presence is desired and required, our force and commitments will remain. For your safety is our safety, your liberty is our liberty, and an attack on your soil is an attack upon our own." [34] And Secretary McNamara has indicated that we would back up our commitment in Europe without regard to consequences:

The term "unacceptable damage" is a relative one. . . . For example, we have made it quite clear that the defense of Western Europe is as vital to us as the defense of our own continent and that we are prepared to back up our commitments there with our strategic nuclear power *no matter what degree of damage might result* should the deterrent aspect of this policy fail.[35] (Italics added.)

Other remarks by the Secretary have indicated that strategic response to invasion of Europe might even be inevitable, or at least feared as inevitable, and hence our threats might even have an automatic quality. He has argued that

. . . the Soviet Union is deterred from a massive attack on Western Europe by the size of our strategic force and the recognition that we are so intertwined in the defense of Western Europe that that force would be brought to bear against the Soviet Union should they engage in any massive attack on Western Europe.[36]

These positions all make it less necessary to procure ABM to support strategic threats. They imply that a credible threat to defend Europe does not depend upon a defense designed to reduce expected American casualties. A "defenseless" posture is still further encouraged by re-evaluations of ground forces that indicate the United States is stronger and the Soviet Union weaker than was formerly believed.[37]

The position of the Joint Chiefs of Staff must also be considered. In the past they failed to achieve unanimity on ABM procurement, and such uncertainty increases the potential impact, on our decision, of a Soviet decision to procure. For instance, in 1963 the Secretary of Defense reported that the Chiefs had been "uncertain" about deploying an ABM system.[38] In General Taylor's word, they were "split." The Army Chief of Staff, General Wheeler, testified that he had received "pretty unanimous" support for his Nike-Zeus program. The Chief of Naval Operations testified that he favored the "early deployment of the improved Nike-Zeus, contingent upon successful progress in system demonstration tests." However, Chief of Staff of the Air Force, General Curtis E. LeMay, said that we were "not quite ready" actually to put Nike-Zeus into operation. He questioned the advisability of "expending that much money for such poor results." He argued for the

CHAPTER ONE

continuation "at full speed" of development, and ventured the belief that "eventually we can arrive at an acceptable solution to the problem." [39] But by November 1965, *The New York Times* was pointing out that the Joint Chiefs were unanimously in favor of deployment.

In short, it would seem that an antiballistic missile program had far more support from the Chiefs than had been the case when General Taylor wrote of their deliberations from a position of temporary retirement in 1959. He indicated then that all the other Chiefs "viewed NIKE-ZEUS as a rival for defense funds" and that he was the sole advocate of procurement funds for it.[40]

The Chiefs have undoubtedly been influenced by the possible Chinese threat, the U.S. slowdown in offensive weapon procurement — which diminishes competition for funds — and the extent to which expenditures on bomber and submarine defenses have been tied with ABM.

But certainly the most important consideration in this decision is the international atmosphere and the perceived risk of nuclear war. In one political climate, the expenditure of tens of billions of dollars for a missile defense can seem to high government officials to be the most incredible nonsense and a pointless waste. But after a few incidents in Berlin, a Soviet ultimatum, and some troop movements, there will be years when nothing will seem more natural than to complement our offensive weapons with defensive ones. In this sense, the ultimate decision whether or not we should buy a defensive system is likely to be made by the Soviets.

This discussion of the likelihood that we shall procure an ABM system is not systematic, but, in the present situation, no very complete appraisal is possible. In 1963 and before, analysis of the question would have been complicated by the absence of any consensus, even in the Department of Defense, on the rationale for a defense of such marginal effectiveness as provided by the then foreseeable terminal-intercept systems.

In 1964, the Defense Department position became fairly firm in associating active defenses with "the limitation of damage upon the United States should war occur." Thus the most obvious justification for the defense was simply prudence, much as it has been the main justification for civil defense programs in the last few years. However, some in the Defense Department undoubtedly believed that the defense would improve the credibility of our threats to risk nuclear war and would impress the Soviets with our technical superiority. Finally in 1965, the Chinese threat became the Defense Department's rationale for ballistic missile defense.

In other agencies and interested departments there might be different attitudes toward ballistic missile defense, for instance, in the Arms Control and Disarmament Agency, The Bureau of the Budget, the President's Science Advisory Committee, and the Department of State. All of these would have a substantial interest, if modest influence, in the outcome of the debate on the building of a defense, if the Secretary of Defense proposed one; with the possible exception of the Department of State, they could be expected to be opposed. It seems, however, that the Secretary of Defense is sufficiently disinclined to rush ahead with defenses to avoid proposing them unless both the political atmosphere and the technical case for them clearly warrant such action. In this situation, considering his extraordinary influence in these matters, he might well get his way for at least a few years.

The Likelihood of Soviet Procurement and the Soviet National Interest

It is, of course, very difficult to determine what the Soviet Union might do. As noted earlier, their progress is thought to be comparable to our own, though some of their statements boast of much more. And their actions may be as dependent upon ours as our actions may be on theirs. The alleged ABM activity near Leningrad has been mentioned; and it should also be noted that interceptors, apparently for an ABM system, have rolled through Red Square.[41] Probably the most important question is whether or not the Soviet Union will procure and deploy batteries to a sizable number of cities, that is, to more than two or three. Lesser deployment is probably more symbolic than it is strategically or politically significant.

In considering this question, it is useful, on the one hand, to examine past experience of Soviet behavior and existing statements of Soviet scientists and decision makers and, on the other hand, to ask ourselves whether, as nearly as we can tell, Soviet procurement of ABM systems is justified in our eyes by Soviet interests. While it is easier to answer the latter question than it is to predict Soviet behavior from past events, that answer may not be very useful for the prediction of future Soviet actions. Not only are we likely to fail to perceive certain valid Soviet concerns, we may also fail to take into account many invalid concerns that are nevertheless strongly motivating.

Nevertheless, this point of view is useful. In discussions with the Soviet Union in which we try to point out "mutual interests," we must make an assessment of what we think is, and is not, in the interests of the Soviet Union. When *their* assessment of *their* interest coincides with our own, we need do nothing. But when this is not the case, and when our assessment of Soviet interest coincides with our own interest, then we must be aware of it and be prepared to persuade the Soviet Union to our view.

Consider an example: it is likely that the Soviet Union procures and deploys defenses as if even highly inadequate and expensive defenses were very necessary to its interests. From our point of view, such defenses seem easily neutralized and a waste of Soviet resources. If we believe that it is in our interest to have the Soviet Union waste its resources, then we need say nothing — the Soviets' perception of their interest would coincide with our own. However, if the attempt to procure inadequate defenses can lead to such unfortunate consequences that this attempt is neither in our interest nor, on balance, in the Soviet interest (as we see it), then we must be prepared to persuade Soviet decision makers to review their policy.

Do the Soviets see even quite inadequate active defenses as being in their interest even in the nuclear age. The answer to this question is probably yes. For example, General LeMay testified that "they are spending a greater portion of their resources by far than we are on defenses." [42]

Among the factors that are sometimes adduced to explain Soviet defense expenditures are: a desire for defense induced by two world wars; a feeling of being surrounded; and Soviet bureaucratic vested interests.[43] Other explanations are even simpler. When asked by Senator Frank Lausche, in apparent reference to the purported Leningrad installation, why the Soviet Union had "deployed an ABM system" if it were not effective, Herbert York, former Director of Defense Research and Engineering, replied: "Some of their scientists or engineers sold them a bill of goods. That happens here, too. I mean, the situations are not all that asymmetrical." Later he added: "Well, there is plenty of evidence that the Soviets have been very strongly defense minded for years. I mean, you know with respect to certain other things they have done. They try very hard in this area. Trying is not enough." [44]

Evidence of this Soviet interest appears in the "authoritative" Soviet work, edited by Marshal Sokolovskii:

> The rapid development of nuclear-armed missiles and their adoption as the basic means for delivering nuclear blows to targets deep within the country have sharply posed the problem, for all states, of creating an effective antimissile defense capable of destroying enemy ballistic missiles in the air. In principle, a technical solution to this problem has now been found. In the future this form of defense must be perfected.[45]

Interestingly, the second edition of this work deleted the final two sentences of this quotation. The implications of this change are controversial. But we must concede a very great Soviet tendency to procure defense.

Consider the Soviet national interest as it might be viewed by an American analyst. We assume that Soviet procurement would trigger an otherwise avoidable procurement by the United States. This is very possibly the case, as indicated previously. But even if it were not, this assumption would be the proper one for us to consider for two reasons. First, Soviet decision makers surely cannot assume that their procurement will *not* be matched. There is too much contrary evidence for this to be a reasonable hope. Hence, putting ourselves in their position, we should assume "matching." Second, it is useful in the present circumstances to consider the case in which the United States wishes to deter Soviet procurement of ABM rather than to procure our own system. This is at least one of the most interesting arms control cases.

If Soviet procurement led to U.S. procurement, would the Soviet Union find its posture improved or degraded by its decision to procure ABM? It would probably be degraded relative to the United States — though not relative to France. This conclusion follows from considering, first, the effect of U.S. deployment; second, the small utility of current Soviet ABM systems; and, third, the corresponding reduction of Soviet efforts to improve their second-strike posture and to maintain their momentum in space exploration.

First, from the Soviet point of view, U.S. first-strike capabilities are large and may already be frightening. ABM systems that defend cities will further strengthen our ability to threaten Soviet forces. In a confrontation between the U.S. President and the Soviet Premier, the President can hint that even some highly invulnerable Soviet missiles will not deter the United States if its vital interests are threatened: ABM batteries will simply shoot down Soviet retaliatory attacks. A U.S. President would certainly feel less compelled to admit, as was done during the Cuban crisis, that "American citizens have become adjusted to living daily on the bull's-eye of Soviet missiles located inside the U.S.S.R. or in submarines." [46] An ABM program is likely to save more lives than a fallout-shelter program alone against city-directed attacks.*

* Studies of potential urban-area casualties from attacks on cities generally show that one-half to three-quarters of the fatalities would be

Although this effect may yet seem small to Americans, it ought not to seem so to responsible Soviet decision makers. If the Soviet Union is afraid that the United States may retain a capacity to strike Soviet forces without risking total devastation, then the Soviets should seek to prevent, not to encourage, our ABM deployment.

Second, if Soviet deployment is the stimulus for U.S. deployment, there would probably be little advantage from the Soviet point of view in balancing the U.S. gain in counterforce capability. Soviet ABM batteries deter virtually nothing. They certainly do not deter attacks upon Soviet forces if those attacks try to avoid cities — one of the options indicated by the Secretary of Defense.* And it is the opinion of Secretary McNamara that ABM systems will not prevent retaliatory attacks on Soviet cities. Thus he argued in 1963 much as he has done more recently:

> But, regardless of the design of any Soviet ABM system, in view of the warhead improvements we can make under the treaty, of the massive U.S. force available to saturate their defenses, and of the array of penetration aids which are being developed and will continue to be developed and improved, by underground

induced by blast, and the remainder would result from fallout.[47] Thus, without ABM or blast shelters, expected casualties from attacking Soviet weapons would remain high independent of fallout protection; with some kind of ABM program that avoids or minimizes blast effects this is no longer necessarily true.

* "In talking about global nuclear war," McNamara pointed out, "the Soviet leaders always say that they would strike at the entire complex of our military power including government and production centers, meaning our cities. If they were to do so, we would, of course, have no alternative but to retaliate in kind. But we have no way of knowing whether they would actually do so. It would certainly be in their interest as well as ours to try to limit the terrible consequences of a nuclear exchange. By building into our forces a flexible capability, we at least eliminate the prospect that we could strike back in only one way; namely, against the entire Soviet target system including their cities. Such a prospect would give the Soviet Union no incentive to withhold attack against our cities in a first strike. We want to give them a better alternative. Whether they would accept it in the crisis of a global nuclear war, no one can say. Considering what is at stake, we believe it is worth the additional effort on our part to have this option." [48]

testing where necessary, the United States will continue to have the capability, and . . . the Soviets will know that we will continue to have the capability — to penetrate and to devastate the Soviet Union if a retaliatory blow is required.[49]

To Soviet decision makers who do not anticipate an attack on American cities or an invasion of Western Europe, the risks of such attacks upon their own cities should appear quite small. In short, ABM batteries deter little and provide protection only against fairly unlikely contingencies.

Third, by comparison to ABM batteries, Soviet retaliatory missiles probably provide the Soviet Union with more substantial strategic advantages, while Soviet space achievements probably provide more substantial propaganda benefits. It is appropriate to compare these three potential enterprises because they require the same limited resources, and probably cannot all be funded in quantity.*

Consider the relationship between ABM and retaliatory missiles. While apparently admitting that a secure Soviet second-strike capability is inevitably forthcoming, Secretary of Defense McNamara nowhere admits that our retaliatory forces are not, at present, capable of disrupting them to a significant degree. He said in 1963:

> In planning our second strike force, we have provided, throughout the period under consideration [1964–1968], a capability to destroy virtually all of the "soft" and "semihard" military targets in the Soviet Union and a large number of their fully hardened missile sites, with an additional capability in the form of a protected force to be employed or held in reserve for use against urban and industrial areas.
>
> We have not found it feasible, *at this time,* to provide a capability for insuring the destruction of *any very large* portion of

* John P. Hardt argues that three priority areas — offensive missilery, missile defense capability, and space exploration programs — "must draw on the same limited military-space supporting industries. The costs of each of the programs must be calculated in terms of the alternative programs. How many ICBM's is a missile defense system for Moscow worth to Soviet leaders? Or will a program to land a man on the moon justify retarding their offensive and defensive missile programs? These are presumably the type of difficult decisions that must be faced by Soviet leaders. . . ." [50]

the fully hard ICBM sites, *if* the Soviets build them in quantities, or of missile launching submarines. . . . Our ability to destroy these submarines before they fire their missiles will be limited *once* the Soviet Union places any large number of them on station.[51] (Italics added.)

That same year, Harold Brown, Director of Defense Research and Engineering, stated: "I do not think it is possible for them to destroy all of our retaliatory capability or for us to destroy all of theirs, *providing that both sides plan carefully.*" [52] (Italics added.)

In 1964, the Secretary of Defense was similarly conjectural. In denying that we could achieve a "full first-strike" capability that would reduce Soviet retaliatory capability to "acceptable" levels, he referred to it as unattainable "on the basis of our estimates of the Soviet nuclear strikes forces in the fiscal year 1967–69 period. . . ."

But the United States is not restraining its procurement to assist the Soviet Union in maintaining a second-strike capability. Evidently, Soviet expenditures on relatively invulnerable retaliatory forces would not be wasted from a purely strategic point of view and would probably be more useful than would analogous additions to our retaliatory forces.

In the past the preponderance on our side has permitted the United States to threaten strategic responses to other than strategic attacks. Our statements have threatened "massive retaliatory power." * We have spoken of "some circumstances" in which we would take the "initiative." [54] In the case of Cuba, President Kennedy stated that "it shall be the policy of this nation to regard any nuclear missile launched from Cuba against any nation in the Western hemisphere as an attack by the Soviet Union on the United States requiring a full retaliatory response upon the Soviet Union." [55] Our superiority has also made it somewhat less difficult to affirm, with conviction, that we will prevent a massive Soviet invasion with such responses. Thus an official White House statement of

* "The basic decision," said Secretary of State John Foster Dulles, "was to depend primarily upon a great capacity to retaliate, instantly, by means and at places of our choosing." [53]

March 27, 1962, reads: "It has always been clear that in such a context as a massive conventional attack on Europe by the Soviet Union, which would put Europe in danger of being overrun, the West would have to prevent such an event by all available means. This has been United States policy since the late Nineteen Forties and it represents no change." [56] Secretary McNamara stated more concretely that "it is our policy to utilize whatever weapons are needed to preserve our vital interests. Quite clearly, we consider access to Berlin a vital interest." [57]

Such pronouncements indicate that the decision to defend Europe is, like a similar decision to defend our own country, not a matter to which computations of risk apply. Nevertheless, all things being equal, the Soviet Union would presumably prefer to make any computations concerning these threats look very sobering.

The Soviet choice between retaliatory weapons and ABM defenses should also be influenced by the probable U.S. response. As indicated earlier, the United States generally seems prepared to see the Soviet retaliatory capability grow without responding by the procurement of more and more U.S. missiles — assuming that these missiles do not threaten us; in any case, it is not clearly U.S. policy to try to maintain an ability to strike Soviet forces. However, substantial numbers of ABM batteries would, at least in principle, provoke the most serious efforts to maintain our all-important retaliatory capability. This might, of course, be done largely with further improvements in penetration aids, but it might also lead to larger warheads and more numerous weapons.

The Soviet decision between offensive missiles and defensive missiles should also be influenced by costs. As noted earlier, a very considerable number of retaliatory weapons can be purchased for the price of an ABM system covering only about twenty metropolitan areas. And defending fewer cities is somewhat pointless, for strategic purposes, when faced with thousands of missiles.

Finally, the entire construction of ABM batteries for twenty or fifty cities could be a complete waste of money in terms of protection provided if war actually occurred. For instance, the United States might build a missile that could elude defenses. Or we might learn exactly how the Soviet system worked and use tactics that nullified it. These and simultaneity of arrival, streamlined (and hence faster) re-entry vehicles, smaller radar cross sections, nonradar reflecting nose cones, and so on, are all being considered.[58] The offense could easily leave the defense hopelessly far behind.

By comparison, several hundreds or thousands of Soviet missiles procured in place of a defense would provide additional deterrent value in any general war. In fact, they would threaten to reduce the critical postwar problems of U.S. passive and active defense to ultimate problems of economic recovery and recuperation. It has been argued, for example, that economic viability of the postwar economy would be an obstacle to recovery after an attack upon the United States of 1,000–4,000 megatons of which 750–2,000 were exploded on nonmilitary targets. This would "create serious to insuperable obstacles to the achievement of [economic viability] . . . unless extensive pre-attack preparations were made to avoid this. Much would depend on whether the attacker did, or did not, attempt to maximize the economic difficulties created by the nonmilitary portion of the attack."[59] Note that even the upper limit requires only 1,000 missiles, with 2-megaton warheads, devoted to urban targets. Threatened by numerous additional missiles, we should probably find that our problems became as insoluble as those that now presumably would face the Soviet Union in an unlimited war.

Next, we should consider the relative propaganda benefits of constructing ABM systems, on the one hand, and achieving space "firsts," on the other. In the long run, there seems to be much wider scope for the latter than for the former. Presumably, space achievements will follow each other for some time to come. By comparison, a deployed ABM system is likely to exhaust its potential for propaganda quickly. And there is a high probability, as indicated earlier, that a one-shot Soviet propaganda achievement in defense would be nullified by the construction of a system by the United States. By contrast, continuing space "firsts" may be possible despite the best U.S. efforts.

From the Soviet point of view, the case for ABM defenses seems stronger as protection against new nuclear powers (Nth countries) than against the United States. The Soviet military establishment probably views the possibility of a future ballistic missile threat from France or Germany as a strong motivation for a defense. Without questioning the legitimacy of these fears — which are naturally of more concern to the Soviet bloc than to ourselves — we may question the legitimacy of an ABM response to the danger. Must a great power, with the capability for complete destruction of a lesser power, take defensive steps to prevent "small" attacks from that country? Or can a great power simply put its trust in deterrence? Finally, is a defense against smaller powers worth an acceleration of the arms race with respect to the other major power? These are some of the questions an American analyst would expect a Soviet specialist in arms control to be concerned with.

Would Soviet Restraint in Procurement Be Risky?

There seems relatively little Soviet risk of "falling behind" in the procurement of ABM systems, and little strategic risk of actually doing so. U.S. procurement requires authorization by Congress, and hence warning is given of our intentions. While the exact period between procurement decisions and various stages of projected deployment may not be known, Soviet decision makers can probably predict these lead times at least roughly. Furthermore, any propaganda advantage that might arise from a first announcement that ABM systems were to be procured by the United States — the "technological triumph" anticipated by General Taylor in an earlier quotation — could probably be nullified by Soviet statements concerning their (possibly fictitious) achievements. Without intelligence information, and possibly even with it, we could not easily determine who procured first: it would be a matter of years between the first completed installation for a city and the twentieth or fiftieth such installation. Neither power can catch the other by surprise, or even credibly claim to have done so, in such a situation.

A more serious problem is the risk that war will occur and, in the absence of defenses, wreak greater destruction than would have occurred otherwise. This assumes that the defenses will actually work and envisions an uncontrolled war or one fought to the bitter end. But it is becoming ever more likely that the destruction caused by the United States in a future strategic war would be determined more by our intentions than by our capability, which for practical purposes is "unlimited." Thus a strategic reserve would probably be maintained, and Soviet cities would be spared to whatever extent American cities had been spared. Such an evolution in doctrine further diminishes the likelihood that defenses would play a significant role. Defenses around cities to be attacked might be overwhelmed with weapons from a large reservoir of such forces, and other defenses might be ignored. (However, a war that involved a spasm of destruction is still possible — especially if Soviet plans provide for no other options. On the other hand, in such a war the Soviet Union might find present and projected defenses of only very, very marginal assistance, if U.S. statements quoted in the previous section are to be believed.)

Would U.S. Restraint Be in the U.S. Interest?

Should we try, as Secretary Rusk wishes, to put some "lid" on a new qualitative arms race? Or should we argue that the only firm basis for our policy is to exploit technology by procurement in old and new areas alike? Shall we seek security through attempts to stay ahead of arms race developments or through attempts to slow them down? Should we discourage Soviet procurement of defenses by threatening to purchase our own in response or encourage it by purchasing them first?

Obviously these decisions involve a host of political issues. Attempts continually to press ahead in the procurement of strategic weapons can be argued to have either good or bad effects on the U.S.-Soviet political relationship. Certainly the decision to press ahead with ballistic missile defenses can be expected to have significant political effects in comparison with other weapons developments.

Undoubtedly, however, a lot depends on the surrounding political climate and the statements issued to accompany the decision. If, as might seem likely, the decision to buy a ballistic missile defense were made in a period of international tension, then the defense would signal precisely what motivated it — increased risk, and fear, of war. If the defense, despite its great expense, were procured in a period of low tension, built slowly, or built in response to a Chinese threat, and if it were combined with increasingly close U.S.-Soviet relations in other spheres, little political harm might be done.

The strategic issues involved in restraint are perhaps somewhat easier to describe. We have at present two alternative methods of limiting damage upon the United States if war occurs. The first involves the construction of a variety of defenses. The second involves the negotiation, or quiet encouragement, of a halt in offensive missile procurement; this is discussed in Chapter Five.

But there is probably little point to restraint in procuring antiballistic missile systems if there is to be no serious effort to establish either an informal or a formal halt in missile procurement. In the absence of such an effort, U.S. ballistic missile defense systems will probably be procured as soon as any one of a variety of events occur over the years. These include a Soviet ballistic missile defense, a new administration more receptive to defense, defensive batteries of higher efficiency, political pressure upon the current U.S. government to do "more," further Chinese progress in weapons development, and so on. In short, restraint, if not pursued vigorously, may not be effective in the long run. Of course, the desirability of restraint depends on the likelihood that it will be effective. If we do not believe that missile defenses can be restrained by treaty, understanding, or unwillingness to make the necessary expenditures, then there is that much less point in trying.

Undoubtedly, the prospects for bilateral restraint in procuring ballistic missile defenses depend first and foremost on the very large expenditures associated with them and on their low expected efficiency. If either one of these factors "improved," the prospects for restraint could be substantially diminished. Second, the prospects for restraint depend upon the perceived risk of war. Third, and considerably less important as a motivating force in either government, is the belief that effective restraints might become possible by treaty or otherwise.

At present, the prospects for success in an attempt to achieve restraint are fairly good in the short run. Both sides probably perceive more clearly than ever before how high the costs of a successful defense might be. This is in part because of experience with large, expensive, and ineffective air defenses. Second, the perceived risk of war is at present low. Many believe that the Cuban crisis was the high-water mark in the risk of nuclear war. Finally, with the U.S. suggestion at Geneva that both parties should consider the possibility of a "freeze" of strategic weapons, the prospects for either informal or formal halts in offensive weapon procurement seem to be improved. In short, restraint might well achieve its objective for a time at least.

What are the strategic objectives of this restraint? We might begin to freeze our present advantage — whatever it may be. We might save tens of billions of dollars required in building defenses and more billions required to achieve the necessary confidence that we could neutralize Soviet defenses. (This last requirement may already have cost us a few billion dollars for the advance development of improvements in Minuteman and Polaris missiles that would otherwise have been unnecessary.)

We might begin to build a relationhip with the Soviet Union that permitted restraint to operate — or deterrence to work — in forestalling other weapon developments, not yet fully perceived, which might become a source of future problems — strategic and political. We might develop a consensus for trying to solve these problems, confidence that the problems could be solved, and some sophistication and expertise as to how this might be done. Many of the subtler of these advantages depend on the way in which the restraint is effected; this is discussed at greater length in the treatment of a freeze in Chapter Five.

A common and somewhat annoying issue is sometimes raised. Should we welcome or fear Soviet prosperity? Most people have resolved this issue in their own minds, but as a nation our position is still uncertain. During the Test Ban hearings, the following exchange occurred:

> *Senator Hickenlooper:* Therefore, if it comes to spending and economic threats we can outspend them and we can go on and really drive them to a position of economic distress if we want to continue with our scientific advancement.
>
> Therefore, who gets what out of this treaty? The Russians — don't they get relieved here from those further tremendous expenditures and charges on their economy, while we abandon that particular advantage . . . ?
>
> *Secretary Rusk:* Senator, I think we could do it but I don't think we could enjoy it.[60]

Should we welcome the possibility that both sides will spend great quantities of money on ABM because we are better at it? Or, as Secretary McNamara argues, should we maintain that "it is very much in our interest to have the Russians expand their educational system and consumer goods distribution. . . ."[61] There is also the possibility that the Soviet Union will procure defenses even if we do not. If they do this for invalid reasons, should we explain the issues to them and try to discourage their waste of resources?

Related Arms Control Issues

There are a number of topics that relate the ABM problems to arms control. Some of these are referred to briefly in turn.

Research and Development in ABM

It is certainly very difficult and not necessarily desirable to prevent research and development in missile defense problems. Antiballistic missilery represents an important area of military interest, and it is only natural that both sides should want to stay on top of development problems. Furthermore, work on defense is necessary for work on offense problems. Many are beginning to believe that this is its main function. During the Test Ban hearings the following exchange occurred.

> *The Chairman* [Senator Fulbright]: If I understand him [Herbert York] correctly, the value of the ABM system is largely in testing the penetrability of our own weapons, and that we should pursue the ABM, but this is its main function.
>
> *Dr. Kistiakowsky:* Yes Sir.[62]

And, in any case, the pressure to continue research is very substantial. For example, in explaining the personal attention which he gives to missile defense, the Secretary of Defense said:

> I do this for a variety of reasons, but among them is to assure myself that every possible action is being taken to accelerate the development. I know of absolutely nothing that was cut back from which we could benefit. I know of no action that could have been taken that wasn't taken during the past year. . . . I met with one of the heads of Bell Labs. . . . on this specific point, to ask him whether there was anything we could do that we had not done to accelerate the program.
> He assured me that all the resources that they could profitably employ were being profitably employed. No additional amount of money could expedite the program.[63]

And of course the Secretary is not merely responding to pressure. Elsewhere he has said:

> Whether we will be successful, I can't predict. But I am not prepared to say that there can be no defense against intercontinental ballistic missiles.[64]

This attitude is entirely appropriate. The development of highly effective ABM systems would not be far more surprising, judged from the vantage point of the parties involved, than the development of ICBM's themselves.

Nevertheless, research and development (R & D) in these areas by *both* powers does not *necessarily* serve our nation's interest. Though it is difficult to know how to prevent or slow it, or even whether we should want to try, several things can be said against R & D. First, the research continues to provide uncertainties and chances for strategic imbalance. Second, if both sides eventually achieve equal chances of making a breakthrough in defense, each will anticipate being at a substantial disadvantage: each may anticipate that it will not itself exploit its periods of defense superiority, but may fear that the other will. Third, whatever breakthroughs are made by either major power are likely to be duplicated, with some time lag, by the other. This has been the course of technology in the past, and it means that each power is, to some extent, working for the other and hence, possibly, working against itself.

A No-First-Procurement Policy

The decision to procure ABM systems is a most important threshold. This is probably the place to hold the line, if arms control considerations argue for restraint. This is because (a) the lead time required for procurement will act as a kind of "firebreak" between a period of no defense (associated with relative strategic security) and a period of defense (associated with possible destabilization of certain weapons systems); (b) the procurement decision is expensive enough to be given full consideration; and (c) present defenses are quite inadequate and leave at least the United States, if not the Soviet Union, very undecided about their effectiveness.

The "firebreak" aspects of a no-first-procurement policy are especially important. A deployed system, unlike a system under development, may suddenly increase in usable effectiveness, or such improvement may be feared. For example, it is clear at the present time that it will take several years to procure *any* system whether it is to defend against one, three, five, ten, or a hundred missiles fired at it simultaneously. Once the system is deployed, however, its capability may be increased, in relatively short periods of time, from being adequate to defend against, say, three missiles to being adequate against ten. This possibility will accelerate the arms race by encouraging procurement of certain nonballistic missiles such as low-altitude cruise missiles. At present, with a "firebreak" of several years, the procurement of such new types of missiles can be continually deferred, so long as major Soviet procurement of missile defense is deferred. In other words, deployment of ABM systems could be expected to accelerate the race by encouraging production and improvement of missiles to cope with offense-defense interactions that would otherwise be considered academic.

Verification for No-First-Procurement Policies

It may be possible merely by using intelligence information to verify that the Soviet Union is not building missile defense batteries. In other words, the United States may be able unilaterally to "police" the Soviet compliance with a no-first-*procurement* understanding. However, some inspection in industrial areas may be required to ensure nonproduction. On the other hand, the verification only of the *nondeployment* of terminal-intercept systems should be simpler and can presumably be done by unilateral U.S. methods.

Advances over Terminal-Intercept Systems

The most important arms race dangers, and the most significant possibilities for protection, will arise from improvements over terminal-intercept systems. The present systems can absorb large amounts of money and encourage further expenditures, but they are unlikely to limit expected casualties to very low absolute numbers or to protect society. Even if the

55

defense drew ahead in terminal-intercept ABM systems, it would still be possible for each side to threaten agriculture, small towns, and so on. But with systems that destroyed enemy missiles in mid-course or immediately after firing, more serious imbalances might arise. Such schemes are always under consideration:

> *Chairman Russell:* You said that we had no alternative to the NIKE family in a defense against missiles. There was a plan at one time, I do not know how far it got, to have some huge missile shot up into the skies [deletion in original]. . . . BAMBI would get all of the decoys and everything else if it would function as it was planned to do.
>
> *Secretary McNamara:* I think we found that the sky was bigger, perhaps, than we anticipated.[65]

Neutralizing these systems may require nonballistic methods of delivery. But a Bambi-type system might be realized at a time when strategic aircraft did not exist in large numbers. While other methods of delivery exist, and some are undoubtedly under development, one side might not be as prepared for such a defense as it would have liked, especially if it had been built quickly. In many ways the real threat to stability of ABM is its potential for just this kind of technological surprise. Some publicly discussed possibilities for such a surprise in ABM systems include the use of cannons for ABM defense and the use of novel offensive weapons effects for the destruction of missiles in their silos.[66] Other notions that Soviet authorities claim to have found in our press include the possibility of throwing up a screen of fine metal fragments in front of missiles, the use of a stream of high-speed neutrons to detonate nuclear warheads of incoming missiles, and the use of electromagnetic energy to destroy or deflect them.[67]

The Arms Race after Deployment

Once terminal-intercept or more advanced systems are deployed, the arms race may very possibly take on a different quality. Each country will be forced, by its opponent's secrecy, to "game" the offense-defense race within its own establishment. This is done to some extent at present. Thus, Dr. Brown testified:

> The United States decided not to deploy the Nike-Zeus because its effectiveness was inadequate against U.S. penetration aids programed for entry into the U.S. inventory before a Nike-Zeus system could be deployed, and we assume the same would be true of Soviet penetration aid capability.[68]

Thus, once deployed, improvements in our missile defense capability would be sought to keep pace with our improving offensive capability, and vice versa; the buying of strategic weapons would be accelerated.

Progress Toward General Disarmament

The procurement of ABM systems may, all things being equal, impede progress toward arms limitation or reductions. We have mentioned the reasons why these systems may accelerate the arms race, and these reasons lend support to our conclusion. There are further reasons, however. Negotiated arms control is complicated by ABM systems. Their effectiveness provides another unknown — an unknown that is particularly hard to assess without very detailed inspection.

We have only just begun to think in concrete terms of the problems of "equalizing" missile capabilities on each side. Should the treaty refer to retained megatonnage, numbers of missiles, gross vehicle weights, or what? But this balancing of missile capabilities may be child's play compared to the problems of balancing defensive capabilities and their relations to penetration mechanisms. The ability of the defense will depend on its tactics, as well as on its radar, computers, types of interceptors, "hardness," complementary civil defense capabilities, and so on. The most detailed inspection and the most complicated negotiations would be necessary to reach a consensus on the comparative utility of a U.S. and a Soviet ABM system — even if measured against a given type of missile. Missiles have many different penetration properties and may be fired in many ways — in salvos, with decoys, with electronic countermeasures, and so on. Again the most detailed inspection would be necessary to ascertain the penetration properties of the adversary's missiles. By comparison, the disarmament problems of balancing the retaliatory capabilities of both sides against undefended cities seem trivial. There will never be any defensive balance as suitable for arms control as no defense at all, so long as mutual deterrence is used to prevent general war.

It is useful to consider defenses as a *form* of disarmament if only to see their disadvantages in a better light. The process of defending one's own country can be viewed as akin to disarming one's opponents. If both sides build efficient defenses, a kind of disarmament will result; but this disarmament would be desired by neither side (at least as concerns its own disarmament), would be unregulated by any control organ, would be subject to the caprices of technology, and would be unrelated to political progress in resolving underlying conflicts. Most important, it would probably be resisted by the defense community in each major power, which has become accustomed to deterring potential enemies with an enormous capacity for retaliatory destruction.

Accidents

One commonly mentioned arms control virtue of ABM systems is their capacity to protect against accidental missile firings. This advantage is generally overstated, however, for two reasons. First, the likelihood that a Soviet or U.S. armed missile will be fired accidentally at a city is very, very small. There has been, as far as I know, no instance of a single missile being fired accidentally. And even if one were fired, the missile might not fire reliably or accurately, and might not be targeted on a defended site. Second, to protect against this threat, scores of ABM batteries would have to be kept on an alert that permitted firing with only a very few minutes warning.

It seems unlikely that the U.S. Department of Defense or the Soviet Defense Ministry would permit so many nuclear warheads to remain on a sustained alert of this kind in noncrisis periods. These short-range missiles, on high alert, probably pose a greater threat to cities than accidental enemy firings — even though their warheads are smaller. The warheads may not be small by the standards of the Hiroshima bomb; hence, an accidental detonation over an urban area, or in a silo, could be very destructive and could possibly trigger actual attacks. Probably, therefore, the defenses would be activated only in crises and would defend only against crisis accidents.

Nth-Country Deterrence

Another argument for ABM systems is that they would be useful for defense against ballistic missile threats from Nth countries. Communist China is generally taken as an example of such a country. Persuasive examples of such a threat in the next decade are harder to find for the United States, though perhaps not so hard to find for the Soviet Union. It is often further argued that while ABM systems may not be sufficient to cope with the threat from one of the two major powers they ought to be capable of effective defense against primitive weapons from less advanced powers. This argument depends upon details.

It might or might not be true that the penetration methods used by a major power would be expensive or complicated. If these methods required small, efficient, light warheads — perhaps to permit large numbers of bombs to be delivered by a single missile — then the necessary techniques might be too advanced for China in the seventies. On the other hand, if penetration could be effected by easily achieved techniques for eluding interception, such as cheap decoys, a country with a few missiles might penetrate quite as easily as one with a large quantity. Since presently foreseeable systems admittedly only "raise the price" to the offense, and since a Chinese threat might concentrate on a few cities, it is possible that an advanced ABM system might be vulnerable to fairly primitive Chinese missiles.

Whether or not the defensive system can protect against a few Chinese missiles or force the Chinese to build twenty missiles rather than two to hold hostage a few defended cities, there will probably remain a large number of undefended sites ranging from cities with a population of a few hundred thousand to such installations as dams, nuclear laboratories, and the RAND Corporation. Hence, the Chinese capacity to destroy probably cannot be denied.

More important, however, than the technical nature of the offense-defense race is an assessment of the situations in which Sino-American relations could call for threat and counterthreat on a level of nuclear violence. Most Asian sources of conflict will either permit direct U.S. defense or involve a low level of violence, with which nuclear threats are not likely to be associated. Thus, we can defend against invasions of Formosa or Japan and, more often than not, will find nuclear strategy irrelevant to guerrilla action in Southeast Asia. As a result, it is difficult to imagine plausible situations in which the United States and China would trade nuclear threats.

Even were these threats to be traded, it is again difficult to imagine situations in which our willingness to take action would depend on the extent to which we had procured a defense against Chinese ballistic missiles. The very best defense would be untried and of uncertain effectiveness. Hence, the President would not be able to depend upon it. The targets that the Chinese selected for their missiles would be unknown in advance, and potential casualties in the United States would be very large in absolute numbers, at least after the initial stages of procurement of intercontinental missiles by the Chinese. Our pattern of action would probably be similar to that of past actions and policies in which we determined the course to be followed relatively independently of detailed calculations of consequences. For some things, we would act as if we would fight to the last man. For others, we would not even take the political risks of adopting a posture of determined resistance. There are probably very few situations in which Presidents calculate the costs sufficiently carefully (and have sufficient confidence in the defense) to make these calculations relevant.

Moreover, whatever the calculated cost to ourselves, the potential cost to our allies will be large. The Chinese cannot fail to perceive the feasibility of directing their threats against our allies in the Far East. Hence, computations of potential cost will be complicated, and our own potential costs will become still less relevant.

It seems that the argument for decreasing expected U.S. losses in order to deter further the Communist Chinese is an application of the now-discredited principles that were applied earlier to the deterrence of Soviet aggression in Europe. As noted then, we do not any longer consider it necessary to have a "credible first-strike capacity" based on our ability to reduce Soviet retaliatory capability to "acceptable" levels in order to deter Soviet threats. These principles of nuclear blackmail are likely to be even less applicable in Asia than in Europe.

Especially important in considering the problem of China is timing. The existence of a Chinese intercontinental ballistic missile threat may be far distant, or it may occur in ten years. At this point it is very difficult to tell. We can build some kind of antiballistic missile system in a few or several years. Since the procurement of defenses is an especially sensitive problem in the development of U.S.-Soviet strategic relations, there is much merit in waiting until the danger is clearly perceived before introducing this potentially disturbing issue. We should avoid being panicked into defenses by the Chinese bomb.

Hard-Point Defense of ICBM's

The discussion has concentrated on the impact of urban defense ABM systems. But ABM's might, in principle, be useful for defending ICBM's. Because ICBM's can more easily be hardened, they are more easily defended with an ABM system than are cities. Nevertheless, such a defense is now considered more expensive than the more efficient multiplication of missile sites. Defense of missile sites would not so definitely encourage offensive weapon procurement as would defense of cities.

Separation of Forces from Urban Targets

Related to the problem of reducing destruction if war occurs is that of keeping or redeploying forces away from urban areas. This might be part of a unilateral or bilateral arms control measure. Point-defense ABM systems (protecting only a city and its surroundings) might discourage this separation by providing a degree of protection for whatever forces might be in or near the city. For example, the deployment of B-58 or F-111 bombers to civilian airfields, as a dispersion operation, could be encouraged in crises by the knowledge that the ABM system defending the nearby city would also defend the airport. However, low-level interception of missiles may not protect delicate aircraft parked in the open or in ordinary hangers.

Destabilization

It is possible that missile defense systems might turn out to be better able to defeat Polaris-type missile systems than ICBM's. This means that a Soviet or U.S. ABM system would have its greatest impact on what has, until now, been considered the most secure part of the strategic force. The effect of such an "undermining" of the strategic posture was indicated in the words of Governor Rockefeller that were quoted earlier in this chapter. By contrast, without ABM, Polaris-type systems would probably guarantee for the present a second-strike capability to whoever builds them.

Inspection

It could be as important to keep secret the locations and workings of ABM systems as it is to keep secret the locations of missile sites. An adversary might want to attack ABM installations or to know which targets are not protected by them. And it certainly would be useful for an enemy to know specific characteristics of the system if it is to neutralize it. Therefore, Soviet procurement of ABM systems might encourage, and seems likely in no significant way to discourage, Soviet secrecy. This has implications for many other disarmament agreements.

Nuclear Diffusion and the Denuclearization of Europe

If ABM systems become efficient, particularly against IRBM's, there may be some interest in deploying them around European cities. Whether or not the warheads of interceptor missiles could be kept under U.S. control is not clear. If the weapons were maintained on alert and the systems were owned by the European powers, it might be necessary to relinquish control of the warheads. Conceivably, this difficulty might be avoided, but if it were not, it would constitute nuclear diffusion. In either case, denuclearization policies would be defeated by European ABM systems unless special provision were made for ABM interceptor warheads. While there is no particular theoretical reason why this exception cannot be made, the matter would probably be, at the least, a source of difficulty in negotiation.

Qualitative Acceleration of the Arms Race

At the present time, efforts to neutralize the defenses of terminal-intercept systems emphasize the saturation of the defense with decoys or the simultaneous arrival of missiles. This need not remain the case, and it is certainly conceivable that new weapon effects or large warheads of some kind might be found very effective for overcoming defenses. In this case the procurement of ABM systems could have unfortunate collateral effects on the arms race. The *kind* of effect to be feared could be an increased relative effectiveness of weapons in orbit. Depending on technical details, weapons in orbit might or might not be able to penetrate systems that were designed to counter a ballistic missile trajectory from a particular continent. If these weapons turned out to be cost effective against deployed ABM systems, there would be a temptation to abrogate the present U.S.-Soviet understanding not to put weapons of mass destruction in outer space. Another example might be "dirty" bombs designed to be exploded in rural areas and to cover defended cities down wind with long-lasting fallout.

Catalytic War (Or Unauthorized Behavior)

The procurement of ABM systems seems to decrease the probability of a war initiated by a third party because it makes it more difficult to destroy an urban target in either the United States or the Soviet Union. However, although the catalytic attack itself need not be successful it can cause dangerous strains and hasty actions, and, of course, an attack need not necessarily be on city targets — an airfield might do as well. If malevolence is assumed, as opposed to inadvertence, it may be reasonable to expect an attack sufficiently concerted to achieve penetration. Probably the major benefit of a deployed system is the increased likelihood that Moscow and Washington, viewed as command posts, would survive.

Nuclear Materials Cutoff

There has been discussion of a nuclear materials cutoff. While we cannot be certain without reference to classified information, it seems that the procurement of ABM systems would probably require such large amounts of fissionable material, either here or in the Soviet Union, that a bilateral cutoff would become impossible. After all, thousands of interceptors may be procured.

Test Ban Treaty

It is generally believed (and the Secretary of Defense has so testified) that the United States can procure an ABM system without abrogating the Test Ban Treaty to conduct relevant tests. This may also be true for the Soviet Union. However, it is possible that the Soviet Union would find tests useful to develop an efficient interceptor warhead, and both powers could be tempted to test the system against certain nuclear effects. For instance, the Director of the Los Alamos Scientific Laboratory, Norris E. Bradbury, testified that, although tested warheads existed "on the shelf" for ABM interceptors, "we could look to making better ones . . . ," and General Taylor has stated: "Both sides could achieve an antiballistic missile, but one with less desirable characteristics than would be the case if additional atmospheric tests were conducted." [69]

Classified information should be available to determine whether the development of interceptor warheads can be carried out easily underground. In any case, this problem has obvious interactions with an extension of the Test Ban Treaty to underground tests. Whether a major power might some day announce that its security required it to test an ABM system against atmospheric nuclear effects, it is obviously impossible to say. But certainly the decision to procure and deploy a large-scale system must tempt decision makers to fill any gaps in their knowledge of its effectiveness. Again, classified information may make it possible to determine the significance of such gaps.

What Is to Be Done?

It is quite evident that there is a case for attempting to avoid, rather than to build, ballistic missile defenses and the complementary types of defense that they may require. This case depends, of course, on certain values and estimates. One must decide what one believes about the risk of war, the value of resources, the nature of the U.S.-Soviet competition, and so on. But there is a case worth considering, and it raises the question of what might be done to induce restraint.

There are two quite different ways of avoiding the procurement of ballistic missile defenses and some intermediate possibilities. First of all, we could resort to formal or informal agreement.

A formal agreement prohibiting ballistic missile defenses would almost surely have to prohibit as well an increase in the number of offensive missiles. While it might be possible to imagine an agreement to freeze defenses without an agreement to engage in actual disarmament of missiles, it is very difficult, for political reasons, to imagine an agreement to avoid defenses without even a *freeze* of offensive weapons.

The role of antiballistic missile systems in the context of formal agreements is discussed in Chapters Four and Five. It seems necessary to include restraints on antiballistic missile systems in either a freeze or reduction agreement since, otherwise, the strategic presuppositions of the agreement would change so drastically as to imperil the agreement. However, in some cases, the avoidance of missile defenses could be based on a tacit understanding underlying the treaty. In any case, the restraints on antiballistic missile systems are likely to be the most important and valuable aspects of either the freeze or the reduction agreement in terms of resources saved and strategic stability ensured.

Leaving the discussion of formal agreements for later, the question arises as to whether there are useful ways for maintaining tacit restraints on deployment and procurement. Whether or not these restraints could be effective for a long period, they might well be useful in the short run.

The most important way of discouraging the procurement of ABM defenses is to make them unlikely to work. We should spend the money necessary to ensure, so far as we can, that the Soviets will think ballistic missile defenses are ineffective. And we should emphasize the impact of their actions on our own.

For example, it might be of interest for the Secretary of Defense to discuss, in open testimony, his estimates of (*a*) Soviet costs to procure an ABM system of a type being considered by them; and (*b*) the costs to the U.S. strategic system to ensure penetration. It is quite possible that the Secretary of Defense is better able to compare these costs than any person in the Soviet Union. The comparison may be revealing — and it may be observed by important members of the Soviet bureaucracy who would otherwise not be shown such discouraging information.

It might also be useful to point out that very large systems are required to guarantee the recovery of a country. In particular, we should not permit a Soviet defense ministry to persuade relevant civilian decision makers that it is useful and significant to protect ten or twenty large cities, if in fact it is not. In other words, we might indicate that the costs are going to be quite high if anything is to be gained.

It seems that there is sometimes a very serious doctrinal lag in the Soviet system. This might be documented and discussed publicly by U.S. officials. Such discussion could discredit Soviet authorities and Soviet departments responsible for procuring useless defenses in the past. Although existing documentation would be classified, it might be declassified at little "cost" on the authority of high civilian officials in the Department of Defense. The policy of documenting Soviet procurement mistakes might be extended into a policy of ridiculing Soviet defenses and emphasizing their inadequacy. Our statements might be as specific or unspecific as seemed desirable. (This tactic could of course have undesired consequences, and should be considered with much more care than we have yet given it.)

Still stronger action might call for explanation in general terms of the penetration capabilities necessary to avoid the Soviet defense. For instance, if our missiles have very advanced techniques, we might point out that certain decoys will easily saturate the Soviet system, clearing the way for U.S. missiles with even more advanced capabilities. Some Congressional testimony is already close to this. And these statements would increase the credibility of our assertion.

Another method for deterring Soviet procurement is to threaten action that will more than re-establish our existing advantage. We could point out that Soviet procurement might just tip the scales toward U.S. procurement. This would degrade the Soviet offensive missiles or require the Soviets to expend additional resources to keep up. If it were clearly U.S. policy to "match" Soviet procurement of ABM missiles for a substantial number of cities, this inevitable response could be passed along. In fact, if it were our policy *not* to procure the present ABM systems under any circumstances, it might even be useful to say this forcefully, as it would presumably underscore any accompanying statements attesting to the worthlessness of Soviet procurement. Another way to threaten dramatically to maintain an advantage is to propose procurement of a substantial number of nonballistic missiles in response to a Soviet ballistic missile system.

It might also be useful to describe the arms race in terms that indicated the incompatibility of defense and deterrence. We might point out that another "round," once started, would continue and lead to risks and costs for the Soviet Union that cannot be clearly visualized at present. Space-based systems might be pointed out as a destabilizing possibility.

Finally, most of the methods just described for discouraging Soviet procurement could also be used by the Soviet Union to discourage procurement by us. Thus, the Soviet Union could threaten to match our procurement, offer to restrain their own, warn that bilateral procurement would assist their posture, and so on. In addition, the Soviet Union could, by offering various kinds of inspection, very substantially increase the feasibility, from the American point of view, of a no-first-procurement policy. Such inspection might only have to take place in or around urban areas. This would minimize its conflict with the demands of Soviet military secrecy.

Current Prospects

A year after the reports appeared of Soviet missile systems around Leningrad, there seemed to be little further indication of Soviet progress. The rumors of such defensive systems may have been of the kind that periodically sweep the defense community. For example, in January 1965, John A. McCone, Director of the Central Intelligence Agency, briefed Congressional committees that dealt with defense, foreign policy, and atomic energy, and a UPI report expressed the change in emphasis like this:

> Some Congressional leaders expressed concern about Russia's progress on a missile killer when the limited nuclear test-ban treaty was debated nearly two years ago.
> At that time there were reports that antimissile-missiles were being deployed near Leningrad. The concern has not abated, but it now involves possible Russian progress *in the art* of intercepting and destroying ballistic missiles.[70] (Italics added.)

Evidently, the risk has diminished that the Soviets would greatly encourage our procurement of a missile defense by a premature attempt to claim that their own system existed.

In part for this reason, but also for reasons about to be described, the crucial question seemed to have become whether the United States would, without such provocation, set about building some kind of missile defense anyway. The growing likelihood that we might initiate such a new round in procurement was given credence by a variety of signals.

When the fiscal 1965 budget was introduced (in early 1964), the Secretary of Defense began to justify our rather large missile force by emphasizing its capacity to "limit damage" by striking Soviet forces after our own had been attacked. This doctrine seems to have been shaped by a desire to deny our capacity to strike Soviet forces first — the much debated "counterforce capability" — while justifying an otherwise apparently excessive number of missiles. This was the first time since the civil defense controversy that the United States was thinking in terms of limiting damage if war occurred and it had some unexpected aftereffects. It was immediately obvious to the cost-conscious Defense Department that there were a variety of competitive and complementary methods for limiting damage. If one was to be tried, others also had to be considered. Perhaps civil defense was more effective than the use of missiles to attack Soviet residual forces. If so, civil defense would have to be given a higher priority. More generally, missile defense, bomber defense, and antisubmarine defense had to be considered closely and in relation to one another.

The effect of this perception was to give some impetus to the idea of ballistic missile defense but also to undermine the damage-limiting notion itself. If damage limiting implied ballistic missile defense, then the latter seemed more reasonable and the former potentially more expensive than had been formerly believed.

As a result, many studies were evidently done on ballistic missile defense. When the Secretary of Defense testified on the fiscal 1966 budget, he discussed damage-limiting capability at some length. The main impression given by the testimony is that the degree to which we should aim to protect ourselves against the possibility of war is still very much undecided. The testimony shows an increased awareness of the ability to buy different amounts of defense; this tends to increase the likelihood that some will eventually be bought and hence that more will be procured later.

One of the most interesting parts of the testimony was the following table, which depicts the results of a Soviet attack in the early seventies. The "Early Urban Attack" assumes that cities are attacked at the outset. The "Delayed Urban Attack" assumes that attacks on cities are sufficiently delayed to permit us to attack Soviet forces effectively. The table illustrates the effects, in reducing casualties, of successively larger expenditures in initial investment. The first $5 billion would be

ESTIMATED EFFECT ON U.S. FATALITIES OF ADDITIONS TO THE
APPROVED DAMAGE-LIMITING PROGRAM
(BASED ON 1970 POPULATION OF 210 MILLION)

Additional Investment	Millions of U.S. Fatalities	
	Early Urban Attack	Delayed Urban Attack
0	149	122
5	120	90
15	96	59
25	78	41

spent for fallout shelters. The $15 billion investment would add some ballistic missile defense and some bomber defenses, and the $25-billion investment would add more of each.

The emphasis on damage-limiting seems to have changed somewhat in its rationale from the previous year. In 1964, the Secretary of Defense had claimed that studies continued to show the utility of attacking Soviet forces after we had ourselves been attacked. These were described as residual forces that could not be launched at once. In the more recent testimony, the use of missile attacks for effective damage limiting seemed to depend primarily on a Soviet delay in attacking American cities, a delay that was described parenthetically as "an unlikely contingency." [71] Part of this change of emphasis stemmed from the fact that the more recent testimony considered Soviet forces in the early seventies, while the previous discussion was associated with Soviet forces in the late sixties. For whatever reason the change was made, it tended to diminish the justification for damage-limiting expenditures.

As for the central item in the defense package, Nike-X, the Secretary planned to "reexamine the question of production and deployment of the NIKE-X system again next year." He noted:

> Considering the vast amount of development, test and evaluation work still to be accomplished, deferral of this decision to the FY 1967 budget should not delay an initial operational capability by many months beyond what we could expect to achieve if we were to start production in FY 1966.[72]

Thus the situation remained quiescent, but the United States could hardly be expected to avoid a decision forever. It is particularly important to appreciate the fact that figures based on Soviet capabilities in the early seventies could be most misleading if our estimates were too high. In the absence of a treaty prohibiting, among other things, procurement of ballistic missile defenses, the United States could eventually find that its reasons against procurement had been undercut by a Soviet decision to relax their efforts.

Among the arguments for buying a missile defense, one achieved especial prominence in 1964. The Chinese explosion of a bomb encouraged the argument that an ABM system was required for defense against a possible forthcoming Chinese intercontinental missile. However, Secretary McNamara noted that studies showed "the lead time for additional nations to develop and deploy an effective ballistic missile system capable of reaching the United States is greater than we require to deploy the defense." [73]

There is another level on which the prospects for ballistic missile defenses can be dimly perceived. This is in the dialogue between the two major powers, which invariably contains echoes of the changing likelihoods that one side or the other will push ahead. This dialogue is carried on through articles, papers, and pronouncements of various kinds. In early 1965, two interesting Soviet commentaries appeared.

The first, an article by General N. Talensky on "Anti-missile Systems and Disarmament," appeared in the Soviet journal *International Affairs*. It referred to Western writing and considered many of the themes just presented. General Talensky minimized the danger that an effective antimissile system in the hands of an aggressive state could intensify the danger of an outbreak of war. In this he was in agreement with a variety of American strategists who did not believe that the literal "stability" of the situation was imperiled by prospective defenses. General Talensky went even further and argued that stability might be *enhanced* by the resultant shifts in emphasis between defensive and deterrent weapon systems.

The Soviet officer conceded that the possibility could not be ruled out that "the side lagging" in the construction of defensive systems might build up its attack capabilities, thus accelerating the arms race. This is probably the crucial point to be communicated to Soviet decision makers (as well as to our own — but they know it). Somewhat illogically, however, he maintained that the side which made a "spurt" in the means of attack as a response to defensive measures would instantly expose its aggressive intentions and stand condemned as the aggressor. The general further maintained that the early implementation of general and complete disarmament was the one reasonable alternative to a race between antimissile systems.

In short, this declared Soviet view seemed to reserve its position on defensive systems, to assert its right to push ahead, and to deny our right to respond with further procurement of offensive weapons. It did not rule out the possibility, however, that it would respond in this way to our procurement of defensive systems. Perhaps most interesting, it did not contain the usual Soviet assertion that a Soviet defense already existed.

The possibility of a race in the procurement of antiballistic missiles is conceded; the implementation of general and complete disarmament is held out as an alternative to the procurement race. If such progress is put off "indefinitely," while the means of nuclear attack are built up, then a peace-loving state could not forgo the creation of its own defense.

All in all, this Soviet approach is a considerable step forward over other Soviet positions. Although it denies most of the Western premises at least once, it also concedes most of them at one time or another, and it obviously understands them.

A second Soviet scientist, Academician V. Emelyanov, also

devoted some space to this topic in an interesting paper, "What Scientists Say," in *New Times*. Most of the paper is devoted to conversations that Emelyanov had with Americans.

In these conversations, one American says that antimissile systems will not work and goes on to add that "if the whole thing is taken over by Big Business, arms spending will grow to monstrous proportions." Emelyanov's self-quoted remarks show him to be fiercely skeptical of the possibility of avoiding defense. But comments interspersed into the reported conversation say approvingly:

> The problem of anti-missile missiles has been the cause of much concern among the American scientists. If Big Business comes into the picture it will be hard to stop their production. For it is a profitable business and no capitalist is likely to forfeit his profits.

It is possible, therefore, that Soviet spokesmen may become sober and responsible in their statements on ballistic missile defense. Premier Khrushchev referred to the Soviet ability to hit a "fly in the sky," but the days for such words from Soviet leaders may be over. Spokesmen such as Marshal Sokolovskii continue to say: "We have successfully solved the complex and extremely important problem of intercepting and destroying enemy rockets in flight." [74] But in February 1965, an editorial in *Kommunist* declared that forces in the United States "want to exhaust the Soviet Union economically by imposing a new arms race on Moscow." [75] These apprehensions may well inhibit Soviet statements and actions that would encourage such forces.

BOMBER DISARMAMENT: UNDERLYING CONSIDERATIONS, 1964

Introduction

THIS CHAPTER deals with bomber disarmament as a partial measure that might be agreed upon by the two major powers in the absence of more general progress toward disarmament.

The conclusions are simple and can be summarized here. The U.S. proposal for reciprocal destruction of obsolescent B-47's and outdated Soviet Badgers does not go far enough.* Such an agreement might well prevent further bomber disarmament for political reasons and would, from a strategic point of view, do little more than would result from a few more years of obsolescence. On the other hand, the Soviet suggestion that all airforce bombers throughout the world should be destroyed seems — if taken literally — to be both ill-defined and unworkable.† This chapter proposes instead something that is likely to be desirable on strategic grounds, although it may be politically infeasible either here or in the

---

* William C. Foster, Director of the U.S. Arms Control and Disarmament Agency, and Secretary of State Dean Rusk broached this possibility informally to Soviet officials on the occasion of the signing of the Test Ban in Moscow.[1]

† The Soviet proposal was contained in a memorandum presented to the Eighteen Nation Disarmament Conference on January 29, 1964. The Soviet Union has since suggested that there is a possibility of "agreeing to start with the major powers," has promised to be "flexible" in negotiating, and has indicated that it will come forward with a series of proposals.[2]

Soviet Union. Both sides might simply phase out (and destroy) B-47's and Badgers and begin proportional (heavy) bomber disarmament by phasing out (and destroying) Soviet Bears and Bisons along with U.S. B-52's over the next few years. The U.S. case for heavy-bomber dismantlement is surprisingly strong. It would not only eliminate the Soviet bomber threat, but it would also free missiles now tied down by the need to target Soviet bomber bases and air defense installations. Savings would result from smaller air defense efforts and from the elimination of bomber maintenance costs. And bombers are playing an ever more marginal role in U.S. strategy — hence their dismantlement is not a great loss.*

U.S. Bombers and Soviet Air Defenses

Composition of the U.S. Bomber Force

The United States has several thousand planes capable of dropping nuclear weapons. Since very small tactical nuclear weapons exist, almost any plane could in principle deliver a nuclear weapon if no penetration or range problems existed. Moreover, carrier- and European-based fighter-bombers carrying nuclear weapons could reach targets at varying distances within the Soviet Union. With the procurement of the F-111

---

* As of late 1965, some of the U.S. B-52's are being used for conventional attacks in South Vietnam against areas under Viet Cong control. This and related uses of B-52's for conventional attacks (such as for bombing China, if need be) are of controversial utility. For those who are persuaded of their merit, the following further arguments for dismantlement of bombers should be considered. First, bilateral destruction of heavy bombers would preclude analogous Soviet actions in support of North Vietnam or China. Second, the agreement itself might influence Soviet ability and willingness to push for a termination of the war in Vietnam. Third, other aircraft might substitute for the B-52's (unless one assumes that their maintenance is required for strategic purposes, which this chapter rejects, the costs of using B-52's in Vietnam are very high). Fourth, a limited number of B-52's might be retained, for example, 200 instead of 700.

It should also be noted as this book goes to press, that the B-47's are no longer in the operational inventory. This has little effect on the argument, which can refer to destruction of mothballed B-47's instead.

(TFX), the distinction between fighters and strategic bombers will be still further clouded. This plane will be capable of flying to Europe without refueling. It is known to have a non-stop ferry range of 3,300 miles and a bomb load capability of 10,000 lb.[3] It will cost "less than $3 or 3½ million per plane," according to Harold Brown, Director of Defense Research and Engineering.[4] It will be capable of aerial refueling.

There is little likelihood of eliminating these tactical bomber capabilities from the U.S. arsenal in any agreement that does not simultaneously have far-reaching implications for many other weapon systems. Such planes are designed for limited war, particularly for limited war in Europe. There is relatively little uncertainty in the Department of Defense concerning their utility. This is in sharp contrast to the controversy over strategic aircraft. For instance, Dr. Brown testified:

> In the case of tactical aircraft, Senator Thurmond, I think that the need will continue, so far or as far forward as I can see, 10 years, 20 years, indefinitely.
>
> For strategic aircraft it is harder to say. I am pretty sure the strategic aircraft will be important and useful as bombardment vehicles for at least another 5 years. They may be important for another 10 years, but I am not so sure about what happens then or after then.[5]

Therefore, while it is highly likely that tactical aircraft would be treated in detail in a general disarmament agreement, it seems equally clear that any partial measures or first steps that are to involve bombers *alone* should emphasize strategic aircraft.

As of 1964, the U.S. force of strategic bombers fell into three fleets:

1. About 630 subsonic B-52 (Stratofortress) heavy bombers. These planes have a best range of 10,000–12,500 miles and are capable of aerial refueling. Some carry only multimegaton free-fall bombs, but others, alternatively or in addition, carry two Hound Dog (4 megaton) missiles capable of traveling a distance of about 600 miles (gross weight: 450,000–488,000 lb;

typical performance: 600 mph at 50,000 ft). These planes became operational in the period 1955–1962.

2. About 700 subsonic B-47 (Stratojet) medium bombers. These planes can be refueled in flight. They have a best range of 3,200 miles (gross weight: 200,000 lb; typical performance: 600 mph at 40,000 ft). These planes became operational in the period 1952–1957.

3. About 80 supersonic B-58 (Hustler) medium bombers. These planes can be refueled in flight and have a range of more than 5,000 miles at their cruising speed (gross weight: 160,000 lb; for short distances they can travel at twice the speed of sound. These planes became operational in 1960.[6]

The B-52 subsonic heavy bombers make up the largest and the most important element in the strategic bomber force. A B-52 can fly from the United States to the Soviet heartland with a 10,000-pound bomb load and return without refueling.[7] These bombers are *not* being phased out of the existing force, and decline in their numbers projected by the Defense Department for the period 1964–1968 is based on expectations of attrition. In all, 744 of these aircraft have been procured. No further procurement is planned, and it is estimated that 630 will be in the force in 1968.[8] (Since there are 45 planes in a wing, this represents 14 wings of B-52's.) However, the last B-52 was procured in 1962, and the production lines have been closed down. There are no serious advocates of further procurement of B-52's, although there is some uncertainty concerning their expected lifetime. For instance, the Air Force Chief of Staff was asked how long the B-58's and B-52's could be kept in operation. He replied:

> This is very difficult to answer . . . ; everyone assumes that these airplanes are going to go on indefinitely, that we will be able to fly them indefinitely. This may not be the case. They may wear out sooner than we think they are going to wear out.
>
> There is a lot that we don't know about fatigue in these modern high-performance airplanes. So this bothers me, that we may have to discard these airplanes sooner than we think.[9]

Part of the problem relates to the difficulties that the airplanes are expected to have in penetrating Soviet defenses, should war occur. Expensive modifications (retrofitting) in the B-52 structures have been undertaken in anticipation of these problems. Through 1964, retrofitting had already cost $1.6 billion, with an additional $306 million requested for the fiscal year 1965.

The aging B-47's are gradually being phased out of service on a schedule that has not changed since fiscal year 1962. The schedule called for the last B-47 to leave active service in 1966. In early 1964, there were still about 700 such planes in the operational force.

The B-58 bombers are not being phased out of the force, but no more are likely to be procured. It is estimated that, as a result of attrition, there will be 72 B-58's in the force in 1968. These bombers have had problems of reliability, as evidently all bombers do. For example, in 1955, three years after the first procurement of B-47's, they had an in-commission rate of only 65 percent.[10] Secretary McNamara recalls being at Omaha on a day when "almost literally all of our B-58 bombers were unavailable for alert status because of mechanical failures." Later testimony indicates that these reliability problems have eased. But the unit cost of B-58 bombers has been high ($10 to $12 million), and since B-58's have a smaller bomb-load capability and shorter range than a B-52, they are not especially favored.[11] The generals LeMay, Power, and White would all prefer to buy additional B-52's rather than B-58's, and Secretary of Defense McNamara concurs with this judgment.[12]

U.S. Attitudes Toward Bombers

One school of opinion in the United States is concerned that the manned bomber will disappear, and believes that a new fleet of bombers would be useful. In part this belief seems to stem from a conservative view of what constitutes utility in strategic weapons. For instance, General Maxwell Taylor explained in 1959 that the other Joint Chiefs did not agree with him that we then had "an excess number of strategic weapons and weapons systems in the atomic retaliatory force." They felt, according to him, that "there are so many incalculable factors that you can never overinsure in this field." [13]

But the urge to maintain bombers also arises from other factors, not all of which are especially subject to strategic analysis. Bombers are tried and true, but missiles are not, in the eyes of their supporters. Often there are evident personal attachments to bombers. The top Air Force generals and even some of the senators most concerned about bombers have had long personal experience in flying or directing them. Their concern is associated almost invariably with the "flexibility" that would be lost if there were no manned strategic system. Evidently any manned system will do, no matter what its purpose.*

Perhaps a more fundamental obstacle to bomber disarmament, however, lies in the accumulated influence of the Strategic Air Command (SAC) and its bomber forces as a result of its prime responsibility for deterrence during the fifties. For instance, in *On Thermonuclear War*, Herman Kahn compares the British Empire's dependence on the British fleet with the U.S. dependence on the SAC bomber fleet.[15] Those who once molded this all-important force are naturally reluctant to see it disbanded. And the apparent efficiency of the Strategic Air Command officers in discharging their responsibilities has, over the years, heightened their influence both in Con-

---

* Secretary of the Air Force Eugene Zuckert testified: "We believe that as the general [LeMay] has pointed out, that our proper strategic posture demands some kind of a manned system because of the flexibility it gives you. If the B-70 proves to be a blind alley for any reason, we have to explore all the other methods because we have to come up with a manned system, in our opinion." He then referred to B-70 (a 2,000-mph supersonic bomber devoted to reconnaissance), Dromedary (a long-endurance, large, slow airplane designed to fly up to 48 hours, but not to penetrate defenses at all), and a low-altitude penetrator.[14]

gress and elsewhere. This only begins to indicate the political obstacles to bomber disarmament.

The Strategic Role of U.S. Bombers

The strategic role of our bombers is severely limited by four characteristics. Bombers are vulnerable on the ground, slow to target, of uncertain penetration capability, and they must be committed at a very early stage in a war.

First, the bomber force cannot be depended upon for a high rate of survival from a surprise enemy attack because of its great vulnerability on the ground. In normal periods, in order to minimize this vulnerability, half of the SAC bomber force is maintained on a fifteen-minute ground alert with a small number on airborne alert. The fifteen-minute warning is supposed to be provided by BMEWS (Ballistic Missile Early Warning System) stations in Clear, Alaska, Thule, Greenland, and Fylingdales, Great Britain.[16] Such notice would not be given if missiles were fired over the Antarctic — a widely discussed possibility that was mentioned by Premier Khrushchev (but which would be expensive in accuracy and in pay load) — or if submarine-launched missiles were used. Similarly, the Cuban missiles would have "outflanked" the warning system.*

The submarine-launched missiles, especially, pose a potential threat to ground-based bombers. Secretary McNamara believes that "toward the latter part of this decade . . . we must anticipate that submarine-launched missiles or others coming with very little, if any, warning will very probably destroy the majority of aircraft on the ground." [17]

Against such problems the Department of Defense has maintained the capability to fly one-eighth of the B-52 force

* If there had been no heavy bombers in the U.S. force, the strategic concern over Soviet missiles in Cuba would have been diminished since the missiles would have had no highly profitable targets. This indicates one of the ways in which bomber disarmament will have a stabilizing effect.

on airborne alert for about one year. (The Air Force had asked for one-fourth.)[18] And the number of SAC bases has steadily grown in number. SAC now presents 55 domestic air-base targets and 13 foreign targets, and, in times of immediate emergency, the force can be dispersed to 100 fields.*

Even after such dispersal, however, SAC would still provide a first-priority target. Consider, for instance, the situation in 1964. General Maurice Preston testified in 1960 that SAC's ultimate goal was one squadron (one-third of a wing of 45 bombers) of B-52's per base and one wing of B-47's per base. Since, in 1964 figures, there are about 15 wings of B-47's remaining (the 700 planes noted earlier), 42 squadrons of B-52's (the 14 wings noted earlier), and about 6 squadrons of B-58's (the 80 planes noted earlier), this would require 63 bases. Since the 55 domestic and 13 foreign bases referred to exceed this number, the goal has evidently been effectively achieved. Nevertheless, the "bonus" to enemy attack that catches the bombers on their bases would be somewhere between 15 to 1 (heavy-bomber bases) and 45 to 1 (medium-bomber bases), even assuming that the bombers carry nothing more than the single H-bomb that Secretary McNamara indicated would destroy every bomber on its base.[20] With 100 fields, the average bonus would be at least 14 to 1 since there are about 1,400 bombers. It should be emphasized that the bombers with their expected BMEWS warning would not represent an adequate deterrent in the absence of protected missile systems. In this sense, they do not provide adequate backup protection for a situation in which our missiles could be successfully attacked.

* Such dispersal plans were described to Congress as far back as 1956.
"*Colonel Nichols:* Now we have a dispersal plan in SAC. It works like this: Each one of our bases, let's take the base at Fairchild, we have two wings there, each wing will have a plan and the plan will have the aircraft say take off from Fairchild and come down to these green areas. They are what we call orbit areas.
"At that position the aircraft will circle. He will await then instructions from his home base if it is not destroyed or from another source if his home base is destroyed, and then he will either land at what we call our dispersal base or go back to Fairchild, depending on what he is told." [19]

The second limitation of bombers is that they are slow to target. If a bomber has a top speed of 500 mph and must travel 2,000, 4,000, or 6,000 miles, it will take 4, 8, or 12 hours to reach its target. Several different missile salvos can take place in this time. This means that bombers are especially unsuited to the "damage-limiting" strategy advocated by the Department of Defense. Only a "very, very, very, low percentage" of the effective forces will be bombers, despite the fact that they are capable of carrying a much larger number of megatons than are existing missiles. This was discussed by Secretary McNamara:

> *Secretary McNamara:* What percentage of the force that destroys the Soviet Union is delivered by bombers? The answer to that is a very, very, low percentage. . . .
>
> *Mr. Ford:* If that is the case . . . why do you keep bombers in the force at all until 1968?
>
> *Secretary McNamara:* Because they add some insurance and because certain targets may be more effectively destroyed by bombers assuming the bomber can get there before the targets have been launched against the United States, *and that is quite an assumption.*[21] (Italics added.)

The third limiting characteristic of bombers is a "substantial range between the optimistic and pessimistic estimates" of the number that will penetrate the Soviet air defenses. (This uncertainty is itself undesirable since we should prefer to have our deterrent capability unequivocal.) And in both cases, "a higher proportion of the Minuteman force than of the B-52 force can be counted upon to reach targets in a retaliatory strike." Bombers are also rated lower in "systems dependability," by which is meant that the uncertainties associated with them are harder to estimate. Thus the Secretary of Defense has noted that "we can predict the results of a missile attack with greater confidence than those of a bomber attack." [22] The extent of these uncertainties has been indicated by General Thomas White, who asserted, a few years ago, in reference to U.S. bombers: "All might get through in one case and then there might be a great loss in another." [23]

Speaking more generally of free-fall bombing, the Secretary of Defense termed it "nearly impossible" by the end of the sixties.* This means that planes would have to be dependent upon their own guided missiles which would permit an attack from a distance. But a missile of this type, Secretary McNamara noted in canceling one (the Skybolt),

> . . . could not make a worthwhile contribution to our strategic capability since it would combine the disadvantages of the bomber with those of the missile. It would have the bomber's disadvantages of being soft and concentrated and relatively vulnerable on the ground and the bomber's slow time to target. But it would not have the bomber's advantageous payload and accuracy, nor would it have the advantages usually associated with a manned system. It would have the lower payload and poorer accuracy of the missile. . . .[25]

The Secretary of Defense indicates as a fourth limitation that bombers must be "committed . . . very early" in a war and cannot be used "in a controlled and deliberate way." [26] In particular, the widely used argument that bombers can be "recalled" is quite misleading: invulnerably based missiles do not need to be fired in advance and hence the ability to be recalled is not an issue with them. Furthermore, recalling bombers is dangerous and difficult. They are not, in fact, very "recallable." The recalled fleet has tired, if not exhausted, crews, and somewhere in the system there must be low, if not empty, fuel tanks. If the recall is a mistake, the bombers may have been effectively neutralized. Bombers are, for this reason, not even very capable of accepting an enemy surrender —

---

* "*Secretary McNamara:* . . . we will be in serious difficulty by the end of the decade if at that point our strategic force is dependent upon free-fall bombs as the primary weapon of attack, because no one in a responsible position at the Pentagon that I am aware of believes that free-fall bombs can be placed over the prime targets in the Soviet Union at the end of this decade.

"*Senator Stennis:* Why?

"*Secretary McNamara:* Because by that time the air defense systems of the Soviet Union will be such as to make it nearly impossible for an airplane to advance to a position over the target so that it would be in position to launch free-fall bombs against that target." [24]

the risk of recalling them to vulnerable bases (if there were no missiles) could make it impossible. Most important, the time for recall is limited. Congress has been told that civilian decision makers would have to make some (recalling) decision within one and a half hours of the time the bomber force was launched toward its targets.[27] (Obviously this does not refer to an airborne alert which might be maintained for relatively long periods.)

As a result of these restrictions, the utility of bombers is limited to certain special uses as "supplementary devices to the main force." * What are these supplementary uses? *Air Force and Space Digest* complained that

> No mention is [being] made of the position that manned strategic aircraft greatly enhance operational flexibility by allowing: recall of an attack; unmistakable displays of resolve, through stepped-up airborne alerts and large-scale maneuvers, such as were used in the Cuban crisis; wartime assessment of target damage; location and destruction of mobile targets; a close matching of the weapon to the target; and, when the occasion calls for it, the use of very-high-yield warheads.[29]

We have discussed recall of an attack. The threatening nature of a fleet of bombers on airborne alert is a more plausible but still quite dubious consideration. It has received wide attention.† In answer to a written question from Senator Margaret Chase Smith, Secretary McNamara said that the SAC bomber

---

* This comment of the Secretary of Defense was reinforced by the assertion that "There is no plan in the Air Force that I know of, or no thought of any plan to substitute air launch for sea and land launch for the great bulk of the megatonnage." [28]

† "*Senator Cannon:* When we get to the point that we are practically phased out without manned bombers under our present program we would have no method of making a visible display of strength insofar as SAC's posture is concerned, would we?

"*General LeMay:* With missiles you cannot do anything except to say, 'I will shoot my missiles,' that is all.

"*Senator Cannon:* You cannot very well take a picture of a man with his thumb about 6 inches above the trigger and say, 'He is going to put it on down if you don't do such and such.' That doesn't give you much of a bargaining point, does it?

"*General LeMay:* That is correct." [30]

fleet's advanced state of readiness during the Cuban crisis was meant both "to avoid the possibility of surprise" and to "impress upon the Soviets our seriousness and determination." [31] In this latter effort it was presumably successful, although this was most clearly only one element among other considerations. In speaking to the Supreme Soviet of the U.S.S.R., Chairman Khrushchev reported on the Cuban crisis as follows:

> Events developed at a swift pace. The American command put all its armed forces, including troops stationed in Europe as well as the Sixth Fleet, in the Mediterranean, and the Seventh Fleet based in the Taiwan area, in a state of complete combat readiness. Several paratroop, infantry and armored divisions, numbering some 100,000 men, were allocated for the attack on Cuba alone. In addition, 183 warships, with 85,000 sailors on board, were moved toward the shores of Cuba. Several thousand warplanes were to cover the landing on Cuba. About 20% of all U.S. Strategic Air Command planes carrying atomic and hydrogen bombs, were kept aloft around the clock. Reserves were called up.[32]

While analysts who emphasize air power tend to argue that the "20 per cent of SAC" was an important consideration leading to Soviet concessions, it is obviously impossible for anyone to say — perhaps even for Premier Khrushchev himself. It should be noted, however, that Soviet attitudes toward such displays of force are somewhat peculiar from an American analyst's point of view. For instance, during the Paris Summit Conference in 1960, Secretary of Defense Thomas S. Gates ordered the Joint Chiefs to institute an alert. This alert involved both the Continental Air Defense Command and the Strategic Air Command. It lasted for seven hours and was said to be justified by the need to check the ability of the President, while abroad, to keep in touch with U.S. forces.[33] (Nevertheless the action seems to have been most provocative. President Eisenhower argued that international negotiations had sometimes been used to conceal preparations for a surprise attack. This tends only to reinforce the seriousness of his act.) The reaction of American strategists, had they been in policy-making positions in the Soviet Union, would have been to put Soviet forces on alert to decrease Soviet vulnerability. Instead, at a Paris press conference, Malinovsky volunteered: "We have not declared any military alert." And Khrushchev added: "Correct. We have not declared an alert and will not declare one. Our nerves are strong." [34]

Whatever the psychological impact of airborne bombers, it can hardly fail to decline rapidly. Our bombers, even from airborne alert stations, can hardly be within one half hour of their targets as our missiles are at all times.* Hence they do not add significantly to whatever threat of surprise attack exists. And even the implied threat deliberately to initiate a nuclear war will wear very thin in the face of the increasing invulnerability of Soviet forces.

The merits of most of the remaining arguments for bombers — wartime assessment of target damage, location and destruction of mobile targets, use of very-high-yield warheads, and so on — depend in part on U.S. strategy and in part on a host of cost-effectiveness considerations. The present strategy is a "damage-limiting" one.† The intention is to preserve the option of striking at many Soviet forces, after being attacked ourselves, so as to limit the size of a follow-on attack. Secretary McNamara argues, without giving details, that "comprehensive studies" show "under a wide variety of circumstances . . . forces in excess of those needed simply to destroy Soviet cities could significantly reduce damage to the U.S. and Western Europe." It can be assumed that the studies are based, in particular, on the assumption that a nuclear war will be fought to a finish. (For instance, the Secretary intends to attack weapon *storage* sites with bombers. This "limits" damage only if the war is not likely to be terminated quickly.) On

---

* Congressman George Mahon, hypothesizing a situation in which war occurred after the bombers were approaching their targets, suggested that "probably the missile would hit its target before the bomber." General Curtis LeMay replied: "Under most circumstances, yes." [35]

† "Thus, a 'damage-limiting' strategy appears to be the most practical and effective course for us to follow. Such a strategy requires a force considerably larger than would be needed for a limited 'cities only'

the assumption that the Soviet Union achieves secure second-strike capabilities — a widely heralded expectation — these studies will become outmoded. The emphasis must then turn, in one way or another, to "war-termination strategies." If our enemy has secure second-strike forces, we will not be able to justify plans to eliminate quickly the residual forces of an aggressor. The tendency to do so now is reinforced by Soviet relative weakness, which permits the Secretary of Defense to state that "today, following a surprise attack on us, we would still have the power to respond with overwhelming force, and *they would not then have the capability of a further strike*." [37] (Italics added.)

When the Soviet Union can retain the "capability of a further strike," two different tendencies will discourage the use of bombers even if they exist. First, it will become relatively less likely that a Soviet attack would include American cities — since the Soviets would want and be able to hold these cities hostage with their secure force. (Our own policy takes this form.)* Hence an unrestrained U.S. response to attack would not be in order. But bombers are difficult to use in a restrained fashion primarily because of penetration problems.

Second, there would be far less motivation to maintain the capability for such "bitter end" activities as assessment of target damage, destruction of weapon sites, location and destruction of mobile missiles, use of very-high-yield weapons, and so on.

Finally, there is the question of a "proper mix" in our offensive weapons. While such a mix is highly desirable, it is in-

---

strategy. While there are still some differences of judgment on just how large such a force should be, there is general agreement that it should be large enough to ensure the destruction, singly or in combination, of the Soviet Union, Communist China, and the Communist satellites as national societies, under the worst possible circumstances of war outbreak that can reasonably be postulated, and, in addition, to destroy their warmaking capability so as to limit, to the extent practicable, damage to this country and to our Allies." (Secretary McNamara)[36]

* See Secretary McNamara's Ann Arbor speech: *The New York Times*, June 17, 1962.

evitably going to be a mix of missiles in the view of the Secretary of Defense.* But missile-carrying bombers do not provide an especially good way to vary our missiles systems, for the reasons given previously.

In short, I believe that clearly foreshadowed changes in defense thinking will further reduce the utility of bombers, as Soviet second-strike capability increases. But in any case, it is clear that bombers are, by far, the most expendable portion of the strategic forces, whether judged by existing or anticipated doctrine. The bombers are simply insurance of a highly generalized kind. They have some unusual properties, which are not especially impressive. None of these calls for the approximately 700 bombers that will be in the force even after the B-47's have been phased out. From a strategic point of view, the United States should definitely be asking, "What can we get in return for dismantling our bombers?"

Future Manned Bombers

Among the considerations involved in bomber disarmament negotiations will be the likelihood that the United States will wish to procure a new manned bomber or more bombers of an existing type. This likelihood is small if it refers to a new type of bomber procured in large numbers, but not so small if the bomber is to be procured in relatively small numbers — for instance, three. Already in 1963 journalists were reporting that "even the Air Force is said to be losing faith" in the

* "I do not believe it is proper to infer . . . that I am sponsoring for all time a mix that includes missiles and manned bombers launching gravity bombs. Rather, I am talking about a mix of systems. It could be a mix of missile systems. As a matter of fact, I believe it will have to be a mix of missile systems under any circumstances, each system with characteristics different from the other systems and, therefore, adding in total to the problem of the defense." Elsewhere he remarked: "No other airborne vehicle that I have heard described for us in the 1970's depends on anything other than a missile for its striking power. So it seems to me that all of the technical developments point to the use of missiles, and it is simply a question of what kind of missile and how many and where they should be located." [38]

manned bomber furthest along in development, the B-70.*

B-70's were due to be produced for about $50 million each. For each such plane, it would be possible to procure and install about 12 Minutemen in hardened silos. Similarly, a wing of 45 B-52's procured and operated for 5 years costs at least as much (well over $1 billion) as 250 hardened and dispersed Minutemen.[40] This illustrates the unfavorable cost effectiveness of new or existing expensive bombers and emphasizes how unlikely it is that they will be procured in large numbers. No new procurement of any such bombers is now planned.

In addition to the low-level penetrator (LAMP) noted earlier, there is the Dromedary. It is also in too early a stage of development to be of concern in any disarmament negotiations. After he described its long endurance, slow speed, and stand-off characteristics, General LeMay was asked whether we had not been studying this aircraft "for at least a decade." He admitted that it had been discussed "off and on" but argued that the Air Force was taking "another look . . . because of what has been brought about by the cancellation of the B-70." However, this plane was to stand off and fire "14 to 17" improved Hound Dog missiles from as much as 1,000 miles away.[41] Probably the cancellation of Skybolt has discouraged the development of the required missile.

In short, it seems very unlikely that large numbers of any manned bomber will be procured under the Johnson administration.† However, there is always the possibility of very substantial changes in technology which, when coupled with a specific use for a bomber, could make its procurement feasible.

* See Jack Raymond, "New Strategic Bomber Gains Favor in Pentagon," *The New York Times*, December 26, 1963. The *new* strategic bomber referred to is a low-level penetrator, but it developed in a later column that the "favor" which it had gained was simply a $5-million research contract. This plane is apparently the LAMP (Low Altitude Manned Penetration aircraft) designed to fly at supersonic speed a few hundred feet off the ground below the beams of defensive radar.[39]

† Other administrations might well be different. Barry Goldwater said that one reason he was running for President was to maintain a proper "mix" of bombers and missiles.[42]

Such advances might be in variable-sweep wings, engine developments, penetration aids, and laminar-flow control. (The last is a method of changing the lift/drag ratio of aircraft and permits substantial reductions in size for fixed performance.)[43]

Nevertheless, this having been said, it is relatively feasible on technological grounds to argue for, or tacitly accede to, a cutoff in the production of "fleets" of new bombers. Such a cutoff would not be very restricting with present technological expectations.

Soviet Air Defenses

Soviet defenses have been characterized as "tremendously increased" in effectiveness since 1960. They are thought to include both high-altitude (SAM-II's) and low-altitude (SAM-III's) surface-to-air interceptor missiles around key points in Russia. The number of persons engaged in air defense activities is thought to be very large. In 1956, there were 550,000 people in Soviet air defense, or about four times the number engaged in U.S. defenses at that time.[44]

It is impossible, but perhaps unnecessary, to be very precise about the extent and costs of Soviet air defenses. There would apparently be great savings in defense costs to the Soviet Union if all U.S. bombers could be dismantled in a disarmament agreement. More limited agreements, such as a trade of Badgers for B-47's, would *not* permit this saving. And, to the extent that the Soviet Union intends to maintain air defenses against a growing French, and possible future German, threat, the savings would also be diminished. However, only a part of the present Soviet air defense operation would probably be necessary as a defense against French bombers. For instance, force targets, of whatever nature, and cities deep in the Soviet Union might not need protection if the U.S. bomber threat were removed. (We assume that British bomber disarmament would be part of any U.S.-Soviet agreement to scrap all strategic bombers.)

91

CHAPTER TWO

Soviet Bombers and U.S. Air Defenses

Composition of the Soviet Bomber Force

As is the case with the United States, a great many Soviet aircraft could carry nuclear weapons of one kind or another for varying distances. Again, it seems appropriate, in considering bomber disarmament as a separate measure, to restrict our attention to the Soviet strategic bomber force. This is thought to consist of the following:[45]

1. Seventy turbo-prop Bears (Tu-20), range about 7,000–8,000 miles, capable of carrying two short-range air-to-ground missiles or one large winged missile with range about 1,000 miles (gross weight: 330,000 lb; maximum speed: 580 mph). Became operational in 1956.

2. The supersonic delta-wing 4-jet Bounder, not now in production, a possible replacement for Bison (gross weight: 300,000 lb; maximum speed: 700 mph).

3. One hundred and twenty 4-jet Bisons (M-4), range about 6,000 miles, equipped for aerial refueling, capable of carrying a winged missile (gross weight: 250,000 lb; maximum speed: 600 mph). Became operational in 1956.

4. An emerging twin-engined supersonic medium bomber, Blinder, similar to the U.S. B-58, capable of aerial refueling, with a long-range air-to-ground missile. Possibly a strike/reconnaissance aircraft (gross weight: 150,000 lb; maximum speed: 1,000–1,030 mph). Became operational in 1962.

5. One thousand twin-jet medium-bomber Badgers (Tu-16), range about 3,500 miles, capable of carrying a single air-to-ground missile like the U.S. Hound Dog with range about 450 miles (gross weight: 150,000 lb; maximum speed: 610 mph). Became operational in 1955.

The Secretary of Defense has announced that "latest national intelligence estimates indicate there will be a decline in the Soviet bomber force and one far earlier than a decline in our force." [46] The Defense Department has also estimated the bombers which the Soviets "could place over this country, on two-way missions," as "no more than approximately 120 heavy bombers plus perhaps an additional 150 medium bombers, the targets for which would be limited to Alaska and the northwest areas of the United States." [47] Discussion of *two-way* missions indicates a doctrinal lag and underestimates Soviet capabilities for a first strike.

Soviet Attitudes Toward Bombers

Khrushchev stated, with the launching of Sputnik in 1957, that the era of the bomber had passed and that bombers were in the "twilight of their existence." By 1960, he stated, "Almost the entire military air force is being replaced by missiles," and he suggested that probably he would "further reduce and even discontinue the production of bombers and other obsolete equipment." During this period, the Soviet Union was, or was thought to be, ahead in missile capabilities and behind in bombers. With the development of Soviet stand-off, air-to-surface missiles, there was renewed support for the Soviet Air Force, which Khrushchev said the Soviet Union was "continuing to develop and improve." Some Soviet Air Force spokesmen — First Deputy Commander of the Soviet Air Force, Air Marshal S. Rudenko, and A. Tupolev, the Soviet aircraft designer — have spoken of the bomber in much the same terms used by U.S. Air Force spokesmen. [48]

Marshal Sokolovskii's *Military Strategy* takes a position very similar to that of our own Department of Defense. While conceding that long-range bombers are "rapidly yielding first place" to ballistic missiles, it asserts that this replacement may take "a long time" and that aircraft have not yet "completely exhausted their combat potential." Reference is made to specific missions, such as striking mobile targets, and so on. [49]

CHAPTER TWO

The Strategic Role of Soviet Bombers

In order to appreciate the strategic role of Soviet bombers, it is necessary to understand the general Soviet strategic posture as it has emerged over the years. This posture is exceedingly defensive in orientation — surprisingly so to many American analysts. There are various possible reasons for this of a technical, social, political, economic, bureaucratic, or other nature. They need not concern us here. But some history is appropriate.

When the United States had the only significant strategic capability, it threatened massive retaliation and built forces that were quite capable of accomplishing the destruction of the Soviet Union whether or not such an action was preceded by Soviet provocation.* Part of the Soviet response was to emphasize defenses. General LeMay testified that "they are spending a greater portion of their resources by far than we are on defenses." [51] Another part of the response was, of course, to procure strategic retaliatory forces. In fact, it was feared, especially during the missile-gap period, that the Soviet procurement of missiles would be more than sufficient to attack simultaneously all U.S. strategic weapons. Concern among strategists was genuine. For example, the present U.S. preponderance of strategic forces is precisely the reverse of the situation repeatedly anticipated in Herman Kahn's *On Thermonuclear War*. This book was written in 1959 after the author had worked for a decade at the RAND Corporation.

* In answer to questions which seemed to reflect on Air Force capabilities by emphasizing American casualties in a general war, General LeMay testified, somewhat petulantly: "I wish that there was some way, Mr. Chairman, I could guarantee fighting a war without getting anyone killed on our side. Unfortunately, I cannot do that at this time. There was a time when I was commanding SAC that I think we could have retaliated with the strength we then had and destroyed the greater part of Russia and the loss rate would have been the loss we would have suffered from the normal accident rate of that many hours' flying time. This situation no longer exists because they have built up their defenses and they have an atomic capability of their own." [50]

94

The size of the anticipated gap was enormous. The number of Soviet missiles thought to be in existence in mid-1961 was only 3½ per cent of the number that had been anticipated two years earlier for that same date. Bomber misjudgments were only slightly less dramatic.[52]

Very large numbers of relatively invulnerable missiles were ordered. Hence, when Soviet procurement ceased to be as large as anticipated, the Soviet Union's capability for attacking our enlarged forces became extremely ineffective. The U.S. capability for striking Soviet weapons became significant, however, and, as has been noted, remains sufficiently large to respond to a Soviet attack in such a way that, theoretically, no *further* Soviet attacks would be possible. (Obviously this statement is an approximation.) This "damage-limiting" capability is not shared by the Soviet Union.* Instead Soviet spokesmen emphasize 100-megaton bombs in relatively small numbers. These are better suited for an attack on urban areas than on military targets.

As a result of these considerations, the role of bombers in Soviet strategy seems to be even smaller than the role of bombers in our own strategic posture. In the first place, the relatively great capability of the United States to strike vulnerably based bombers decreases the utility of such forces to the Soviet Union. Second, the fact that the Soviet Union is not in a position to attack U.S. forces effectively at any stage in a nuclear war sharply diminishes "special purpose" reasons for retaining bombers. For instance, if the Soviet forces are insufficiently large to attack more than a small percentage of our Minutemen, what need is there for Soviet strategic reconnaissance? Similarly, a capability for attacks on U.S. land-based mobile missiles — of which there are none at this time — be-

---

* Secretary McNamara has said that "the relative numbers and survivability of U.S. strategic forces would permit us to retaliate against all the urgent Soviet military targets that are subject to attack, thus contributing to the limitation of damage to ourselves and our allies. . . . [This] damage-limiting capability of our numerically superior forces is, I believe, well worth its incremental cost. It is a capability to which the smaller forces of the Soviet Union could not realistically aspire." [53]

comes relatively pointless if a large number of other types of forces cannot be attacked.

These conclusions indicate that bomber disarmament of a suitably balanced kind should be quite advantageous to the Soviet Union.

Future Manned Bombers

There seems to be little public evidence of a new Soviet bomber, except for Blinder, which is thought to be a replacement for Badger.[54] However, information on Soviet research and development plans is obviously difficult, if not impossible, to come by. Hence no firm conclusions can be reached.

U.S. Air Defenses

In assessing the strategic value of Soviet bombers, the effectiveness of U.S. defenses against bombers must be considered. We should also consider those costs of maintaining defenses that might be saved under a bomber agreement.

As far as effectiveness is concerned, U.S. bomber defenses cannot be assessed unless there is a war. They were not built with a clear notion of expected effectiveness. For instance, in 1956, General Partridge, then Commander in Chief, Continental Air Defense Command, testified as follows:

> *Senator Symington:* Do you think you could knock down 50 percent of the attacking force?
>
> *General Partridge:* I would not hazard a guess.
>
> *Senator Symington:* 75?
>
> *General Partridge:* The way to evaluate our air-defense system is to try to think of it as insurance which you carry for years and hope the house will not burn down.

>   .   .   .   .

> *Senator Symington:* You just don't know what you could do?
>
> *General Partridge:* No, Sir; I have no basis on which to guess, but. . . . There is a terrific difference to the enemy between

operating against some defenses and operating against no defenses.

If the enemy knows that we have no defenses, he can come in, cruise around the country, go anywhere he wants to, bomb one airplane at a time. If he does not like one approach, he can go around and make another one. He could use his fighters and just strafe up and down the streets, do anything at all.

On the other hand, if he knows we have some defenses, no matter how meager they may be, he must do many, many things which General LeMay so very effectively outlined on his chart. He must use large formations or large numbers of bombers, and he must come at night and in bad weather and so on and on and on, carry defensive weapons, perhaps carry fighters with him and so on. So his offensive capability is tremendously degraded just by the fact that there is an air defense, even if we shoot down not one bomber.[55]

The general went on to testify that it was almost impossible to get a "realistic" test of the system and that "as we build further to the North and put the sea flanks on it is going to be impossible. . . ."[56] This continues to be the case. Asked what percentage of kill our antiaircraft defenses would have, the Secretary of Defense replied that "the answer depends upon a large number of factors that are in themselves unknown."[57]

In fact the system has many inefficiencies. Herman Kahn suggested in 1960: "One way not to make a reputation as an analyst in the last five or ten years would have been to find a hole in our air defense system . . . ; people mostly think of it as being full of holes."[58] It very probably should not have been built in its present form — a form in which efforts are made to defend, essentially, the entire North American continent. And it is useful to note that this is the view of the Chairman of the Joint Chiefs of Staff, General Taylor. He suggested in 1956 that "the concept of area defense in great depth . . . has not proved feasible, in my judgment, either technically or economically." He preferred an extended "point" defense under which large urban and strategic complexes would be protected.[59] The deficiencies in our present defense should encourage attempts to negotiate bomber disarmament. At the present time, the United States plans no very strenuous efforts to improve defenses unless the Soviet Union deploys a new bomber.* Instead, the "main thrust" of our defensive efforts will be redirected to meet the rising missile threat, although so long as the Soviet Union continues to maintain a force of manned bombers capable of reaching targets in the United States, "we must continue to support a defense against them." [61] Supporting this defense costs about $2 billion each year. Not all of this could be saved even if every last Soviet intercontinental bomber were destroyed, but a fairly large proportion of it presumably could.

Third-Country Bombers

Wars involving aerial bombardment can be divided usefully into two categories. In the first category, at least one of the major powers, Communist China, the United States, or the Soviet Union, is at war. In the second category, none of these powers is directly involved. In the latter case, the conflict can be expected to involve neighboring and relatively small powers; hence, relatively small numbers of easily improvised bombers are likely to be quite suitable for bombardment. As a result, bomber disarmament is hard to define for such powers, and it is not considered further in this chapter.

Another assumption made here is that Communist China will not participate in any general dismantling of its bomber forces, because of its political posture and the fact that it has no bombers of the size discussed in this chapter. The largest bombers known to be in mainland China are Il-28 (Beagle) light bombers. Although Soviet Badgers have been sold to

---

* For instance, in discussing interceptors, Secretary McNamara stated: "We still plan to retain the existing interceptor aircraft in the force, but the number of aircraft will decline gradually because of attrition. We believe that this force will be adequate against what we presently foresee as a declining Soviet manned-bomber threat. However, if the Soviets should deploy a new long-range bomber, we would have to reconsider the size and character of our interceptor force and particularly the need for modernization." A somewhat more detailed statement was made by the Director of Defense Research and Engineering, Harold Brown.[60]

Egypt and Indonesia, apparently none were transferred to China.[62]

As a result, it seems worth considering bomber disarmament only for the United States, the Soviet Union, Britain, France, and Germany. The Federal Republic of Germany has no bombers of the size discussed here. Hence its bomber disarmament must logically await disarmament of tactical fighter-bombers.

Having made the assumption that British bomber disarmament will not become an obstacle to major-power bomber disarmament — a reasonable assumption on general political grounds — we are left with the problem of the French "Force de Frappe." This force of Mirage IV, twin-jet supersonic light-attack bombers, is supposed to grow to 22 in 1964, with another 22 delivered in 1965.* The force will hold several million Russians "hostage," assuming it is capable of penetrating Soviet air defenses: most experts agree that it can (according to Hanson Baldwin).[64]

Although the French are considering Polaris-type systems for the post-1970 period, it would be premature for them to consider even "phased" bomber disarmament schemes. Hence, without a change in French political and strategic intentions, French participation in bomber disarmament is not possible. This has, of course, far-reaching political implications for Soviet participation in a general agreement to dismantle all strategic bombers. The Soviet Union may well oppose divesting itself of types of weapons that a particular Western ally wishes to retain.† It should be emphasized, however, that there are no good *strategic* reasons for this refusal — although

---

* The planes are to be based in southwestern France, and some will be kept on air alert. The French argue specifically that an attacking Mirage IV will be detected by radar at a distance of only 1½ miles — the plane will be 100 to 300 yards above the ground — and that, at 1,500 miles per hour, a SAM-III battery will have just one, quite inadequate, second to fire at it. Other penetration aids are also envisaged.[63]

† But it is worth noting that the Mirage IV is a small 66,000-lb bomber and would not be of the size being dismantled unless and until the United States and the Soviet Union discussed tactical bomber disarmament.

there might be bargaining rationalizations. From a strategic point of view, Soviet bombers are not useful either for attack or defense against French bombers. Nor are they necessary for retaliation in response to a French bomber attack.

Conclusions

This section describes some likely effects of bomber disarmament by giving conclusions with relatively self-contained explanations. These conclusions in no case follow *directly* from the preceding material, and in all cases rest largely on the author's judgment of a variety of factors. Two different possible kinds of agreements are discussed. The first is a limited one involving the destruction of obsolescent Soviet Badgers and U.S. B-47's. The second is much more extensive and would accomplish the phasing out of long-range bombers as well.*

Two General Issues

1. *Neither limited nor extensive bomber disarmament agreements will have much direct effect on the probability of war.* Such agreements would reduce the likelihood of accidents, incidents, and unauthorized behavior, but none of these is very probable, and certainly none is very likely to cause a war on its own. Nor is reciprocal fear of surprise attack, induced by vulnerable bombers, an important possibility in the present and anticipated strategic context. However, bomber disarmament would eliminate certain kinds of fears associated with vulnerable targets — such as the "outflanking BMEWS" fears evident during the Cuban crisis. And favorable *indirect* effects

* The designation "long-range" is used in a technical sense defined in the 1958 Surprise Attack Conference in Geneva. It refers to aircraft with a radius of action of over 2,000 nautical miles (n.m.) and would include at least B-52's, Bisons, and Bears. Badgers and B-47's would be medium-range aircraft — those defined as having a radius of action of 750–2,000 n.m. It is not clear whether B-58's and Blinders are medium- or long-range.[65]

on the likelihood of war are quite possible, such as those that arise from the relaxation of tension.

2. *Extensive — but not limited — bomber disarmament agreements could substantially reduce destruction if war occurred.* Whether or not the total quantity of weapons that can be delivered (deliverable megatonnage) is increased or diminished after a bomber disarmament agreement depends on missile procurement and on the remaining bombers. Measured by deliverable megatonnage, extensive bomber disarmament agreements are preferable to limited agreements, all other things being equal. Limited agreements — Badgers for B-47's — would diminish deliverable megatonnage only slightly, if at all, if these planes were in fact obsolete and incapable of delivering most of their weapons. Extensive agreements would do a good deal better. However, these questions of deliverable megatonnage are less important than those of targeting and war termination. Extensive — but not limited — disarmament of bombers would remove basing or staging airfields from a military target list and hence would widen the potential separation of forces and cities. Furthermore, extensive — but not limited — bomber disarmament would substantially increase the likelihood that war could be quickly terminated, for such disarmament precludes the destabilizing possibility of committing entire fleets of bombers.

U.S. Issues

3. *A limited bomber disarmament agreement may well prevent further bomber disarmament, for domestic (and perhaps also Soviet domestic) political reasons.* It has often been stated that comprehensive agreements are no more difficult to achieve than partial agreements.* One price of the atmos-

---

* Thus, P. M. S. Blackett has said: "To justify the labor of negotiating any agreed reduction and to offset the undoubted strains and disputes that will inevitably arise from the operation of any inspection and control system, the negotiated reduction must be a major one; in fact, of

pheric Test Ban was the elimination of all immediate hope for the total Test Ban Treaty. In order to pacify the critics of the agreement, President Kennedy committed himself to a "vigorous series of tests." [67] This commitment was very explicit.* In the same way, an agreement to destroy B-47's for Badgers would probably lead to renewed assurances from Secretary McNamara that the B-52 and B-58 fleets would remain in the force indefinitely. There may be similar political problems in the Soviet system, but the available information is insufficient to determine whether or not this is so.

4. *An extensive bomber disarmament agreement would probably release considerably more "survivable" and deliverable U.S. weapons from bomber-related assignments than would be eliminated by destroying U.S. bombers.* Secretary McNamara has indicated that a few hundred Minuteman missiles have been procured for air-defense suppression to substitute for the canceled Skybolt missiles.† Furthermore it is quite evident that quick-to-target missiles rather than slow-to-target bombers must be used to attack airfields on which Soviet bombers are, or might be, based. Therefore, an extensive bomber disarmament agreement could shorten target lists by eliminating these categories. It would presumably release a few hundred missiles for other purposes. Only 315 B-52's are even on ground alert, and only about 80 of these can be kept

---

such magnitude as to change qualitatively the nature of the relative nuclear postures of the two giant powers." [66]

* The Deputy Secretary of Defense in a "Safeguards" communication drew together the commitments made by the Chairman of the Atomic Energy Commission, by the Secretary of Defense, and by the President. Among four commitments, and given first, was "The conduct of comprehensive, aggressive, and continuing underground nuclear test programs designed to add to our knowledge and improve our weapons in all areas of significance to our military posture for the future." [68]

† For instance he suggested that Skybolt would have cost "nearly $3 billion," that "incremental initial investment cost for a Minuteman missile, complete with its blast-resistant silo" was "very close" to $4 million, and that a substitution of Minuteman for Skybolt would save about $2 billion. This suggests that about 250 Minutemen were to be procured for this purpose. [69]

aloft for long periods of time.[70] In either case, many of these bombers presumably would not penetrate the Soviet air defenses.* Hence relatively few "survivable" and penetrating bombers might be lost by an agreement.

5. *The missiles released from bomber-related assignments would be more effective in the U.S. damage-limiting strategy, now and in the foreseeable future, than would the bombers destroyed.* First, consider the previous conclusion. Second, as we noted earlier, the Secretary of Defense is dubious whether our bombers can reach the Soviet weapons before these have been launched against us as part of a Soviet attack. Missiles are far more useful to exploit the raggedness in any such attack. More generally, war is not likely to occur in ways that call for all-out spasm bomber attack whether directed at forces or cities. This and the other arguments against bombers are becoming stronger as the strategic context unfolds. Thus, bombers are becoming more vulnerable, more likely to interfere with real prospects for war termination if war occurs, less likely to penetrate to targets, less likely to reach targets in time to limit damage even if penetration is successful, and less necessary as a supplement to growing missile forces.

6. *An extensive — but not a limited — bomber disarmament agreement will remove the Soviet bomber threat.* The present bomber threat cannot be adequately defended against, and can be removed in no other way than by an extensive disarmament agreement of some kind. Such an agreement is truly "defense through disarmament."

7. *An extensive — but not a limited — bomber disarmament agreement would substantially reduce U.S. costs in air defense and in maintenance and operation of bombers.* Bomber maintenance and operation costs will not be greatly reduced by destroying obsolescent bombers, since the costs would ordi-

---

* General Power has remarked that "in one weapon system, say a B-52 out of New Mexico going against the Soviet Union, if your realistic war games are thorough, you have a 50% confidence factor for destroying that target with a given weapon." [71]

narily be eliminated in any case. Nor would it be possible to diminish the annual $2-billion air defense costs if many Soviet bombers remained. However, an extensive agreement might permit a sizable reduction in air defense expenditures and also save several billion dollars in bomber costs.*

8. *An extensive, rather than a limited, bomber disarmament agreement would most improve the relative superiority of the United States over the Soviet Union as measured in existing delivery vehicles.* Recent estimates indicate that our missile superiority is about 4 to 1 or better.[73] The elimination of heavy bombers would trade about three U.S. bombers for one Soviet bomber. The elimination of B-47's and Badgers would trade approximately even numbers of bombers. Hence, according to this almost purely symbolic measure, we should eliminate bombers completely to most increase our relative superiority in delivery vehicles.

9. *There would be no important inpection problems associated with either a limited or an extensive bomber disarmament agreement.* Soviet knowledge of the size of our bomber fleet is, of course, complete. And our appreciation of Soviet bomber capabilities can be little inferior. Many public estimates of the older Soviet bombers are given to the nearest multiple of ten (for example, 70 or 120). No Soviet government could assume that bombers could be kept secret, and there would be little incentive to do so, since they are in no sense a decisive weapon.

10. *The main obstacles to extensive bomber disarmament are probably U.S. political problems, and these are substantial.* The strategic case for extensive bomber disarmament is strong, but probably only the present Secretary of Defense would have any chance of persuading Congress of it. It would take a good deal of courage in various parts of the government even to propose dismantling the SAC bomber fleet.

---

* The maintenance and operation of the B-52 force costs $820 million each year. Phasing it out steadily over three years instead of keeping all B-52's until 1969 (as the present program anticipates) would save $2.8 billion. The cost of modifying the fleet would also be saved — this is $306 million for fiscal 1965.[72]

Soviet Issues

11. *No advantages comparable to those of Conclusions 4 and 5 would accrue to the Soviet Union in an extensive bomber disarmament agreement, because Soviet force posture and strategy differ from those of the United States.* The Soviet Union would not release many missiles from bomber-base targeting, because its force is not sufficiently large to follow a "damage-limiting" strategy and is "at the present time . . . as Khrushchev has outlined it, a strategy directed primarily against our cities and our urban society," according to Secretary McNamara.[74] Similarly, it is unlikely that ICBM's from a small Soviet supply would be used to suppress partially effective air defenses to improve the penetration qualities of a 190-plane heavy-bomber force. Instead, air-to-ground missiles would probably be used. Therefore Soviet ICBM's would not be released from air-defense suppression assignments.

12. *Nevertheless, an extensive bomber disarmament agreement would be very clearly in the Soviet interest.* First, from the Soviet point of view, the Soviet Union would share in the benefits discussed in Conclusion 2 — less destruction if war occurs — and would have eliminated the potential U.S. bomber threat, at the cost of giving up vulnerable Soviet bombers. The advantages referred to in Conclusions 4 and 5 (the release of U.S. missiles from bomber-related duties) should not discourage agreement unless the Soviet Union wishes to use airfields to draw "fire" or to encourage procurement by us of additional missiles.* Conclusion 8 (increase in the relative advantage of the United States) has only symbolic significance. The dismantlement of the SAC bomber force will seem to Soviet officials to be the end of an un-

---

* The United States can be encouraged to procure additional missiles even with its present large superiority. For instance, Secretary McNamara's testimony includes the paragraph: "We have tentatively programed the funding of additional MINUTEMAN II silos after fiscal year 1965, but the actual number to be started will depend upon the situation prevailing a year or two years from now." [75]

fortunate era of American strategic dominance. Possibly they will view it as a rebuke to U.S. Air Force generals whose unauthorized behavior may have been feared in the past. A bomber agreement, even a limited one, might encourage the Soviets to attempt to dislodge the United States from overseas bases that could become superfluous in the absence of aircraft. Bomber maintenance costs would be saved. And unless French bombers and the U.S. TFX prevented it, much of Soviet air defense costs would be saved. The fissionable material in Soviet bombs could be used in Soviet missiles if it were in short supply. (A limited agreement would be of no greater assistance than obsolescence in this regard.) Bombers are not useful to the Soviets for purposes of deterrence, because they are vulnerable, as noted before, and also hard to hide and less reliable. Finally, a major disarmament agreement would represent a large part of that *détente* which is evidently the current interest of the Soviet Union. For propaganda purposes the extensive agreement could be claimed by the Soviets to be nearer to their proposal than to the U.S. informal and limited suggestion.*

What to Do?

13. *I believe it would be good disarmament strategy for either or both sides to hold out for an extensive bomber disarmament agreement.* Conclusion 3 indicates that a limited agreement might prevent further bomber disarmament. In any case the nonsymbolic results of such an agreement will soon accrue from obsolescence. (For example, the U.S. B-47's will be phased out in 1966, and the Badger force is as old.)[77] The argument that the bombers will be prevented from falling into third-country hands is not persuasive. The United States con-

---

* It would also comply effectively with the Soviet draft resolution, introduced in the Security Council on April 21, 1958, that called upon the United States "to refrain from sending its military aircraft carrying atomic and hydrogen bombs toward the frontiers of other States for the purpose of creating a threat to their security or staging military demonstrations."[76]

trols the B-47's, and if the Soviet Union wished to, it could sell light Il-28 bombers to its friends and allies. Extensive bomber agreements make much more sense than limited ones. As noted in Conclusions 2 and 7, only extensive agreements will substantially reduce destruction if war occurs and reduce U.S. air defense and bomber costs. As noted in Conclusion 6, only an extensive agreement will remove the Soviet bomber threat. And, as noted in Conclusions 4 and 5, an extensive agreement alone will *strengthen* U.S. retaliatory forces by releasing missiles from bomber-related duties. Conclusion 12 indicates a real Soviet interest also in extensive agreements. A decision to try for such extensive agreement does not create an all-or-nothing obstacle to disarmament; extensive bomber disarmament agreements will eventually become feasible, if only because the heavy-bomber fleets will get older and less desirable. In time, if nothing is done earlier, offers will be made to trade obsolete B-52's for obsolete Bears and Bisons. Are we capable only of agreeing on disarmament through obsolescence (without a freeze), or can doctrine, analysis, and an enlightened attitude toward national interest in both major powers shape the destiny of already procured, and still usable, forces? This is the question posed by bomber disarmament.

BOMBER DISARMAMENT: PROSPECTS, EARLY 1965

Introduction

IN THE FALL of 1964 the first signs appeared that B-52's were to be phased down unilaterally. These and some other observations are discussed in this chapter. It examines more closely Department of Defense bomber policy, and suggests that B-52's will decline in number as the TFX planes are phased in. This clarifies the possibilities for arms control. These include a cutoff in heavy-bomber procurement, destruction of some B-52's, Bisons, and Bears, and offers to destroy heavy bombers in conjunction with a halt in missile procurement.

A U.S. Follow-on Bomber

A new heavy bomber still seems unlikely. First of all, Harold Brown, Director of Defense Research and Engineering, testi-fied that the Air Force had examined — in addition to multi-purpose strategic reconnaissance systems, such as B-70, and a long-range bomber that would launch stand-off missiles — "what now seems to be the most promising concept, an ad-vanced manned precise-strike system, AMPSS." [1] The name of the system has changed frequently and now seems to be "AMSA" (Advanced Manned Strategic Aircraft), but the con-cept remains fairly stationary. Richard Fryklund described the leading candidate by saying that such a plane would fly toward Russia at about 600 miles an hour, descend almost to the ground as it passed Red defenses, fly at tree-top level to its target (probably at 700 or 800 miles an hour, though an all-subsonic mission is under consideration) and then cruise back to a safe base.

The AMSA would launch large numbers of small missiles (with about 200-kiloton nuclear warheads) at enemy targets 50 or 60 miles away with great precision.[2]

This plane has two serious problems. First, it would take seven years to build. General Robert Friedman testified in early 1964 that December 1971 was the "most optimistic date" that a new follow-on bomber could be expected.[3] Second, it is too expensive — $9 billion to build some 200 bombers, according to the Defense Department. And on August 24, 1964, Richard Fryklund suggested in the *Washington Star* that the fleet would cost "roughly $1.5 billion a year to maintain and operate according to rule-of-thumb experience with past bombers." (A lower estimate was given in the preceding chapter.) Hence, assuming an eight-year life, the decision to adopt such bombers involves about $20 billion in direct costs.

Of course, the procurement of a follow-on bomber depends in large part on the extent to which B-52's and other bombers can fulfill the requirement. The Secretary of Defense has asserted that they can, that

Our current research and development program will make available to us three designs, any one of which could be completed and put into production before our present bombers reach the end of their useful life.[4]

But Harold Brown noted that they might not:

The B-52 has been having structural difficulties which in one sense argues you need a new aircraft soon if you need it, and in another sense it raises the question of reliability of the aircraft. But in any event, we are trying to evaluate what is a reasonable expected lifetime for the B-52.[5]

Since the present bombers were procured over a seven-year period and have had dissimilar use and missions, calculating the expected lifetime for the fleet will be fairly complicated.* Finally in October 1964, Richard Fryklund reported:

> Existing B-52 heavy bombers will be good through 1975 according to an Air Force Defense Department–Boeing Co. study, and with continued modernization, might last into the '80's. Only 200 bombers are needed, according to the Air Force study, and more than that number of later model B-52's are available.[7]

AMSA's chances had declined.

Furthermore, Congress is gradually losing the motivation to force upon the Secretary of Defense additional funds for bomber procurement. Even influential and sympathetic Air Force supporters seem to be having doubts. Senator Richard Russell, chairman of both the Committee on Armed Services and the Subcommittee on Department of Defense of the Committee on Appropriations remarked:

> I want us to move ahead with a new manned aircraft.
> But I must confess that I have some qualms about it. What is the primary consideration in this new aircraft to replace these aging 52's and 58's? Is it speed or altitude or ability to carry long-range missiles, or are you seeking all of these things in this bomber?[8]

And significantly, a recent House Armed Services Committee minority report opposing additional bomber funds expressed disbelief "that the Congress necessarily [had] any commitment in perpetuity to long-range strategic bombers of the B-36 or B-52 type, any more than we had a commitment in perpetuity to the battleship."[9] Congress is therefore not far behind former Deputy Secretary of Defense Roswell Gilpatric who suggested that "all manned bombers" might be "retired from active deployment" in the 1970's in a suitable political environment.[10]

President Johnson is said to hope that the Air Force can find some mission for a new follow-on bomber but to believe that

---

* For example, speaking of the G and H models of B-52, General Bradley stated in 1961: "Actually the G's and H's are the ones that are in the biggest trouble. The reason is that they are carrying a much greater load in comparison to the older one."[6]

one cannot spend $10 billion for nostalgia.[11] The Secretary of Defense himself has asserted that he has not "seen or heard of anything yet that warrants development and production." [12] The *Washington Star* notes that the Air Force has recently asked again to go to the "project definition" phase of aircraft development but that civilian officials believe this "advanced design" work would commit them to "final approval" and hence they will reject it.[13] It is hard to believe AMSA has a chance.

Reductions in the Fleet of B-52's

At the same time, it seems that the B-52's will decline in number — to about 200 planes by 1971. First of all, the studies justifying an advanced bomber generally called for only 200 planes — probably because of the great expense of new bombers; but this factor may have conceded implicitly that no more than 200 planes are necessary. And the study mentioned earlier suggests that this has been accepted.

Second, additional planes are expensive in operation and maintenance costs, and in the crew, tankers, and other resources that might be used for a growing fleet of B-52's. This sort of consideration influenced the phasing out of the B-47's. In 1961, Secretary McNamara testified:

> Since the earlier B-47 medium bombers in the inventory are already approaching the end of their useful life, we propose to phase them out of the force at a somewhat faster rate than originally planned. The crews and other resources thus freed will be utilized to maintain the larger proportion of the force on the 15-minute ground alert.[14]

Third, U.S. policy is already pointing toward a verbal or actual substitution of B-52 with TFX, which will be phased in from about 1966 to the early seventies.* This is indicated

* It is suggested that planes "will start rolling off an assembly line in 1966." [15] Australia is to receive 24 TFX aircraft in 1967. The spending for TFX is expected to be spread over seven years, "with delivery of planes continuing into the 1970's." [16]

in responses to charges that the manned bomber will be phased out. These responses do not commit the Defense Department to B-52's in large numbers. For instance, after Senator Goldwater mentioned manned bombers in a speech to the Veterans of Foreign Wars, the Defense Department replied:

> . . . the idea that all manned bombers are to be phased out is wholly unjustified. Our forward plans now go through fiscal year 1972. Those plans include larger numbers of strategic bombers at every stage. The plans also include a bomber-deliverable megatonnage which is highly classified, but substantially greater than the Senator's statement implies.
>
> No decision has yet been made about our needs beyond 1972, but we are making ample provision: (1) for possible extension of the life of the B-52, (2) for research on new manned systems, and (3) for possible strategic uses of manned systems in production. We will have manned bombers, and plenty of them, just as long as they are needed.[17]

Indeed, the increasing reliance on TFX for a great many duties has been widely foreshadowed. Asked by Senator Mundt whether or not we would be caught short of bombers in 1969 or 1970 if the Chinese attacked India, the Secretary of Defense replied that we would have suitable manned bombers, arguing: "As you know, the TFX has a long range and a very high bomb load, and this is one of the potential missions for it." [18] Whether or not it will be possible to substitute the TFX for the B-52 in missions involving penetration of Soviet air defenses is not clear. For instance, General LeMay testified:

> The main trouble with the TFX is that it is a small airplane, and it will not carry the things you need to penetrate modern defenses and still have long enough range to do it. It is just not a big enough airplane to do this. It is going to do the job fine in a tactical role. . . .[19]

But Richard Fryklund reports:

> [TFX] could carry all of the AMSA equipment (except for an oversized antenna) and could hit almost all AMSA targets most of which are in European Russia.[20]

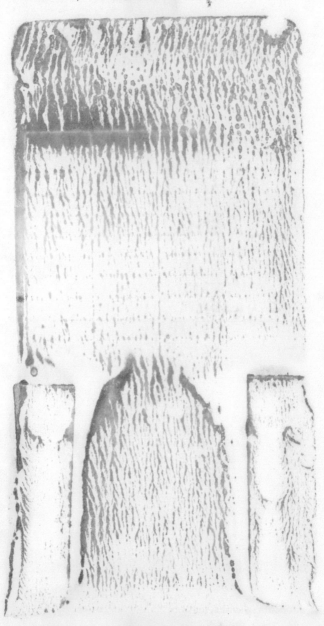

What Might Be both Feasible and Desirable?

Even though we might not be likely to buy a new heavy bomber, we probably would not be willing to say so unilaterally. Defense Department leadership tends to be unwilling to resolve hypothetical or general issues. Like the Supreme Court, it finds a certain protection in dealing with the concrete and the particular. Unless some good reason exists, the Secretary of Defense will not want to explain why *no* follow-on bomber is likely to be procured, and may not be able to.

Moreover all of our bilateral bomber proposals are likely to run into characteristic problems. Not only does the Defense Department prefer to resolve only specific issues, it also prefers to resolve them on the basis of the cost effectiveness of unilateral action. Although bilateral agreements can provide a very real additional "consideration" for actions that would be undertaken in any case, the actions are more likely to come under attack. It is easier for a hostile Congress to question an agreement than to question the application of cost effectiveness. The latter seems a relatively objective criterion, and discussions on these grounds can almost always be won by the Secretary of Defense: he has the information, the background, the staff, and the authority. By contrast, a U.S.-Soviet deal involves a possibly malevolent partner. While we can be *mistaken* in applying cost effectiveness, we can be *tricked* by the Soviets. And a U.S.-Soviet agreement raises certain political questions with which Congress feels as competent to deal as the Department of Defense. It also raises more difficult problems of coordination, since our allies, the State Department, and others must reach at least some consensus.

Such agreements, moreover, may set a dangerous precedent, arouse political pressures for unwise future agreements, mislead the Soviets as to our determination and power, and so on. Because arms control agreements raise these kinds of fears, the combination of unilateral and arms control motivations for a particular action tends to confuse the issues. To the Department of Defense, it will generally seem preferable to leave the Soviets out of its arguments, lest others think that Soviet considerations dominate its deliberations. In the political process it is often the weakest, rather than the strongest, argument that influences the course of the struggle. Finally, the Defense Department would not like to make desirable unilateral actions — such as divesting itself of all bombers — contingent upon Soviet agreement.

For these reasons, Department of Defense policy makers are more likely to expect, and hence to encourage, unilateral rather than bilateral phase outs. Such expectations have certain operational consequences that generally reduce still further the likelihood of utilizing arms control mechanisms.

For example, if it were decided to try for a bilateral phase out of heavy bombers rather than for unilateral action, it would be appropriate to emphasize the strength rather than the weakness of Soviet bomber forces. It is Soviet bomber *strength* that makes a deal worth while, and it is Soviet bomber *weakness* that makes our unilateral phase down of B-52's politically possible. Hence, in the one case, Soviet bomber forces might be described in terms of their effectiveness in one-way flights; in the other case, discussions on two-way flights might be appropriate.

Other, subtler problems arise. If attempts were to be made to induce Soviet acceptance of some bargain, unilateral justifications of our action might have to be muted. Presumably, we should not emphasize too strongly to Congress that TFX can bomb European Russia just as well as B-52's can while persuading the Soviets to give up their capability to bomb the United States. (This is a question of emphasis, however, since the Soviets may understand the political need to "phase" B-52's into TFX's. Moreover, during the Test Ban hearings, they said nothing while the Secretary of Defense spotlighted the unilateral benefits of the treaty.)

These considerations limit the bilateral agreements that are possible and the forms that they may take. Three possibilities remain of interest: the destruction of heavy bombers, cutoffs

of bomber procurement, and the conjunction of bomber proposals with the freeze proposal.

Destruction of Obsolescent Heavy Bombers

A central question involved in bilateral agreements to destroy obsolescent heavy bombers is "Why?" If the bombers
are to be phased out anyway at much the same rate, such
traditional motives for disarmament as "decreasing destruction if war occurs" are absent. Instead, the dominant motivations for heavy-bomber destruction become political. Not all
of these have much to do with bombers per se. Any other
strategic weapon system might do as well.

Presumably bomber disarmament agreements can help prepare for later agreements, perhaps by educating arms controllers on the two sides in the problems of justifying and
drafting formal agreements and by forcing the defense analysts
to think through the strategic and political issues that bomber
disarmament raises.

Decision makers of the two sides would also learn. The
Senate would be exposed to a thorough analysis of the advantages and disadvantages of the agreement. The principle
would be firmly established that strategic computations could
favor disarmament. And many of the questions raised would
be relevant to any substantial agreement that might follow. A
treaty would increase interest in arms control activities and
would stimulate those sympathetic to further disarmament;
the number of people willing to spend time on arms control
would increase and the quality of their efforts might rise. Also,
the Soviet "credit rating" might rise; and the successful destruction of bombers month after month might increase the
political feasibility of further agreements.

This continued destruction of bombers over a period of
years would probably have a desirable effect on the international atmosphere. It would periodically reassure both parties
of the willingness of the other to take positive steps to maintain a treaty. This reassurance would be perceived by both as

inconsistent with the kind of diplomatic pressure represented by Berlin provocations. Each would expect deteriorating relations to be signaled by a halt in the destruction of bombers and each would gain confidence from that perception.

The destruction of heavy bombers might also have favorable effects on aspects of the arms race that involve third parties, such as proliferation. At the least, in nonnuclear countries the supporters of restraint in acquiring nuclear weapons would use the prospect of progress in major-power disarmament as a debating point in their internal councils.

The treaty would be an important test of strength between those who welcomed *détente* and those who feared it. Efforts to gain a favorable consensus on both sides would provoke a great debate. And because the treaty would be strategically innocuous, it would represent a favorable "test case" for those sympathetic to arms control.* After its ratification each could accept the premise that an earnest indication of a national desire for *détente* had been given. And, from a political point of view, the treaty would announce that those interested in further procurement of strategic weapons were in the minority. This announcement could greatly enhance the prospects for a tacit freeze on the procurement of other weapons.

Of course the way in which each spoke about the treaty might influence the expectations associated with it. If the Secretary of Defense had to pacify opponents of the treaty with assurances that *additional* strategic weapons were to be built, he would retard the establishment of nonprocurement understandings. But if he linked the destruction of bombers with assurances that we had enough nuclear weapons, the tacit freeze would be encouraged.

Hopefully, the treaty would add to the U.S.-Soviet strategic dialogue, and improve the insight of each into the constraints

* By and large, it is not feasible in this country to argue publicly against disarmament on political grounds. The desire to achieve disarmament agreements with the Soviets, so long as the agreements are technically sound, is generally conceded in public if not in private. Hence opponents of a treaty are likely to be forced to argue their case on difficult grounds.

under which the other deals with national security and arms control policies. In the long run, this understanding will be the best guarantee of stability in strategic force procurement.

The destruction of heavy bombers by formal treaty could, for these reasons, be of significance even if very few bombers were destroyed. But assuming that 200 bombers were to be retained, and that destruction of less than one-third of the existing force would seem too inconsequential, somewhere between about 200 and 400 heavy bombers could be destroyed.

The destruction of these bombers might best be done over a period of a few years rather than a few months; it could be done weekly or monthly. Four hundred bombers could be destroyed over 4 years if 2 were destroyed each week or 8 each month. The schedule could be arranged to avoid a termination date that would be politically embarrassing to one side or the other, for example, immediately before an election in the United States.

Equal numbers of bombers might be destroyed; a two-thirds reduction of our heavy-bomber force (or 400 bombers) could be matched by a two-thirds reduction of the Soviet heavy-bomber force (or 120 bombers) coupled with the demolition of 280 medium bombers. One purpose of adding medium bombers to the destruction would be to prevent giving the impression, month after month, that the United States was destroying more than the Soviet Union. The destruction might otherwise be susceptible to politically motivated criticism. Since the medium bombers threaten our European allies quite as effectively as the heavy bombers threaten us, it is easy to rationalize the trade and useful to establish the possibility. When and if reductions are made in numbers of missiles, the same explanation would apply to bargains in which medium-range ballistic missiles were destroyed in exchange for our ICBM's.

If each side had already announced its decision to divest itself of heavy bombers, the treaty would be a "pseudo-agreement," a term used by the political scientist Fred C. Iklé to designate agreements that do not record any new settlement.[21]

117

ССHAPTER THREE

But there would still be some strategic motives for the treaty. As in the U.S. proposal to destroy B-47's and Soviet Badgers, it could be argued that the planes might otherwise be returned to service, although, unlike the B-47's, the renovated B-52's would not be purchased by third parties; they are simply too big and expensive to be of interest to most of the world, which could make do with TFX. The return to domestic service of "mothballed" planes is a real consideration; the Air Force would probably object to burning bombers on these grounds.*

If a formal treaty is impossible, we should have to settle for portraying the separate unilateral actions of the two powers as instances of reduction by "mutual example." This would have a certain amount of political impact and might be the best we could get.

Cutoff of Heavy-Bomber Procurement

An agreement is unlikely to be negotiated formally for a cutoff in heavy-bomber procurement. It does not have the appeal of physical disarmament, the urgency of a cutoff in missile procurement or of a test ban.

But a phase down of the bomber force would eventually take the steam out of desires for a follow-on bomber. And as the focus of the debate turned from a new bomber toward the retention of old ones, the arguments for getting each side to refrain from further heavy-bomber procurement would re-appear. Hence, bomber destruction agreements can encourage a tacit agreement against bombers. So also can the desire to cut back air defenses.

Once we or they dismantle air defenses, it will be that much harder to buy a new bomber. Each side would be politically embarrassed by the re-emergence of bombers after the adop-

* "*Mr. Stafford:* [Nominally active bombers] could be returned to active service if conditions indicate?

"*Secretary McNamara:* They could be [deletion in original]. As to their usefulness, General LeMay has asserted: 'I think the B-47 in the hand of professionals could deliver weapons in the year 2000.' " [22]

tion of a policy of phasing down air defenses. Hence for each side to engage in small decreases in air defenses may be, in some sense, to exchange political hostages.

Any Soviet leader interested in reducing air defense expenditures would probably want as many indicators as he could get of our intention not to procure a new heavy bomber. Cutting back Soviet air defense will probably run into strong opposition from the most entrenched of bureaucracies. And Soviet air defense enthusiasts would want long-range assurances of our intentions to justify their cutbacks; air defense systems are not rebuilt in a day.

We might have to avoid buying Soviet air defense by not stationing the relatively long-range TFX in Europe and Japan where it could attack the Soviet Union. And in phasing out B-52's for TFX, we would have to emphasize the irrelevance of strategic bombers in general war rather than the capacity of TFX to substitute for them.

We might also encourage the Soviets to dismantle their air defenses by phasing down our own and stressing those explanations for our action that would also apply to the Soviet Union.

Finally, we might wish to give the Soviets a political rather than a financial stake in our nonprocurement of a follow-on bomber. We could suggest to them that the question of bombers is one over which the civilian leadership in the Defense Department could lose its position. With such a loss, increased prestige, influence, and authority would accrue to those arguing for less restraint in the arms race.

Bomber Disarmament and a Halt in Missile Procurement

One important possibility is to treat bomber disarmament in the context of a halt in missile procurement such as the one discussed in Chapter Five. That proposal for a freeze contains a provision that is probably properly characterized as an error. The error reveals the extent to which the freeze proposal either was not taken seriously or was prepared hurriedly, and is related to the pressures arising from the debate over the retention of bombers.

As it stands, the freeze proposal advocates, for missiles and bombers alike, that "the immediate objective of the freeze on numbers should be to maintain the quantities of strategic nuclear vehicles . . . at constant levels," and the "objective of the freeze on characteristics should be to prevent the development and deployment of strategic vehicles of a significantly new type." [23] With respect to bombers, a prohibition of vehicles of a "significantly new type" is a prohibition on any follow-on bombers since such a bomber would certainly satisfy this description. Hence additional B-52's would have to be procured to maintain a constant level.

But maintaining the level of our present bombers by systematic replacement of old B-52's with new ones is a contingency that we are not now considering and probably never would, even under a freeze. We should have to reopen old production lines at great expense. And for what? The arguments against a follow-on bomber apply a fortiori to an older bomber not designed for the rigors of the seventies. Their lifetime would depend on the defenses of the Soviet Union.[24] Penetration problems could not be avoided by developing stand-off missiles — designed to let bombers stay outside of defenses — since a freeze would not permit their development. And, to the extent that the United States continued to use ICBM's for defense suppression (that is, to attack defenses and open a corridor for bombers), valuable missiles in a frozen force would be required for an otherwise unnecessary job.[25] The requirements for a bomber in the seventies are basically still open to question. Finally, much of the political motivation for a new follow-on bomber could not be sublimated with more B-52's. A follow-on bomber, but not more B-52's, would add to our knowledge, procure something new and exciting, and show our determination to be second to none in the aircraft development field. For all these reasons it is not likely that we would exercise our option to maintain existing levels of bombers.

If, indeed, the United States would not even exercise its option of "one-for-one replacement by externally similar vehicles" in the case of bombers, its insertion in our proposal was an error. The Soviet Union might be willing to maintain its heavy bombers indefinitely. This would have a number of unfortunate consequences. A potential Soviet bomber threat would force us to incur otherwise avoidable air defense costs and to assign missiles to Soviet air bases. And a potential Soviet bomber preponderance would have unfortunate political considerations that might induce an otherwise undesired purchase of B-52's. Finally, retained Soviet bombers would maintain a threat against our cities that could not be effectively neutralized.

In other words, the United States should have proposed, at the least, a freeze in missile procurement combined with the *nonreplacement* of heavy bombers. It would not want to buy the heavy bombers that the U.S. proposal permits. And it might have proposed an agreement more acceptable to the Russians if it had called for a phasing down of heavy bombers — a phase down that would in any case occur in a few years. Such an agreement would combine the freeze desired by the United States with the bomber disarmament proposed by the Soviets — some "arms control" with some "disarmament."

The Future

When the Soviets proposed the disarmament of all bombers in early 1964, they touched upon a sensitive nerve in Defense Department planning. Although the Soviet proposal was obviously impractical, it did reflect the relative obsolescence of heavy bombers and had the power to stir up debate over the manned bomber in the United States. The maintenance of the heavy-bomber force through the late sixties was probably the most obvious and significant deviation from cost-effectiveness considerations that existed in the entire strategic weapons program. The prospects for its phase down were relatively good.

When the Soviet proposal was made, the U.S. heavy-bomber fleet had been programed to be maintained intact until at least 1969. By the next year, in early 1965, the fiscal 1966 budget revealed that the Department of Defense planned to phase out, during that year, two squadrons containing the oldest model of B-52, the B-52B's. These were ten years old. At the same time, $300 million was requested to continue the program to extend the life and improve the capabilities of other B-52 strategic bombers. Detailed plans were not made public.

In December 1964, the Soviet Union sent to the President of the U.N. General Assembly a disarmament memorandum discussing "measures for further reduction of international tension and limitation of the arms race." It suggested eleven measures, many of them emphasizing "mutual example" and referring to agreements with political rather than strategic impact.

On the subject of bombers, the Soviets went even further than they had previously. They called the destruction of bombers "undoubtedly ready to be put into practice." The Soviet government was prepared to discuss "the phasing of the destruction of bombers *in terms of types* within an agreed over-all time limit for the destruction of all bombers." (Italics added.) The Soviets proposed that a formula be worked out under which the large powers would be the first to eliminate bombers.

Thus if a willingness on the part of both parties to reach agreement is assumed, the bargain indicated by the two positions would involve (*a*) U.S. agreement in principle to the ultimate destruction of all bombers, much like our agreement in principle to general and complete disarmament; and (*b*) U.S. and Soviet dismantlement of bombers as they were phased out. The prospects for this agreement are not especially good. Conceivably they might improve if it became obvious that a few hundred B-52's were to be phased out; this could occur in the presentation of the fiscal 1967 budget in early 1966.

Whether we or the Soviets would be willing to design a statement describing unilateral reductions as instances of mutual example is impossible to predict. But the prospects for our procuring a new heavy bomber have clearly declined still further. The testimony given in preparing the allotment of funds for fiscal 1966 argues that it would be desirable to keep open the option of developing a replacement for the B-52's when they have to be retired. But this almost admits that they might never be replaced at all.

MISSILE DISARMAMENT

Introduction

THE PROSPECTS for negotiated reductions in missiles are poor, for reasons that are discussed in the conclusions and that will become apparent in the body of this chapter. Nevertheless an examination of the problems of missile reductions can be educational in sketching the existing state of affairs in missile procurement — procurement that involves three different contests between the major powers — and in providing an appreciation of missile force computations. This chapter assumes that the problems are better understood by considering the situation than by reading arguments about it. The conclusions are mainly devoted to an analysis of the general disarmament plans. Many political issues have been ignored because the plans are so unlikely to be implemented.

If there is any over-all positive conclusion to this chapter, it is a formula, interesting at least in the abstract, whereby the United States could justify acceptance in principle of a Soviet position so as to permit more detailed discussions. The Soviets have demanded agreement in principle for a reduction to "mutually agreed and strictly limited" numbers of missiles before proceeding with technical discussions at a working level. The United States, notwithstanding its prior agreement in principle to the more radical "general and complete disarmament," has objected. Part of the disagreement stems from our general disinclination to agree in principle; there seem to be differences in attitude between ourselves and the Soviets on how bargaining is conducted. (There may also be a disinclination on one or both sides to talk in detail.)

In any case, it will be observed that the United States missile force is now improving very considerably in effectiveness per missile and that, despite these increases, the strategic force is likely over time to become incapable of attacking Soviet forces effectively. These facts provide interesting properties for a plan involving proportional missile reductions in a first stage of disarmament, and reductions to strictly limited and mutually agreed numbers of missiles in a second stage.

During the first stage, the over-all effectiveness of the U.S. force could increase, notwithstanding the reduction in numbers, because of improvements in the efficiency of the remaining missiles. Meanwhile, the Soviet threat would generally decrease. During the second stage, or thereafter, the United States would find itself gradually losing the relative advantages provided in part by the first-stage agreement and in part by its former preponderance. This may not be a fatal objection since, over the period of time required for the two stages, these advantages would probably have been lost without disarmament and would be lost under any kind of very substantial reduction.

It is difficult and unrewarding to describe the problems involved in substantial reductions. Some, but by no means all, arise from the speed with which weapons technology changes. As an introduction to present changes, it may be interesting to point out how quickly the arms race has changed in character since the end of World War II. The U.S.-Soviet arms race had just begun in 1949 when Vannevar Bush remarked:

What would be the nature of all-out war if it came at a time when great belligerents faced each other over adequate stockpiles of atomic bombs, capable of reducing both to relative impotency soon after the storm broke? The condition may never arise. Before it can come about, there is another type of contest: the race to be prepared, in which we are now engaged. If we lose that race decisively we alone shall be devastated and there will be no atomic war between substantially equal contestants. We have to win that race. Worse than that, we have to stay well ahead at all times as the race goes on. If we do there need be no atomic war of the fully devastating sort we study.[1]

Seven years later, Admiral Robert Carney testified:

> After VJ Day, our enemies had been swept from the land, from the sea, and from the air; the scales were very steeply tilted in our favor.
>
> Later, with a monopoly on atomic weapons and a means of delivering them, we had reason to feel in any major showdown the scales were even more strongly tipped in our favor. And then came the very disconcerting realization that the U.S.S.R. was not just a land of untutored peasants; the underestimated Soviets were making technological strides which we had not been prepared to believe possible. . . .
>
> More recently, it dawned on us that our own native land could be subjected directly to attack, atomic attack.[2]

After another seven years had passed, the Secretary of Defense, Robert McNamara, felt impelled to point out that

> We are approaching an era when it will become increasingly improbable that either side could destroy a sufficiently large portion of the other's strategic nuclear force, either by surprise or otherwise, to preclude a devastating retaliatory blow.

Fifteen years after Bush's statement, it seems that the major powers will soon, if they do not now, face each other "over adequate stockpiles of atomic bombs, capable of reducing both to relative impotency," fairly independently of the course of the war. We have not lost "the race to be prepared." In fact, the Secretary of Defense would argue that "Deterrence of deliberate, calculated attack seems as well assured as it can be. . . ." Can much more than deterrence of deliberate attack be achieved unilaterally? Evidently not a good deal more. Mr. McNamara has stated, without contradiction, that "no responsible Pentagon official, certainly none of the Joint Chiefs of Staff," has proposed "a strategic force that would enable us, if we struck first, to so reduce Soviet retaliatory power that the damage it could then do to U.S. population and industry would be brought down to an 'acceptable' level. . . ."[3] The conditions that produced these admissions encourage U.S. consideration of disarmament.

These conditions have operated to improve the prospects for Soviet agreement as well. Marshal Malinovsky announced:

We have no special need for increasing the numerical strength of our rocket forces and our weapon stocks. The next stage is no longer the stockpiling of weapons, but their routine perfection and renewal of stocks.[4]

And there are domestic signs that the time is ripe to consider a halt. There are the presidential comments about "How much is enough?" There is the wide acceptance of the notion of overkill. And there are the signs of strain in the justifications of the Department of Defense for the procurement of so many weapons — the construction of which was initiated in anticipation of a missile gap that never arose. Shortly after these weapons were programed, a Congressman provoked the following exchange:

> *Mr. Minshall:* At what point do we reach the absurd stage of these missiles? How many missiles do we have to have before we get that ridiculous?
>
> *General Irvine:* I think we are going to have an interesting discussion with this committee in about 1963 on that subject.[5]

That discussion is somewhat overdue.

The Major Procurement Contests

The three major procurement contests of the mid-sixties all involve ballistic missiles. Speaking as Director of Defense Research and Engineering, Harold Brown has characterized the major contests as

> one between penetration aids and ballistic missile defense, one between antisubmarine efforts and attempts to insure that ballistic missile submarines cannot be detected or attacked before they launch their missiles, and a third between hardening and missile accuracy. . . .[6]

The rate at which the contests develop surprises even the participants. In 1964, Secretary of the Air Force Zuckert evinced surprise at our own progress:

> It seems to me that we too often forget that it is — it just happens to be this month — 10 years since the committee

headed by the great von Neumann concluded that a rapid ICBM program was practical. Today, the first generation missiles are already being replaced.[7]

And General Walsh, showing surprise at Soviet progress, suggested in 1961 that "the pace is something. You could say they have come in 5 years where we came in 10 in weapons."[8] (Another indication of this same ratio is suggested by the fact that we believe the Russians took 4½ years to build the Bison, compared with 8½ years for our construction of the comparable B-52.)[9]

There is no one in the world who knows what the shape of these contests will be twenty years hence. Without arms control and disarmament, perhaps even with them, the strategic balance facing the next generation must be assessed as highly uncertain. Neither we nor they can answer the question put to General Eisenhower by Premier Bulganin in 1957:

> First of all, who can guarantee, if the present competition in the production of ever newer types of weapons is continued and assumes still greater proportions, that it will be the NATO members who are the winners in such a competition?[10]

Ballistic Missiles

At the end of World War II, ballistic missiles were science fiction: science fiction that very much annoyed those with some grasp of the then existing capabilities. Dr. Bush told the Senate Committee on Atomic Energy in December, 1945:

> We have plenty enough to think about that is very definite and very realistic — enough so that we don't need to step out into some of these borderlines, which seem to me more or less fantastic. Let me say this: There has been a great deal said about a 3,000-mile high-angle rocket.
> In my opinion such a thing is impossible and will be impossible for many years.[11]

Even after four years had passed, Dr. Bush was still able to argue (a) that "there need be little fear of the intercontinental missile in the form of a pilotless aircraft, for it is not so effective from the standpoint of cost or performance as the airplane with a crew aboard," (*b*) that "we would have to pay millions of dollars for a single shot," (*c*) that a 2,000-mile rocket could only be "depended upon to hit within 150 miles of its target," although "perhaps within ten miles" with "sights and homing aids" and perhaps even within a mile or two if all went very well indeed, (*d*) that its warhead would have to be the "scarce and highly expensive" atomic bomb which could not be trusted to a "highly complex and possibly erratic carrier of inherently low precision," and (*e*) that even the atomic bomb would not be sufficiently powerful to permit its use with such inaccuracy.

Time has destroyed the presuppositions of these arguments, especially in the production of the hydrogen bomb warhead without which the intercontinental missile would indeed have remained science fiction. Edward Teller testified:

> . . . the development of the missiles has in actual fact, and at least to a very great extent, waited for the realization of a warhead. We did not go ahead and undertake a very vigorous program of developing long-range missiles before the time at which it was reasonably clear that a warhead was available.[12]

With an A-bomb warhead, the missile could not be of really practical use unless its precision of guidance was increased "by a factor of 100" over that required to put a satellite in orbit. With a hydrogen bomb warhead this requirement could be reduced by a factor of 10.[13]

In February 1954, after the detonation of a hydrogen bomb, a Strategic Missile Evaluation Committee headed by John von Neumann recommended an urgent "go-ahead" for the ballistic missile program and predicted, "A period of 6 to 8 years should . . . permit the attainment of the beginnings of an operational capability." [14]

Two years later, the AEC was able to advise the Department of Defense that a substantial reduction in warhead weight and size could be obtained. This made feasible a sufficiently small — hence easier to handle — solid-fuel missile. The Navy promptly sought approval for a submarine-launched

Polaris program and the right to cease participation in the Jupiter liquid-fuel program sponsored with the Army.[15] By 1956 development of both land- and sea-based ballistic missiles was underway in the forms deployed today.

Land-Based Ballistic Missiles

Three different land-based missiles have been procured or programed for strategic attack upon the Soviet Union should war occur.* The earlier of these, scheduled by the Department of Defense to be phased out in fiscal 1965 are

Atlas D: 27 missiles in 3 squadrons, liquid-fueled, 3 megaton yield hardened to 2 psi; entered service in 1959.

Atlas E: 27 missiles in 3 squadrons, liquid-fueled, 3 megaton yield, hardened to 25 psi; entered service in early sixties.

Atlas F: 54 missiles in 6 squadrons, liquid-fueled, 3 megaton yield hardened to 100 psi; completed entering service in December 1963.

Titan I: 54 missiles in 6 squadrons, liquid-fueled, 4 megaton yield hardened to 100 psi; entered service in 1961–1962.

The later missiles, to be kept in service, are

Titan II: 54 missiles in 6 squadrons, storable liquid fuel, 5 megaton yield hardened to 100 psi; evidently in the force indefinitely.

Minuteman I: 750 missiles in 5 wings, solid-fueled, 1 megaton yield of undeclared hardness; entered service between October 1962, and June 1965.

Minuteman II: 150 missiles in 1 wing, solid-fueled, funded in 1964.[16]

The missile force has become increasingly secure as the Minuteman missile has been deployed; especially important

* These land-based missiles are part of the Strategic Air Command (SAC) of the Air Force. Their explosive power or "yield" is measured in millions of tons of TNT equivalent, or in megatons. The hardness of their silos is measured by the number of pounds of pressure per square inch (psi) that these can withstand.

have been the efforts to disperse controls over the force. Each of the 3 squadrons in a wing has 5 launch control facilities, controlling only 10 missiles each, located peripherally around a launch center. Hence the 50 missiles in a squadron are not controlled in the final stages from a single point. Each launch facility is connected to at least one other launch facility, providing a redundant communications link to the launch center. In addition, the launch center can fire all 50 missiles.[17] The control points are protected by "extreme hardening." [18] Finally, as a further precaution, it is possible to fire Minuteman systems on the basis of a signal sent out from an aircraft. According to Dr. Brown this arrangement eliminates dependence upon "survival of the launch control centers" or "survival of their cable connections to the missile site," thus also eliminating "any effect of vulnerability of launch control centers or of control cabling." [19]

The missiles themselves are still further dispersed around the control points. They are generally 18–20 miles apart.[20] And each of them is embedded in a hardened silo "designed to withstand thermal and pressure effects and ground motion effects of typical Soviet weapons detonated at relatively close quarters." [21] It gives an idea of the degree to which the missiles are protected to note that an explosive cartridge blows the lid off the Minuteman silo before firing so that the debris that may have accumulated from the impact of a foreign missile nearby can be removed.

In short, the missile force has been built with the aim of retaining, after a nuclear attack, the capacity to achieve a retaliatory blow. It has also been designed to reduce the possibilities of accidental or unauthorized action, which has been said to be "so close to being impossible as to be of negligible importance to us."

As important as the degree of dispersal and protection of the Minuteman force may be its growing flexibility. While the first wing of Minuteman (Wing I) could carry only one target, Wings II–V will have more than one target and can be switched from one target to another by, "in a sense, pressing a button." [22] This greatly improves the strength of the force for retaliatory purposes, since one can target the missiles surviving an attack on a variety of points instead, in effect, of letting the enemy attack determine the pattern of retaliation.

The growing flexibility of the missile force will be combined with much greater efficiency as Minuteman II gradually replaces Minuteman I. Since the life of a missile is generally taken to be five years, it will presumably not be much longer than that before the force is composed primarily of the newer missiles. According to Secretary McNamara, Minuteman II "will be more than eight times as effective against the best-protected military targets as its predecessor [Minuteman I]." [23]

The missile force is presumably also gaining in reliability, but it is difficult to estimate the extent to which a high reliability of firing can be maintained. Some years ago, Secretary Donald A. Quarles noted that "very complicated" missiles that had been "in operational use for a matter of years" had achieved a reliability on the order of 70–75 percent. He suggested that "if we got to 90 percent, we would consider that very excellent engineering." [24] It is important to note that these reliability problems apply to bombers and other weapon systems as well as to missiles. Secretary McNamara has testified:

> I don't wish to leave the conclusion with the committee that these reliability problems in the missiles are any different than the reliability problems in our manned aircraft systems. They are essentially the same. They require the application of the same technology to correct, and I believe it is fair to say that many of our missile systems today are as reliable as some of our aircraft systems today.[25]

Finally, the missile force is improving in accuracy. Originally, it was estimated that Atlas and Titan missiles might fall within 5 nautical miles of their target about 50 per cent of the time, that is, have a probable circular error (CEP) of 5 nautical miles. However, by 1960, successful Atlas launches were reaching within 2 nautical miles of the predesignated target, and the President suggested that U.S. missiles had a

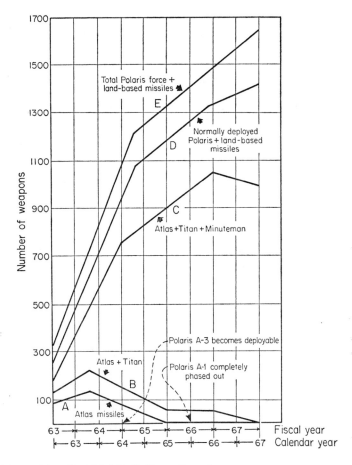

Figure 4.1. The U.S. Missile Force Growth.

Curves A and B show the Atlas, and Atlas plus Titan missile forces. They incorporate the decision of early 1965 to phase out Atlas and Titan I. The latter curve assumes that Titan II will be phased out in fiscal 1967.

Curve C adds the Minuteman force to curve B. It assumes that all Minutemen will be in place in fiscal 1966.

Curve D adds the normally deployed Polaris force to curve C.

Curve E adds the total Polaris force to curve C.

All curves are based upon the data presented either in Chapter Four or in the annual reports of the Institute for Strategic Studies.

CEP of less than 2 miles.[26] Now it has been announced that Minuteman II will have one-half the CEP of Minuteman I.[27] It is difficult to estimate the extent to which accuracies may yet improve.

The growth of the U.S. missile force is shown in Figure 4.1.

Soviet Land-Based Missiles

Presumably the Soviet force is growing in efficiency and security like our own, but information on Soviet intercontinental missiles is obviously hard to come by. The Institute of Strategic Studies suggests that there are two operational models:

1. A liquid-fueled, 10 megaton ICBM weighing 300,000 lb, capable of traveling over 8,000 miles; in service since 1955.
2. A storable liquid-fueled ICBM carrying in excess of 30 megatons; in service since 1963.

The possibility that the Soviets have lagged behind us in developing efficient solid-fueled missiles comparable to our Minuteman is corroborated by both General LeMay and Secretary McNamara, who testified that "we should recognize the [deletion in original] advantage we have in the solid propellants over the Soviets." This is a sizable advantage in simplicity of handling, speed of firing (that is, short countdown), economy, and perhaps in other ways as well. Secretary Zuckert testified that "I would rather have the solid-fueled POLARIS and MINUTEMAN than any liquid-fueled missile that I can imagine." [28]

Estimates of the numbers of Soviet intercontinental missiles have risen surprisingly slowly. In July 1962, Hanson Baldwin claimed that Soviet ICBM's "in operational readiness and in advanced stages of construction" apparently numbered considerably less than 100. Four months later, in November 1962, Stewart Alsop wrote:

> "According to the current estimates, their 100th long-range missile became operational only a few weeks ago. If the current

intelligence estimates are accurate—and on this score McNamara says that he is absolutely convinced.' . . ."

A year later, in November 1963, Hanson Baldwin estimated Soviet ICBM's as "one-fourth to one-fifth" of our own 500 (that is, 100 to 125). Three months later, in February 1964, he suggested that the Soviet Union had "only about 150 intercontinental ballistic missiles." [29] In April, the Secretary of Defense gave an estimate implying a force of less than 187

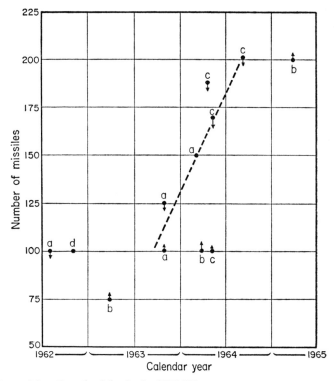

Figure 4.2. Growth of the Soviet ICBM Force.

This chart is based upon data provided in the text. The arrows indicate upper and lower estimates. The estimates are related to their sources as follows: *a*, Hanson Baldwin; *b*, Institute for Strategic Studies; *c*, Secretary of Defense McNamara; *d*, Stewart Alsop. The dotted line indicates a plausible linear estimate of the increasing numbers of Soviet ICBM's.

missiles, and shortly thereafter, on April 26, Mr. Baldwin suggested the numbers 100 to 170. On August 17, Secretary McNamara gave an estimate of our superiority which implied that the Soviets had fewer than 200 ICBM's. Figure 4.2 plots these estimates. The dotted line indicates the growth that would occur if, in fact, the Soviet Union did have "about 150" on February 14, 1964, 170 by April 26, and continued to build at that rate through the next few years. This results in almost exactly 100 missiles per year.

The Soviet Union also possesses large numbers of medium-range (MRBM) and intermediate-range (IRBM) missiles deployed in the Soviet Union and aimed at targets in Western Europe. These are thought to have explosive yields measured in megatons, and to number about 800.[30]

For a variety of reasons, Soviet land-based missiles are probably relatively vulnerable if their positions are known. First, there are indications that the missiles are clustered in groups of "eight or more," sometimes with two missiles for each launch site.[31] Furthermore, in 1962, reports indicated that hardening was just beginning. It was said to be comparable to the intermediate stage of hardening for Atlas missiles, which are neither in the open nor in a silo but are set horizontally in "coffin-type" installations.[32] This suggests a hardness of approximately 25 psi, if the coffins are comparable to our own. The most recent comments by the Secretary of Defense on Soviet hardening do not indicate any very great changes, although they do indicate some.

For example, Secretary McNamara noted in early 1964, "As I pointed out last year, the Soviets are hardening some of their ICBM sites. . . ." It is possible that the very large Soviet missiles are not easy to harden. Furthermore, the liquid-fueled missiles have a slower reaction time than do solid-fueled missiles. This encourages the Secretary of Defense to believe that "it is probable that the launching of their bombers and missiles would extend over a sufficient period of time for us to receive the first blow, and to strike back not only at Soviet cities, if that be our choice, but also at the elements of their forces that had not yet been launched." [33]

A still more explicit statement of this type was made by General White:

> For years to come there are going to be a considerable number of their missiles that will not go, as there will be with ours, and it is highly useful to knock the ICBM force out. Now the trick is to find out which ones did not go.[34]

In order to protect this force, the Soviets are relying in part "on concealment and on active defence. . . ." [35] For instance, General Talensky notes:

> Most of these installations, if not all the decisive ones, are reliably concealed and consequently to hit them would require the pinpointing of a target from a launching site thousands of kilometers away. Part of the means for delivering a retaliatory blow are mobile and it would be difficult to hit them at an exact spot. Lastly, a substantial part of the means of attack would inevitably be diverted to sham targets.[36]

Vulnerability of Land-Based Missiles

Strictly speaking, land-based missiles would be much less vulnerable if they could be fired upon warning of attack but before enemy missiles had detonated. In the late fifties, when missiles were highly vulnerable, there was talk of launching missiles on warning, that is, of anticipating the arrival of Soviet missiles, indicated on a warning screen, by launching our own. But since the missiles could not be recalled or destroyed in flight, such a suggestion involved great risks of inadvertent war. Furthermore, as General White pointed out, we could not afford to fire much of our deterrent lest the warning were false and the missiles needlessly exhausted. In 1960, General Power, then Commander in Chief, Strategic Air Command, told the Economic Club of New York:

> The survivability of the missile poses a somewhat different problem from that of the bomber and must, therefore, be solved by different techniques. Since a missile cannot be recalled once

it has been launched, it would be too risky to fire it until there is incontestable proof of aggression. Therefore, our ICBM's probably would have to "ride out" the initial attack. This problem is taken into account in our later missiles which will permit launching from silos deep in the ground, thus providing good protection or "hardening" against the effects of near-misses.[37]

It is now accepted doctrine that the missiles should "ride out" a surprise attack, although the question continues to arise.* Whether the Soviets would fire missiles on warning is difficult to answer conclusively. However, the reasons given for our hesitation to fire on warning still apply to the Soviets. It should also be recognized that the Soviet system has been extensively spoofed (that is, alerted unnecessarily) by the Strategic Air Command, whether by accident or design.† After such experiences, a Soviet leader is probably loath to fire on warning. For these reasons, the invulnerability of land-based missiles must rest upon their ability to ride out an attack.

Thus, our Minutemen are likely to survive a straightforward attack in which one or more missiles are fired at each. Even the "most pessimistic view . . . suggests a vulnerability ratio for our hardened, dispersed Minuteman sites of less than two sites killed on the average by a single very-large-yield Soviet missile." [41] Hence so long as our forces are numerically superior to those of the Soviets no ordinary attack upon them could be launched. Our vulnerability problems are likely to

* For instance, in discussions of the fiscal 1965 budget this conversation occurred:

"*Chairman Russell:* What percentage of these missiles could have been launched prior to the arrival of an incoming salvo from the Communist bloc?

"*General LeMay:* I think we could launch the bulk of our missiles within the 15-minute warning time that we would allow. Our alert missiles, I think, would be launched in that time." [38]

† Thus Premier Khrushchev reported: "Take the case of General Power, who heads the U.S. Strategic Air Command. In November 1961, after a false alarm he ordered bombers stationed at all U.S. bases to head out for the Soviet Union. He did not even bother to inform the U.S. President, that is, the Supreme Commander of the country's armed forces, about it. For all of twelve and a half minutes the American Strategic Air Command was virtually in a state of war with the Soviet Union." [39] Whatever the facts of the incident reported by Khrushchev, "flushing" U.S. bombers is within the authority of the SAC Commander.[40]

arise only through esoteric methods of attack. And even these problems are diminished in significance by other weapon systems such as Polaris. In any case, a special technique would have to destroy more than one missile with each attacking weapon. One such method that has received wide publicity involves the use of "electromagnetic standing waves." Produced by the fireball of an explosion, the waves might be "of such intensity that any electrical conductors, such as wires and cables, that are strung on poles or buried in the ground in straight lines, would have currents of thousands of amperes induced in them, resulting in their destruction by melting." [42]

The Soviet vulnerability problem for land-based missiles, from a strategic point of view, may be a good deal more elemental. If the United States has learned where the smaller number of Soviet missiles are located — through reconnaissance, defectors, or spies — each such Soviet land-based missile could be attacked by several of our missiles. Thus, 300 one-megaton missiles with a CEP of three-quarters of a mile and a reliability of two-thirds could attack 100 targets of 25 psi hardness and be expected to leave less than 5 intact. [43]

In the long run, especially if the numbers of land-based missiles become comparable, increasing accuracies may become a matter of concern to both sides. One study of an arms control agreement suggests that "The problems to be encountered would be considerably alleviated if CEP's do not improve so that they are less than 3000 feet." * But in 1964 General LeMay testified that the Air Force was "optimistic" over the prospect of achieving "greatly improved accuracies with ICBM's. . . ." [45]

Sea-Based Ballistic Missiles

At the present time, most analysts would argue that the question "Can retaliatory forces survive?" may be answered in the affirmative, primarily because ballistic missiles can be

* This study by Air Force Brigadier General Glenn A. Kent assumes hardened and dispersed emplacement. It treats only land-based missiles under an arms control agreement. [44]

based on or under the sea. Much more attention would now be paid to the destabilizing possibility that "hard" (invulnerable) missile sites could suddenly become "soft" (vulnerable) were it not for the fact that these land-based systems are backed up by sea-based forces that are difficult to attack.

U.S. *Polaris Submarines*

Each Polaris submarine costs about $115 million, exclusive of its missiles. A submarine carries 16 missiles, and each missile must cost $3 million, since the cost of a submarine with missiles has been estimated to be $150 to $160 million.[46]

The operating cost of a Polaris submarine is somewhere between $5.5 million and $7.5 million a year.* This would indicate the costs over five years to maintain a Polaris missile on station at somewhere between $14 million and $23 million, or from three to five times that of keeping a Minuteman missile on target.†

The procurement schedule for Polaris has not changed since fiscal 1963. There were 12 Polaris submarines in June 1963, and the schedule called for the twelfth to the twenty-ninth Polaris submarines to be delivered at the rate of one a month and the thirtieth to the forty-first to be delivered one every two months.[49] In other words, about 24 by June 1964, 29 by November 1964, 33 by June 1965, 39 by June 1966, and 41 by the end of 1966.

The submarine itself should last for fifteen to twenty years if its experience is similar to that of other submarines. Its missiles are cost accounted, as are other strategic missiles, on

* The cost of operating the submarine may be computed as follows. Since Minuteman costs $4 million to install and $100,000 to maintain, procurement of, and operational cost for, 250 Minutemen for five years is about $1,125 million. This has been said to be comparable to the cost of operating and procuring 6 Polaris submarines for five years. Subtracting the cost of procurement gives this result.[47]

† These figures assume that half the submarines are on station, that each cost $115 million, and that the life of a missile is five years.[48] The lower figure assumes that the Polaris system will work for fifteen years; the upper figure depreciates the submarine over five years.

a five-year basis.[50] The lifetime of the system, assessed against technological breakthroughs, is also at least five years. For instance, Secretary McNamara testified:

> At the present time we see no reason to believe that the PO-LARIS will lose its invulnerability in the near future. When I say "near future," let's say 5 years. I don't see any reason to believe we will lose it after that, but I don't want to even hazard a guess as to the period after that. However, none of the techniques that might possibly cause the POLARIS to be vulnerable appear to be in the state of development so that they can be deployed within a 5-year period.[51]

The submarines each have two crews totaling 224 men, and the crews are alternated every 3 months. Of the 3 months, each submarine is in port for about 30 days and at sea for about 60.[52] It is interesting to note, especially in considering the possible growth of the Soviet submarine force, that we have been having some problem supplying the necessary crews. Personnel in the submarine force have tripled from 1960 to 1965 (from 8,000 to 25,000), and the needed men cannot be trained quickly.[53] For instance, it requires 42 months of training for men concerned with nuclear-propulsion and about 2 years for the men concerned with guided-missiles.[54]

While at sea, the submarine and its crew are highly isolated. Communication between submarine and submarine, or between submarine and surface craft, cannot be achieved "securely." [55] There is no two-way communication to shore.

Far more important, however, is the ability of the submerged Polaris submarine to receive messages from the base. However, Admiral Ignatius Galantin testified in 1962: "We still have maintained a record of 100 percent solid coverage of all traffic sent to them, and this includes numerous surprise drill messages the operations commander will send. . . ." [56] Whether or not this situation would hold during war, in particular after an attack, is not so clear. After considerable discussion of the appropriate phase, Admiral David McDonald affirmed that it was "possibly . . . but not likely" that communications with Polaris submarines could be knocked out with high-yield weapons.[57]

Not all of the Polaris submarines are maintained in a location that permits firing at once. It is often said that of the deployable submarines, we can count on "approximately 2/3 . . . being on station at all times." [58] This figure is based on the previously noted fact that each submarine is at sea only 60 days out of 90, or two-thirds of the time. However, former Secretary of the Navy Paul Nitze has remarked that the present deployment rate is "extremely high," because presently deployed ships have not yet reached their first overhaul period. Eventually, of the 41 submarines to be built, "7 would be in overhaul, 34 deployable." [59] Hence, if two-thirds of the deployable submarines were on station, about 22 submarines could be relied upon at all times. However, Admiral George Anderson has pointed out: "We also have the option of increasing the number of boats on station, if, for example, we feel that there is a particular period of tension, such as we did during the Cuban operation." [60]

When the Polaris submarine is on station, it need not be at a "fixed known location." Instead, "Each captain is free to roam at will in his area as long as he maintains his target coverage. . . ." In short, "nobody in this country knows where any one of our deployed submarines is." [61]

Since a submarine need not fire from a fixed point, it clearly has the capacity to fire at any points it wishes within its range. According to Admiral Levering Smith: "The target choices are made in the fire control system either when he receives the message or when he goes into a preselected area. As he goes from one area to another area it is current practice to shift his target." [62] Evidently the missiles are kept trained on targets which may be changed systematically as the submarine passes out of range of some points and into the range of others.

The range of the submarine-launched missiles varies. There are three different models of the Polaris solid-fuel missile. The models A-1, A-2, and A-3 have a range of 1,200, 1,500, and 2,500 nautical miles (1,380, 1,700, and 2,800 statute miles), respectively. The first five Polaris submarines are equipped with the A-1, the sixth to the eighteenth will be equipped with the A-2, and the nineteenth to the forty-first will have the A-3. Eventually, the first five submarines will have their A-1's replaced with A-3's. (The A-3 became deployable in mid-1964. The A-1 will be phased out in early 1966.) A fourth missile, the B-3, is under consideration, but according to the vice-president and general manager of Lockheed's Missile Systems Division, which would build it, the B-3 concept is still "pretty much in people's headbones." If the B-3 emerged, it would be installed in place of the A-2's.[63] (The B-3 has recently been renamed the "Poseidon.")

The significance of these ranges depends of course on the distance of Soviet (and Chinese) targets from the sea. Fairly deep penetration of the Soviet Union with a 1,200-mile missile can be achieved from the Baltic and Barents Seas and along the extended, exposed, Arctic and Pacific coast lines. With the A-2, a Polaris submarine could be on station in the Norwegian Sea (or in the Eastern Mediterranean) without being restricted to border or near-border targets. The A-3 would permit relatively deep attacks from the Atlantic off the coast of France.

Another way of looking at the situation is to note the extent to which the sea area has been increasing from which targets could be attacked. For example, the A-2 would generally double "the water area from which the submarine would fire with A-1." This has the effect of assuring for each submarine an operating area that is never smaller than "the state of Texas." (Texas has an area of 260,000 square miles; a circle with this area would have a radius of 290 miles.) The change from A-2 to A-3 will have a further impact in increasing this area. Admiral Galantin noted:

> With the A-2 missile, the area in which a submarine can be deployed and cover its important targets is about 6 million square miles. With the A-3 missile, it is going to be a little over 15 million square miles.

In fact, the A-3 missile can hit any spot on earth from the sea.[64]

Besides the range of the missiles, several other characteristics are of importance. In particular, the yield and accuracy of the missile can, in principle, determine the sort of targets for which it would be useful. There have been a variety of speculations concerning the utility of the Polaris missiles for force targets, and there has been some feeling that they are accurate enough only for city targets. In particular, their accuracy has been widely portrayed as inferior to that of the Minuteman missiles. However, in 1963, Dr. Brown said that the Polaris CEP depended "mostly on the navigation error, which is still being reduced." [65] In other words, improvements in locating the position from which the submarine would fire would improve the accuracy of the missile itself. The yield of the missiles is not thought to be smaller than that of the Minuteman missile. It is estimated at 0.7 megatons.[66] However, the B-3 or Poseidon missile will improve in yield and accuracy very substantially.

The reliability of the missile force does not seem to be in question. According to Dr. Brown, the Polaris A-2 "reached the assurance of [deletion in original] percent reliability which had been set by the Joint Chiefs of Staff as the goal," thus eliminating the need for further scheduled tests. Evidently the A-3 is following the same course. Admiral Anderson testified that its flight-test program was "on schedule" and that all indications confirmed that it would "meet or exceed the high reliability goals established for it." [67]

Finally, the readiness of the missiles is extremely high. While on patrol, all 16 missiles of each submarine have been "ready to fire on instant notice 95 percent of the time and 15, 99.9 percent of the time."

A measure of the power that these characteristics provide was given by Secretary of the Navy Nitze, who used current reliability figures for the 8 on-station submarines of an average day to conclude that these forces could eliminate most of the war-making capabilities of the Soviet urban industrial complex and kill 25 to 35 million people.[68]

The Polaris submarine is not the only possibility for hard-to-detect sea-based missiles. Although, as we have suggested, no one sees any immediate threat to the "invulnerability of Polaris," other weapon systems are being explored that would substitute for it. For instance, the Air Force is said to be exploring "Orca, a notion of constructing encapsulated, unmanned, and generally immobile missiles . . . which might be deployed at random over the earth's surface — in isolated wooded areas, arctic wastes and oceans and obscure waterways." One method of deployment might have these missiles floating "just below the ocean's surface, much like a naval mine." Lockheed has proposed "Turtle," a submerged, manned missile complex "capable of long-range mobility at very slow speed." Meanwhile, the Navy is test-firing a "Hydra" concept of launching rockets from "free-floating vertically positioned platforms at sea." Other studies refer to secreting platforms below the surface in inland or easily accessible waterways.[69]

Soviet Missile-launching Submarines

The development of nuclear submarines by the other side seems to be far behind our own in numbers and efficiency. In 1963–1964, the Soviet Union was said to have "at least" 30 missile-carrying submarines, of which 20 were nuclear powered.[70] The Secretary of Defense has asserted, "We know that the Soviets are building nuclear-powered submarines, both missile-firing and attack, but there are a number of uncertainties concerning these forces." [71]

One uncertainty seems to be the rate at which the Soviets will achieve operational status in the firing of missiles from under water. In April 1964, Secretary McNamara corroborated the fact that no Soviet missiles yet had operational firing capability under water. The key word here is probably "operational," since a Soviet Polaris-type missile named "Snark" was first displayed in Moscow as early as November 1962. And even a few months before, Hanson Baldwin had stated: "Russia's first submarines capable of launching missiles from submerged positions are just being built, and one of the first submerged missile-launchings was recently held." [72]

Until submerged firings are possible, the Soviet Union must rely on surface-launched missiles, with ranges from 100 to 400 miles, which became available in 1959. Whether or not the Soviets find this very restricting is not clear. There is some evidence that the submarine is not yet thought of as a strategic weapon. Reference to its use in Sokolovskii's *Military Strategy* is sketchy. For instance, after discussing the characteristics that Soviet submarines should possess, *Military Strategy* states: "These qualities will permit the submarine forces to engage in successful combat with an enemy navy and, if necessary, to deliver nuclear strikes to coastal targets." [73] Changes made in the second edition of this work have tended somewhat to eliminate this oversight.[74]

Surface-Deployed Ballistic Missiles

As of 1965, ballistic missiles of either major power are not at all likely to be deployed on the surface of the sea except perhaps in the proposed Western Multilateral Fleet (MLF), which may never materialize. The MLF would represent a relatively substantial barrier to missile disarmament: first, because of Soviet objection to the idea and, second, because of the increased number of parties who would be signatories to a missile reduction treaty.

Vulnerability of Sea-Based Forces

If the sea-based missiles of the United States and the Soviet Union were highly invulnerable and sufficiently numerous, the prospects for reductions in land-based missiles would be improved, assuming the absence of effective antiballistic missile defenses against sea-based missiles. The land-based forces would be unnecessary for a sure retaliatory force, and their use against other land-based targets if war broke out would be deterred by the existence of sea-based forces that could not be struck. Hence a close look at the prospects for antisubmarine warfare (ASW) is warranted. It should be mentioned that these remarks would have to be qualified if the missile defenses discussed in Chapter One were built.

It may be that both we and the Soviets would be better off if there were no effective antisubmarine defenses, since their construction could lead to renewed procurement of forces and perceived insecurity. Nevertheless, the United States sees no alternative to seeking such a defense, and, indeed, it is not clear that an effective defense could be matched eventually by an effective Soviet defense. The problem of defending against submarines is not a symmetrical one for the two major powers.

In any case, very little restraint in ASW procurement could be expected on the grounds that technology *should* be slowed. Present policy shows no uncertainty concerning the importance of ASW efforts. The Secretary of Defense has testified:

> In ASW I have one ground rule and that is that money is no limit whatever on research and development projects associated with increasing our ability to detect, track and kill Soviet submarines, including particularly Soviet missile launching submarines.[75]

Of course, procurement is another matter. In the testimony on the budget for fiscal 1965, Secretary McNamara indicated that, in view of "a number of uncertainties" concerning Soviet missile-firing and attack submarines, "the ASW force structure which we are now proposing for the latter part of the program period [1965–1969] must be considered highly tentative." Despite these uncertainties, the Secretary believes that the Soviet submarine will be "one of the major threats" by 1968.[76]

However, this threat is evidently not yet overwhelming. For example, Hanson Baldwin suggests that, during the Cuban crisis, "six Soviet submarines — all conventionally powered by diesel engines for surface cruising and electric batteries for submerged operations — were sent to the vicinity of Cuba." He viewed the possibility of other submarines as "unlikely," noted that they had been "more or less" continuously tracked "without too much difficulty," and speculated that in a state of war they "probably" could have been destroyed. This was confirmed by the Chief of Naval Operations, Admiral Anderson, who noted that the Navy had been able to identify six submarines by photographs and that "if weapons instead of camera films were employed, these submarines would surely have been 'killed.'" [77]

In addition to technical problems, the Soviets have difficulties in deploying submarines. The Atlantic and the Pacific are basically Western seas. Admiral Charles Weakley described the problems of a Soviet submarine commander in this way:

> For example, coming around the North Cape there, he has about 500 friendly miles. He has 4,000 of increasingly unfriendly miles. Coming out the other way he has about 600 friendly miles, and he has about 4,400 of increasingly unfriendly miles.
>
> Now any time he is in water[s] which are hostile to his presence, he cannot, for example, run his fathometer to check the depth of the water, he cannot use his radio for communications, he cannot do anything which reveals his presence. He must be awfully careful about charging batteries, that type of thing, because anything he does renders him liable to detection by our forces. [78]

Evidently other Western advantages exist also. Commenting on a confused newspaper article entitled, "New Submarine Finder Project Will Blunt the Role of the Polaris," Admiral William Raborn suggested:

> I think the man got himself mixed up a bit. That is designed against enemy submarines and not POLARIS submarines. I would like to point out to the writer and those who might be interested in this program that it takes friendly real estate to establish this rather comprehensive system, and the North Atlantic basin is under friendly control, and not available to potential enemies for such stations. I would think that these are facts which will become rather apparent upon thought. [79]

If future hostilities occur, a submarine fleet would probably face difficulties similar to those met by the World War II surface fleet. For instance, in 1958 Admiral Arleigh Burke described ASW efforts in time of war by saying:

> We will mine the exits and narrow channels through which the enemy submarines must pass.

We will augment the barriers.

We will have hunter-killer groups operating — constantly searching — in areas of probable enemy submarine concentrations.[80]

Of course, there is more to ASW for the United States than "bottlenecks." There are distinct problems of detection, classification, location, and destruction.

First, consider detection. The Secretary of Defense has maintained that "we are continuing a very ambitious research and development effort in the submarine detection area." At least in 1957, the Navy considered this problem "the most difficult in antisubmarine warfare . . . the one in which we have the least confidence." * In 1961, research and development efforts in submarine detection apparently emphasized the use of sound in (*a*) variable-depth sonar to provide detection ranges below the ocean thermal layer comparable to those that our new hull-mounted sonar give above the thermal layer; and (*b*) a new sonar promising further improvement in detection ranges.[84] The thermal layer referred to was described by Admiral Burke in 1959 in the following terms:

> One problem which has confronted ASW since its beginnings is that of the "thermal layer." This is a layer of water within the ocean depths where a significant change of temperature exists. This layer is usually found between the "surface" water and the water of greater depths, and forms a virtual mirror for sound waves. Sonar pings generally bounce off it. Submarines have long known this and have been hiding just below the layer. One of the major advantages of the ASW submarine is its ability also to get below the "thermal layer" and listen there where the noises travel. Surface ships have not been able to reach below "the layer." However, variable depth sonar is under development which is designed to probe at the best listening depth beneath its parent destroyer.[85]

* Admiral Burke indicated, however, that the detection range had been extended "4 to 5 times," presumably over World War II ranges.[81] By 1960, the Navy was speaking of Project Artemis, "a research program to establish the feasibility of ocean-area active sonar surveillance."[82] This would sound ambitious indeed. A year later a "closely related" program, Project Trident, was described as a research and development effort "aimed toward the development of equipment with which an effective ocean-area surveillance system can be made from shore."[83]

After detection come problems of classification and location. These call for mobility. Carriers, shore-based aircraft, helicopters, attack submarines, and so on, all play a role. They carry expendable sonars (sonobuoys) that increase "considerably the speed at which an area can be searched for submarines. These contain radios which transmit submarine information back to the parent aircraft. New sonars, planned for use on surface ships or submarines or on the sea bottom, are expected to increase substantially the distances at which submarines can be detected." [86]

The classification problem is an especially difficult one. For instance it was testified that "you have not only to distinguish a friend from a foe, but you have to distinguish the submerged object and identify it as a submarine rather than a fish, marine life, rocks, and everything else that has been classified as submarines." [87] One device used to distinguish submarines from whales, and one that indicates the kinds of subtle technical problems involved, is the magnetic anomoly detector (MAD), which senses the "distortion of the earth's magnetic field caused by the passage of a submarine." However, this device is said to have "very little growth potential" because, although accurate, it is "extremely limited" in range.[88]

After detection, classification, and location, there is the problem of destroying the target.

Many weapons are available: ASROC, an outgrowth of the rocket-assisted torpedo (RAT), used on surface ships; SUBROC, used on submerged submarines to provide them with a long-range antisubmarine attack capability (according to *The New York Times* [December 5, 1963] this range is 30 miles); and mines, delivered from the air and from submarines.[89] As progress is made in long-range detection of submarines, the demands for improved methods of destruction are increased. Admiral Lloyd Mustin pointed out that "as our sonar ranges increase, the 'time late' of target location information, longer weapon run time and opportunities for target evasion also increase, and we find that we must either provide midcourse guidance for our missiles en route to the target, or have 'weapon-carrying vehicles' that can be accurately controlled to the target and the weapon dropped within its homing range." [90]

It is clear that we have made great strides in antisubmarine warfare, a field described by the Secretary of Defense as "one of the most complex fields of development in the entire area of defense weaponry." [91] Nevertheless, the Soviet submarine threat has not diminished. Admiral Hyman Rickover has testified:

Our antisubmarine program from its inception in 1917 has been a hit-and-miss proposition, different people coming in nearly every year. . . . I think we are no better off today relative to the Russian submarines than we were in 1941 relative to the German submarines.[92]

And in 1964, Admiral McDonald testified in these revealing terms:

I frankly think that before we solve this problem we are going to have to come up with something that we probably are not even dreaming about now.[93]

Soviet progress in ASW seems to have been inferior to our own. The Secretary of Defense believes that "we are way ahead of the Soviet Union in this specific field." [94]

Keeping up with every submarine development is an even greater problem for the Soviet Union than it is for us, since our submarines are so much more advanced than theirs. For their part, they do not even seem to have taken the problem seriously. The editors of the RAND translation of *Soviet Military Strategy* remarked that it was interesting that the authors placed destruction of enemy carrier units ahead of destruction of missile-launching submarines.

As must be evident from the material discussed so far, no single technological breakthrough is at all likely to neutralize Polaris. It is not true, as was put so graphically by Senator Clair Engle, that, "If the Russians ever get a breakthrough on being able to see underwater, the Polaris will be just like a turtle going across a hot road." It is not "a weapons system that is wholly dependent upon one proposition: namely, you can't see underwater." [95] Even if it were easy to detect Polaris, it would still be necessary to separate the submarine's signal from that of other sources. Were this to become relatively simple, it would then be necessary to determine a relatively precise location — as indicated earlier, "kill" radii are measured in fractions of a mile. Since a submarine location can change rapidly, the destruction of even a single Polaris is not assured if it is located only at long range. Finally, the probable destruction of not one but most or all Polaris submarines relatively simultaneously would be necessary to decrease their utility as part of the U.S. military posture. And meanwhile, the range of missiles carried by our submarines increases, as we have noted. For example, since the system was initiated about eight years ago and has already doubled the range of the initial 1,200-mile missile, the range of the A-3 could easily be multiplied by a factor of 5 during the seventies, presumably in some new-model submarine. This would permit worldwide deployment in approximately 125 million square miles of ocean.

It is not necessary to discuss the vulnerability of surface-based ballistic missiles in too much detail since, with the exception of the MLF, which may never be formed, neither major power seems to be planning such a force. However, it is probably true that such a force would be highly invulnerable from a practical point of view, though vulnerable by comparison with the Polaris force. In a sense, fewer technological breakthroughs and fewer new weapon systems would be required to decrease its utility. On the other hand, new devices are always being developed to improve the security of a surface fleet.*

---

* For instance, in 1960, Secretary of the Navy William Franke suggested that aircraft carriers were considerably harder to detect than one might think. Showing a radar picture of 196,000 square miles in the Western Mediterranean, he noted that it showed "less than 25 percent of the total number of ships which were actually at sea in the area at the time." Nor was it possible from the "ideal" radar picture to pick out the two attack carriers mixed amongst other ships of the Sixth Fleet.

Ballistic Missile Defense

We have now discussed some of the elements of two of the three contests that were referred to earlier — contests between attempts to ensure survival, on the one hand, and destruction, on the other, of land-based missile systems and sea-based missile systems. Superimposed on these contests related to missile basing is another related to missile delivery. While the late fifties and early sixties posed the question, "Can retaliatory forces survive?" the late sixties and seventies could conceivably pose the question, "Can retaliatory forces penetrate?" At the present time, most believe that the offense has a substantial lead over the defense. In 1962, General Burchinal testified ". . . some scientific judgments, Dr. Von Karman's among them, . . . show we have a 2- to 4-year lead time in the offense over the defense — missile offense over missile defense." [97] But this gap may be narrowing; it is difficult to tell. This third contest was discussed in Chapter One.

Targeting

The three procurement contests under discussion culminate in the targeting of missiles and bombers on urban-industrial sites and on bomber and missile installations. The basic idea behind our strategic force targeting, if not behind that of the Soviets, is to target several weapons on each site until the probability that it would be destroyed is sufficiently high. Dr. Brown testified:

> And in every case the commander of SAC, if we are talking about strategic vehicles, and the Joint Chiefs of Staff program extra vehicles; they program extra aircraft, they program extra

Furthermore, if a "chance guess" located the carrier, Secretary Franke estimated that it would have moved 30 miles "before the necessary information could be collated, introduced into the launching system and the enemy missile reach the objective area." Further complications could have been introduced with the aid of "defensive electronic countermeasures." [96]

missiles, so as to raise the probability of striking the target high enough to be militarily acceptable. And, of course, that probability is different depending on what the target is.

The more important the target is militarily the higher they want that probability to be and as a consequence the more aircraft or the more missiles or the more of both they program to strike that target.[98]

Once a satisfactory likelihood of destruction of these targets has been achieved, plans are drawn up that permit selective attack. Thus General LeMay reported to Congress that the Kennedy administration wanted many options in their war plan:

We have tried to comply by producing as many as possible. I am talking about our strategic plans now. We have options now that can be exercised by the President in going to war. We also want to hold out a reserve. Whether this is desirable to do under the conditions that might exist or not remains to be seen. But I certainly have no objection to having those options.

The discussion that follows is motivated by an attempt to discern the ways in which improvements in missile efficiency might make it possible to achieve missile reductions. This theme is continued in the conclusions and should be introduced.

Improvements in the efficiency of individual types of missiles are very difficult to prevent technically and politically. And they might justify comparable reductions in missile numbers. These reductions might encourage further reductions, and the agreements might have important political effects even if the reductions themselves had little effect on force efficiency. In any case, other justification for reductions must be superimposed on that arising from improved efficiency.

Missiles improve in efficiency as they become more dependable: as the frequency improves with which a missile — surviving an initial attack — can be expected to accomplish its mission. Dependability arises from reliability (of successful firing), accuracy, yield and readiness, its ability to penetrate defenses, and such other factors as the hardness of the enemy target.

If missiles have low reliability, a great many have to be targeted on a single site. If their reliability is higher, fewer are necessary. For instance, if a missile destroyed its target whenever it was reliably fired, and if the missile has a reliability of 50 per cent, the target would be threatened with an 87 per cent probability of destruction when three missiles were fired at it. If the reliability of the missiles were increased to 70 per cent, there would be a 90 per cent probability of destroying the target with only two missiles. If reliability were 90 per cent, only one missile would be required. Evidently improvements in missile reliability can be very important for achieving high probabilities of destruction — such as 90 per cent. We do try for high probabilities of destruction. General Power has suggested that "we have a better than 90 per cent confidence factor that what we call the hard targets, important targets, will be destroyed." [99]

While an increase in missile reliability could substantially reduce the U.S. force size for fixed performance, this is not so clearly the case for the Soviet Union, if the Secretary of Defense is right that

> Given the small number of weapons they have today, the probability is they would use them primarily against urban areas. This is the theme that runs through that book on Strategy [*Soviet Military Strategy*, Sokolovskii, ed.] that you referred to. [100]

For such a countercity strategy an increase in reliability from 50 per cent to 90 per cent increases force effectiveness by .90/.50.

Of course, a single reliably fired missile may or may not destroy its target, depending upon its yield and accuracy. The effectiveness of a missile is generally assumed to improve in proportion to increases in the fraction $(\text{yield})^{2/3}/(\text{CEP})^2$. Thus, if the yield of a Minuteman went up, over the years, by a factor of 5, its efficiency as a weapon would go up by about $5^{2/3}$, or about 3. If, simultaneously, its CEP were halved, as testimony indicates would be the case if Advanced Minuteman replaced Minuteman, force efficiency would go up by an additional factor of 4, or 12 times over-all. While this does not indicate that our force could be cut by a factor of 12 — probably no target has 12 missiles aimed at it — it does indicate that substantial reductions could take place while greater probabilities of destruction were achieved.

Improvements in reliability, yield, and accuracy can have a significant impact upon the dependability of the force, but improvements in the ability of the force to be retargeted can permit more flexible planning. In particular, the ability to reassign missiles to targets for which the initial firing has failed will permit firing just one missile at a time while at the same time maintaining a small reserve. This avoids firing several missiles at each target simultaneously. These gains are somewhat complicated to characterize abstractly, and their application depends on details, but they can justify substantial reductions in force size. For example, if we want to achieve a 99 per cent probability of destruction with missiles that each have a 90 per cent likelihood of destroying their target, we would ordinarily assign two missiles to each target. If certain missiles can be retargeted, however, plans could call for firing one missile at each target and a second missile at only the 10 per cent that survived the first salvo. This would call for an average of 1.1 missiles instead of 2. It is true that there are difficulties in determining whether or not a target has survived, but if most of the uncertainty of destruction arises through the unreliability of the launch, we might simply observe the launch and estimate from its success the likelihood of destruction.

Whether or not missiles can perform their mission depends also on their ability to survive attack or, in the jargon, on their "survivability." But so long as the Soviet force is small, the survivability of U.S. land-based missiles is really very little at issue, since Soviet missiles would hardly be directed against individual Minutemen. In fact, at present, air bases would be far more attractive targets for counterforce attacks. In any case, the Secretary of Defense has noted that "the most pessimistic view . . . suggests a vulnerability ratio for our hardened, dispersed Minuteman sites of less than two sites killed on the average by a single very-large-yield Soviet missile." [101] If this average decreased from 2 to 1, then for each 100 Soviet high-yield weapons there would be an abstract gain of 100 U.S. Minutemen surviving.

Of course, such improvements in our force effectiveness could be diminished or nullified by decreases in force effectiveness arising through Soviet force improvements. Soviet forces might become better hardened, although existing Soviet forces seem to be of the type that the United States finds difficult to harden. (Our comparable first-generation liquid- or storable-fueled missiles were finally hardened, but to no more than 100 psi.) Improvements in Soviet hardening on this order would reduce the lethal radius of an attacking missile by a factor of about 2. But this could be offset, for example, by halving our CEP's or by some combination of yield and CEP in our missiles that increased the efficiency — that is, the fraction $(\text{yield})^{2/3}/(\text{CEP})^2$ — by a factor of 4.

The Soviet Union might attempt to defend force targets with active defenses. Or it might multiply the numbers of points at which targets were located. If the United States attempted to target Soviet forces, the latter would probably be the most effective thing for the Soviet Union to do, if it were not prohibitively expensive.

Conclusions

Prospects for Negotiated Missile Reductions

1. *The negotiation of general disarmament is virtually impossible in the foreseeable future.* While some kind of general disarmament under international law may be a possibility in time, nuclear weapons, the capacity to deliver them, and the knowledge required to make further nuclear weapons are a permanent part of the strategic landscape. The weapons themselves can be hidden, and the capacity to make and deliver them cannot be eradicated.

2. *The prospects for any negotiated missile reductions in*

the coming years are very poor. It is obvious from the preceding material that changes in weapons systems have been occurring so rapidly that experts are dissuaded from the necessary long-range planning. And it is not at all clear that any balanced disarmament will be perceived to be a good or fair bargain. The mutual interest in the reductions will be, for the most part, an interest in decreasing destruction if war occurs. Compared with the interest in avoiding war, this particular motivation has never found favor. If observers feel that there is any diminution whatsoever in the stability of the balance of terror, a countervailing decrease in the destructive aspect of war will not be sufficient to make the prospect attractive to them. Nor are reductions in the capacity to destroy likely to be very large unless there is substantial disarmament. A mere 50 missiles can kill 50 million people.

In any case, even if the Soviets reduced their capacity to destroy Americans, would we necessarily decide that we required anything less than a capacity to destroy every Russian citizen as a deterrent against attack? Thus, one side or the other might see no purpose whatsoever in trading reductions in capability.* Either might prefer large numbers of hostages to smaller numbers.

Some of our missiles, those targeted on Soviet missiles, could readily be given up if the same Soviet missiles were destroyed.

---

* For instance, Secretary McNamara testified: "There is general agreement that [our force] should be large enough to ensure the destruction, singly or in combination, of the Soviet Union, Communist China, and the Communist satellites as national societies, under the worst possible circumstances of war outbreak that can reasonably be postulated, and in addition, to destroy their warmaking capability so as to limit, to the extent practicable, damage to this country and to our Allies." [102] Such a goal might not be changed just because the Soviet force declined in strength.

If our goal were changed, however, it might reflect the view of former Deputy Secretary of Defense Roswell Gilpatric. In discussing the 1970 requirements for strategic retaliatory forces, he said: "Such a force, comprised of weapons systems invulnerable to surprise attack, would be *capable of destroying the centers of Soviet and Chinese Communist society.*" [103] (Italics added.) This is a much smaller requirement.

Such a trade might be called an iso-targeting reduction — permitting our targeting to remain fixed. It would probably require the power with the fewer missiles (the Soviet Union) to give up more missiles than the power with the greater number (the United States) if there were several Soviet missiles at each target point. In any case, such a trade, if prolonged to its limit, would leave the Soviets with no land-based missiles and ourselves with land-based missiles targeted on Soviet cities. Less extreme reductions along these lines would not be to the Soviet advantage either.

To the extent that a disarmament agreement saved financial resources, both sides might be interested, but, as noted below in considering existing plans, reductions themselves do not save large amounts of resources. Larger costs are involved in developing forces than in maintaining force levels. Also, by and large, the weapon systems that are more expensive to maintain tend to be replaced by less expensive ones. This reduces unilaterally the pressure for bilateral agreements to destroy armaments.

Any negotiated reductions will also raise a variety of political issues that the United States may wish to avoid. Such agreements will provide a target for both sincere and politically motivated attacks. They may be a cause of alarm to the West Germans and a source of dissension with the French. And to a far greater extent than is the case with an agreement to halt procurement, an agreement to reduce armaments raises questions concerning the nature of the relationship evolving between the United States and the Soviet Union.

It may be that the case for reductions in weapons would have to be so strong to overcome these political and strategic obstacles that any weapons satisfying the necessary conditions would be far from essential and could be disposed of unilaterally. Indeed, the agreement to coordinate reductions within the two major powers may prove a liability for attempts to persuade the U.S. electorate that we have particular missiles in excess.

Impact of Existing Plans

Largely for the reasons just sketched, neither major power has considered its plans for missile disarmament very closely. It may nevertheless be interesting to discuss the gross implications of these reasons at the present time and the ways in which U.S.-Soviet differences might be settled if serious negotiations were attempted.

There are two important issues yet to be suitably negotiated. The first concerns the degree and the nature of first-stage missile reductions. Both major powers have proposed plans for general and complete disarmament. The United States proposes proportional reductions on the order of 30 per cent.[104] The Soviet Union has suggested reductions leaving "a strictly limited and mutually agreed number of nuclear missiles which would be at the disposal of solely the Soviet Union and the United States on their national territories." *

The second outstanding disagreement concerns inspection. The United States' current attitudes on inspection are considerably more relaxed than they were previously, if discussion of the freeze is any indication. In the suggestion to limit missile stockpiles to existing levels, the United States emphasized only the monitoring of critical production steps, replacements, and launchings, although it also spoke of inspection for launching-site construction, which presumably would involve inspection that potentially pinpointed Soviet launch sites. But in a proposal to dismantle missiles, the United States might

---

* The Soviet Union has further stated that it would permit the retention of these missiles until the end of the third stage, that is, until the virtual completion of the disarmament process. This is regarded as a concession to Western fears. At Geneva, for example, the Soviets said: "We have agreed to the maintenance of a nuclear 'umbrella' because the Western Powers see some sort of menace to themselves if nuclear weapons were to be completely eliminated. . . ." However, it is admitted that this arrangement "would create additional guarantees for the security of States. . . ."[105] Notice that the wording of the Soviet proposal in the text prohibits both Polaris submarines and the NATO manning of U.S.-based missiles discussed in the Assembly of the Western European Union.[106]

well require greater inspection, if only for political reasons.

The Soviet plan for control over the "nuclear umbrella" would come into effect from the beginning of the second stage of disarmament and "would be established at the launching pads themselves . . . (the number of which should not be greater than the number of missiles retained)." Presumably this rules out Soviet decoy launching pads, if such exist. Both Soviet and U.S. attitudes on inspection are sketched further after Conclusion 12.

Probability of Nuclear War

3. *Either missile disarmament agreement proposed would have little, if any, direct effect on the probability of nuclear war.* The Soviet disarmament plan, to a greater extent than that of the United States, would decrease the stability of the balance of terror, but this stability itself is perhaps of less importance than political factors in determining the probability of war. On the other hand, missile disarmament would reflect, signal, and shape a significant change in major-power attitudes and would therefore have extensive *indirect* effects on the probability of war.

Destruction if War Occurs

4. *The first-stage plan for proportional reduction could reduce destruction in the United States if war occurred but would have much less effect, if any, in reducing the threat of destruction faced by the Soviet Union or Western Europe.* Reductions in the Soviet force will probably save U.S. cities if war occurs. It is, of course, possible, perhaps even likely, that the agreement would permit changes in Soviet force structure — other than numbers — which *increased* its effectiveness. For instance, increases in reliability over the disarmament period or later might increase the number of Soviet weapons that could be delivered despite the disarmament cutback. However, all important opportunities for such improvements

that are provided by the disarmament agreement are available, and at least equally likely to be acted upon, in the absence of disarmament. Hence the Soviet threat would be smaller after the agreement than without it, and perhaps smaller than at present. Notwithstanding inaccurate discussions of "overkill," this conclusion indicates, at 1965 levels of Soviet weapons, an important opportunity to defend the nation through disarmament. On the other hand, Western Europe would continue to be highly vulnerable to large numbers of Soviet weapons; even a 30 per cent reduction in Soviet missiles would leave Europe open to devastation.

The effect of the missile disarmament plan on the threat to the Soviet Union is not large. The U.S. posture emphasizes a reserve force to be withheld as a threat against cities during the course of a war.[107] The missiles dismantled under a 30 per cent decrease in the over-all force would not be taken from this most important deterrent force. And, undoubtedly, the deterrent force is now, or will soon be, quite large.

5. *The Soviet plan for reduction to specified numbers would presumably decrease destruction in both major powers and in Western Europe if war occurred.* The "minimum quantity" of weapons that would be "mutually agreed" to under the Soviet formula would limit sharply the number of cities that either side might attack. No discussion of the exact numbers has taken place. The Soviets have suggested that "if the representatives of the Western Powers would on their part like to indicate a certain figure or figures at this stage, which could be viewed in the light of the principle already mentioned, this would be considered as an indication by the Western Powers of their agreement with the matter in principle." [108]

Economic Savings

6. *Substantial economic savings would accrue to both sides as a result of almost any missile disarmament agreement; but these would result more from the "freeze" in weapons procure-*

ment associated with the agreement than from the forces dismantled. The real savings involved in missile disarmament do not lie in avoiding immediate procurement or in avoiding maintenance costs by dismantling missiles. They are found in stabilizing the arms race, at least for a time. Both sides could easily spend considerably more on weapons than they presently do.* Among the kinds of weapons that might be bought, the antiballistic missile systems would cost "about $16 billion in initial investment, and maybe a billion and a half a year to operating expenses. . . ." [110] The costs saved by avoiding these systems are far greater than missile-related costs at this time.†

It seems reasonable to assume that both sides will find it possible to dismantle only those land-based missiles that are well into their period of useful life. Hence one might estimate the savings associated with land-missile disarmament by computing the difference between the costs of maintaining, year after year, a missile force at two different levels. If we assume that a 30 per cent reduction would eliminate about 300 of our missiles and about 60 of theirs, this would probably save about $300 million per year for us and about $240 million for the Soviet Union.‡

With the submarine maintenance costs conjectured earlier, the "mothballing" of about 10 Polaris submarines would save $44 to $75 million per year in their maintenance, and $100

---

* Department of Defense Controller Hitch has estimated that Soviet expenditures on defense are about equal to our own and, in view of their smaller gross national product, that this represents 50 per cent more of their resources. [109]

† For instance, it appears that the total procurement and maintenance cost for a Minuteman per year, on a five-year accounting basis, is less than $1 million. The operating expenses alone of the ABM system are greater than could be saved by cutting back 1,500 Minutemen — about 500 more than are planned at this time.

‡ The Soviet missiles most nearly resemble our Titan or Atlas, rather than our Minuteman, and these computations have assumed our Titan II costs, simply because these were given earlier; these costs equal $4 million per year for operation and maintenance together. U.S. reductions are estimated at Minuteman costs.

million per year in procurement of the 160 missiles, assuming a five-year missile life. If submarine procurement costs can be salvaged in one way or another — for instance, by changing the submarines into nuclear-attack submarines — this would represent a saving of about $60 million per year, assuming a twenty-year life. This totals somewhat over $200 million. Soviet costs would be different but similarly irrelevant. Other direct savings could be attached to the disarmament agreement, but there is little doubt that the indirect economic savings associated with slowing down the new arms-race procurement provide the important economic benefit.

Stability with Respect to a Technological Breakthrough

7. *The U.S. — but not the Soviet — first-stage plan would increase very little the risks of a destabilizing technological breakthrough.* The U.S. proportional-reduction plan does not eliminate any weapon systems entirely. Hence it provides virtually the same protection against some new and effective method of attack. The Soviet plan, by limiting the basing of retained forces to the countries themselves, would eliminate submarine forces completely. After such a treaty an improvement in missile accuracy might be sufficient to induce fears by increasing the efficiency of attacks on land-based forces.

Either plan might have important *indirect* effects. For example, either could result in a political atmosphere in which it was more difficult to get adequate funding for research and development activities.

8. *A missile disarmament agreement would have to include a freeze, explicit or tacit, on the ballistic missile defense of cities.* The agreements under discussion might lead to further disarmament and to quite different attitudes concerning the role of urban defense. Nevertheless, at the present time, widescale procurement of an antiballistic missile system, no matter how ineffective, would probably be sufficient to lead to abrogation of the agreement by one side or the other. Hence a freeze on antiballistic missile defense of cities must somehow

be included with a missile disarmament agreement.* Considering the long lead time in developing and procuring antiballistic missile systems, their high cost and their low effectiveness, our control over production centers coupled with unilateral intelligence could be satisfactory in preventing clandestine ABM deployment.

Strategic Impact of Existing Missile Disarmament Plans

9. *The Soviet plan for reductions to specified numbers of missiles would — depending on the numbers — probably eliminate whatever U.S. strategic superiority remains; the Soviet plan to restrict retained forces to national territories would diminish the security of the U.S. force by eliminating Polaris submarines.* As noted in the discussion of Conclusion 7, the Soviet plan to eliminate sea-based forces would sharply decrease the invulnerability of the U.S. force. This plan would also be likely to diminish to the vanishing point whatever numerical preponderance the United States may have at present. And, while there can be no objection, in principle, to the notion of eventually restricting retained missiles to anything as vague as "strictly limited numbers" (after all, general and complete disarmament is U.S. policy), there is an objection to undertaking such drastic action in the first stage. This stems partly from common sense applied both to political and to military issues. Confidence in the disarmament process and in the other participants will have to be established first.

10. *Either the freeze of strategic weapons or the U.S. plan for proportional reductions, with or without a freeze on missile characteristics, would almost certainly be more effective in*

* As noted earlier, the U.S. plan for a freeze incorporates this point, as presumably would any of our plans for missile reduction. The Soviet plan does not. Instead, as Mr. Tsarapkin has stated: "The Soviet Union proposes to retain, as a nuclear umbrella, (i) intercontinental ballistic missiles . . . ; (ii) anti-missile missiles; and (iii) ground-to-air missiles. The two latter categories of missiles are proposed for retention in case, as the Western Powers fear, someone should try to violate the treaty and to hide a certain number of rockets or military aircraft or to utilize for an attack existing civil aircraft." [111]

maintaining our superiority than would a continuing arms race; the relative effectiveness of the other possibilities is harder to estimate. In considering missile disarmament, at least a few government analysts would, as a matter of course, consider among others the three possibilities: (*a*) that the Soviet Union strikes first (at cities); (*b*) that the United States strikes second (at forces, in an effort at "damage-limiting"); and (*c*) that the United States strikes first (after a massive Soviet invasion of Europe). In each case, the analyst would consider the effect of a freeze of missile numbers and the effect of missile reductions, both of these with and without a freeze on missile characteristics.*

Thus, the accompanying "table of preferences" summarizes the following reasoning. First, consider Column A. Assume, as is likely, that the probability of a Soviet attack is unaltered by the agreements. We are therefore concerned only with reducing its size. For any specified degree of control over characteristics, a reduction of missiles would be preferable to a freeze of missiles, since the reduction would save some U.S. targets from attack. Similarly, for any specific decision between freezing and reducing numbers of missiles, a freeze on missile and launching-site characteristics would be preferable to the absence of such a freeze. Again the freeze would save some U.S. targets by reducing Soviet force effectiveness.

* We assume that similar computations are made by Soviet strategists, but it is possible that they are not. From a U.S. strategist's point of view, it is hard to believe that the Soviet Union would be willing or able to engage in a detailed and comprehensive agreement until it has confidence in its ability to make such analyses. However, the Soviet point of view lends less weight to strategic considerations. For instance in Sokolovskii's *Soviet Military Strategy,* a statement given enough thought to be redrafted in the second edition now reads: "During a war, strategic concepts often have a reverse effect on policy. Cases even arise when the military factor acquires decisive significance." (While this may be very radical by Soviet standards, it is incredibly understated by our standards.) And sometimes Soviet spokesmen consider these considerations counterproductive, if not immoral; for example, "One cannot allow speculation on the basis of the slogan of 'maintaining the balance of forces' — that is, maintaining the ratio of qualitative and quantitative indices of armed forces and their structure — because that would lead to undermining the cause of disarmament." (Mr. S. K. Tsarapkin).[112]

PREFERENCES AMONG ARMS CONTROL OPTIONS IN TWO CASES
(1 = BEST, 5 = WORST)

	A *Soviet Union strikes first** (at cities) †	B *United States strikes first** (at forces) †
I. 30 per cent reduction; no freeze on missile characteristics	3 or 2	1 or 2
II. 30 per cent reduction; freeze on missile characteristics	1	3 or 4
III. Freeze on missile numbers; freeze on missile characteristics	2 or 3	4 or 3
IV. Freeze on missile numbers; no freeze on missile characteristics	4	2 or 1
V. Continued missile force buildup	5	5

* We have noted earlier the tendency to act as if the likelihood of one's own country striking first is so unequivocally small that the adversary has no right even to consider it. The least controversial way — which we promptly embrace — to justify our consideration is that (*a*) the consideration of a Soviet first strike is the conservative military thing to do for U.S. planners, and (*b*) consideration of a U.S. first strike is desirable only because of the potential threat of a Soviet invasion of Europe that might be repulsed in no other fashion. (Neither preventive nor pre-emptive war is at issue here.)

† Obviously there are other cases to consider — for instance, a U.S. first strike at cities and a Soviet first strike at forces. But we believe our two considerations to be the most interesting from the U.S. point of view because (*a*) a Soviet attack on forces (a "rational" attack) is so well deterred and so much less threatening that a shift of attention to an irrational attack at cities is warranted, and (*b*) U.S. attacks on forces are of more interest than attacks on cities because they are more likely and also because our ability to mount such attacks is influenced far more substantially by disarmament.

Finally, agreements I–IV are clearly better than V in this regard, since the latter permits the Soviet force to improve both in numbers and in efficiency. On these grounds, II is best, and IV and V are next to last and last, respectively. The choice between I and III depends upon details (for instance, the absence of a freeze on Soviet missile characteristics might permit Soviet effectiveness — in percentage of deployed missiles deliverable — to increase by a factor of more than 1.4, thus overcoming the 30 per cent reduction.)

Column B is more complicated, and the rankings are different. Now the most important characteristics of the agreement are not those that restrict the Soviet force but those that fail to restrict our own. The ability to retrofit Minuteman I and Minuteman II (that is, turn the earlier model into the newer one) probably makes I and IV better, from the U.S. point of view, than II and III, which would presumably prevent this. V is the worst, if not in the very short run then somewhat later, as Soviet forces are hardened, based at sea, improved in efficiency, and dispersed.

11. *U.S. proposals for inspection and control, which are embodied in both the freeze and the first-stage proposal, may well be less restrictive if and when the Soviet Union can fire virtually all missiles simultaneously.** From the U.S. point of view it is highly desirable to keep Soviet missiles at a stage of effectiveness or in a state of deployment where they cannot be fired in a single salvo: this increases the ability of the United States to limit damage by striking Soviet forces even after a first salvo of Soviet missiles has struck. But such a freeze requires inspection and control of Soviet launching sites. If, on the other hand, the Soviets are at or near a stage of effectiveness, or a state of deployment, when virtually all of their missiles may be salvoed, the U.S. motivation to freeze the characteristics of launching sites and vehicles will be reduced. Quite possibly, Soviet plans do not call for making full salvos.†

* It is not a new idea to try to control missile characteristics. The Western experts at the Geneva Surprise Attack Conference included in their illustrative inspection system the statement: "An inspection system must be carefully evaluated and continuously re-evaluated not only in terms of present missile 'state of the art' but also in terms of the foreseeable growth potential. These changing missile system characteristics could include new vehicles and new ground support equipment greatly affecting readiness times, accuracy, preparatory activities, and over-all performance capabilities." [113]

† In the U.S., salvo characteristics generally improve — for instance, "Each Titan II squadron will be able to salvo its missiles utilizing less missile areospace ground equipment than that required by Titan I."

Where Could Agreement Be Reached
if Agreement Were Desired?

12. *The Soviet Union might not accept a proposal for a freeze that does not promise disarmament, and it might not accept a proposal that requires inspection of launching sites.* The Soviet government has consistently wished to preserve territorial secrecy during the transition period, if not after, and to permit verification only of the forces destroyed and not of those retained. Its slogan has been "control over disarmament," not "control over armaments." * Then Soviet position indicates that the control organizations would be able to send their inspection team "to any point" only after "the accomplishment of all measures relating to general and complete disarmament."

While there may be many reasons, a strategic reason for this concern is that the Soviets feel they "cannot submit information on the location of armed forces and military installations." The U.S. proposals for control "mean providing opportunities to locate targets for attack." [117] Quite obviously, from a purely strategic point of view, there are many contexts in which this could be so. And furthermore, these situations change back and forth over the years. Several U.S. strategists have tried for years to persuade the Soviet Union that secrecy is too easily

---

Therefore it is of very great interest to note a relevant change in Sokolovskii's *Soviet Military Strategy*. The second edition contains the insertion: "A nuclear missile strike consists of several simultaneous launchings of missiles with nuclear warheads by all combat-ready launching pads." [114] This is consistent with Premier Khrushchev's statements: "We are creating a system which, if one of the instruments assigned to retaliate is put out of commission, will always be able to bring duplicate instruments into play and destroy the targets from reserve positions"; and "We are locating our missiles in such a way as to ensure duplication and triplication." [115]

* Soviet statements, like our own, are carefully worded and must be read carefully. For example, the Soviet Union has announced that it is "ready to accept any proposals of the Western Powers on *control over disarmament* if those Powers accept the Soviet proposals on general and complete disarmament." [116] (Italics added.) In the Soviet view, our control suggestions are often not control over disarmament at all but control over retained weapons.

lost (perhaps through stealing of state documents) to be a useful defense. And because it accelerates the arms race and makes disarmament difficult, they argue that it should be given up. But this view may stem from a failure to empathize sufficiently with Soviet strategists. The Soviet problem, in Soviet eyes, has been deterrence of our attack; and deceleration of the arms race has, in their minds, been secondary to this goal. This position is quite reasonable. Furthermore, even if secrecy were not useful now, it might easily become so later as weapons and reconnaissance possibilities changed their character.

Moreover, an indefinite freeze is similarly in direct opposition to Soviet attitudes and statements. Their disarmament proposals have called for the achievement of general and complete disarmament within four years. Their speeches and rhetoric, far more than our own, view disarmament as an overriding consideration. More important, perhaps, from a "realistic" point of view is that our present missile superiority is at least 4 to 1, and without disarmament the Soviet Union would be frozen indefinitely at a level of inferiority that it might reasonably regard as unfortunate.[118]

13. *The United States is likely to enter into an agreement for missile reductions only if the agreement emphasizes proportional reductions and some inspection from the outset.* The United States has been firmly committed to proportional reductions in the past.* Furthermore, there are political and psychological arguments for inspection from the outset of an agreement.† And finally, there can be no doubt that some in

---

* At the Eighteen-Nation Disarmament Conference in Geneva, William C. Foster said: "Each side . . . presumably has designed its own defense system to meet its own needs. That is how the present balance was achieved. If every major type of armament in the defense system of each side is reduced by equal percentages at the same time, the present rough balance would be retained through the disarmament process. That is the simplest, the fairest and best way to ensure that neither side gains a military advantage over the other during the process."[119]

† With the increasingly large numbers of weapons in the hands of both major powers, it is becoming more and more common to find demands for inspection and control buttressed by such factors — plausible military arguments are more complicated and harder to discover. For in-

the U.S. government feel that Soviet secrecy is, for one reason or another, an ultimate barrier to better relations between the two powers.

14. *A missile disarmament agreement calling for inspection of production centers alone is probably the only logical compromise of U.S. and Soviet attitudes on first-stage inspection.* Conclusion 12 indicates that some limits to U.S. inspection requirements are probably necessary if agreement is to be reached. The U.S. argument for inspecting missile silos has, in the past, been based in large part on the belief that inspection was necessary to verify predisarmament weapons levels. This verification was intended to prevent the threat of surprise attack at some time during the disarmament transition. This rationalization has been a weak one for some time as the invulnerability of our own forces and our knowledge of Soviet strength have both grown. Recently two related admissions by the United States further cut the ground from under this explanation for inspection. First, the Secretary of Defense announced rather precisely the existing Soviet inventories. Second, the U.S. proposal for a freeze did not call for inspection of them. Evidently, we are not overly concerned with fears of surprise attack at the present time. And the Soviet counterforce capability is not likely to increase — independently of inspection clauses — under any agreement that we would accept.

Moreover, we should not overlook, in our emphasis on Soviet secrecy, the utility, to us, of our own secrecy. Many important and useful pieces of information concerning the vulnerability of our missiles, their performance, the performance of missiles to come, the exact locations of our missiles, and so on, may never become known to the Soviet Union. A Soviet agreement, followed by the abrogation of the treaty by one side or the other, would leave our potential adversaries with much useful

---

stance, "If disarmament is to succeed, it is essential that no country *believe* that it has been placed at a military disadvantage as the result of unbalanced reductions." [120] (Italics added.) It is revealing to reflect that a Soviet spokesman would very likely have substituted "advantage" for "disadvantage" in stating this requirement.

information that would not be, as the Soviet negotiators would say, proportional to the disarmament achieved.* Were an agreement in sight — were Soviet negotiators to indicate a willingness to discuss our proposals — these points would, I believe, be understood very rapidly in the United States.

Finally, inspection of launching sites would, in fact, pose many complicated technical and political problems. Soviet inspectors would be examining our own Minuteman missiles and Polaris submarines. Whether or not this has any strategic significance, it must surely have political significance. Disarmament agreements will be complicated enough without introducing inspection where it can possibly be avoided.

15. *A logical compromise between the U.S. and Soviet plans for reduction might call for a first-stage proportional disarmament agreement and a second-stage reduction to a strictly limited and mutually agreed number; in both cases Soviet IRBM's and MRBM's would be included in the reduction.* The phrase "strictly limited and mutually agreed" numbers can certainly be stretched to cover whatever the United States might decide it had in mind for the end of a second stage — this is a 60 per cent reduction. And, from the Soviet point of view, whether or not missile disarmament begins with a series of proportional cuts can hardly be very important. Indeed, as far as land-based missiles are concerned, both major powers have about an equal number: 1,000. The Soviets may wish eventually to destroy enough of the shorter-range missiles to change the ratio between Soviet intercontinental and other missiles. This would work in favor of our allies and would encourage them to back an agreement.

16. *Hence an indicated compromise agreement would be*

* For example, during the Test Ban hearings, George B. Kistiakowsky was able to state in discussing missile silo survivability: "We need to remember in this connection that we undoubtedly know a great deal more about the vulnerability of our sites than the Soviets do, since *we alone are well informed on the nature and structure of the silos* and have performed a number of test explosions relevant to them." [121] (Italics added.) This type of statement might become less plausible after detailed inspection.

characterized by (a) *relatively little control over, or inspection of, missile characteristics;* (b) *control and inspection of missile production facilities;* (c) *proportional reduction throughout a first stage;* (d) *reduction to specified and mutually agreed numbers during a second stage; and* (e) *a freeze on antiballistic missile deployment or procurement.* The Soviet proposal to limit retained weapons to land bases in the United States and the Soviet Union is not ultimately to the strategic advantage of either power, and we assume that the Soviet Union can be persuaded to permit sea-based forces.

The Strategic Impact of this Compromise

17. *Under the compromise agreement, the strength of U.S. missile forces would probably grow absolutely during the first stage.* Anticipated improvements in U.S. force effectiveness and increases in second-strike megatonnage during the first stage would result almost entirely from the substitution of Minuteman II for Minuteman I. In particular, Minuteman II would have increased weight-carrying capability. If the agreement contained an explicit or tacit understanding not to deploy antiballistic missile systems, it might not be necessary to use this weight for penetration aids. This would still further improve the efficiency of the force by permitting large increases in yield.* Furthermore, Minuteman II can be fired from airborne command posts and can be easily retargeted.[123] As we noted earlier, the capacity to retarget adds substantially to force efficiency.

Finally, increases in reliability might well be expected during a disarmament period. Generally speaking, all weapon systems gradually improve in reliability as they enter the force. Even if their reliabilities remain the same, the increased experience permits us to give a good estimate of that reliability. As noted earlier, increases in estimated reliability can have a

---

* If the yield were improved by a factor of 2, the efficiency of the missile would improve (against hard targets) by a factor of about 1.6. Similarly improvements in yield on the order of 3, 5, and 10 would increase efficiency by 2.1, 2.9, and 4.6, respectively.[122]

very substantial effect in reducing the number of weapons needed to target important sites (that is, those that are assigned high probabilities of destruction). The replacement of Polaris missile A-1 with A-3 will be completed in the sixties and this also will improve reliability.[124]

Therefore, it is plausible that a percentage reduction in numbers of land- and sea-based missiles might nevertheless permit an increase in force efficiency. When we add the information that Minuteman II is twice as accurate (and hence as much as four times as effective) as Minuteman I, the conclusion becomes very likely.[125] This improvement alone could, for example, permit the 150 programed Minuteman II missiles to substitute for several hundred Minuteman I and Polaris missiles in maintaining high probabilities of destroying hard Soviet targets. Since many more than 150 Minuteman I's would be replaced by Minuteman II's — there would be 750 more Minuteman I's to replace — the useful improvement in force efficiency might even be limited by the number of high-priority hard targets. This discussion makes it clear why Secretary McNamara referred to his program of "retrofitting a large number of the Minuteman I silos in the first five wings" and "integrating Minuteman I and Minuteman II squadrons into a single system" as one that "will greatly increase combat effectiveness." [126]

Of course, Soviet forces might increase their invulnerability under the agreement — negating some, but probably not all, of the U.S. advantages — but this could also occur without an agreement. The agreement is not likely to provide new ways of making the Soviet force invulnerable. And restrictions on the numbers of U.S. missiles would seem far less important, at present, than either improvements in U.S. missile efficiency — which the proposed agreement permits — or restrictions on Soviet force buildup — which the agreement prevents. Therefore, it is easy to conclude that our counterforce capability would be considerably superior under the first-stage agreement than in its absence.

18. *If the Soviet Union made appropriate efforts, then the*

U.S. counterforce and damage-limiting capabilities would be likely to decrease significantly during or after the second-stage reduction, whereupon the strategic force would revert to a counter-city retaliation function only. Soviet efforts to disperse strategic forces on land and sea would be likely to win eventually a contest against improvements in efficiency of a limited U.S. force, although even this would depend somewhat on the details of the agreement. Certainly there seems to be little opposition to a sea-based force.

19. *Under the compromise agreement, the Soviet ability to strike cities would be likely to decline during both stages; no advantages comparable to those of Conclusion 17 would accrue to the Soviet Union, because its force posture and strategy differ from our own.* The Soviet force seems designed to attack cities; its missiles have fairly large yields and, judging from Soviet space exploits, have sufficient accuracy to strike cities.[127] If this is the case, then improvements in accuracy, yield, reliability, and ability to retarget will not substantially improve the Soviet retaliatory capability. And, the U.S. missile force would still be far too large and invulnerable — some of it based at sea — to be destroyed by Soviet weapons. However, if Soviet weapons initially numbered little more than those agreed upon for the end of the second stage, there might be little change in Soviet capabilities and little U.S. interest in the plan. In that case a freeze could be more to our advantage.

Consistency with U.S. and Soviet National Interests

20. *Nevertheless, the compromise missile disarmament agreement could be in the Soviet interest.* It is quite evident that the Soviet Union does not now anticipate attacking Western Europe. Equally clearly, the Soviet Union has run far greater strategic risks of attack from the United States in the past than it would be running under this disarmament agreement. C. L. Sulzberger of *The New York Times* was quoted after an interview with Khrushchev as saying, "Quite blandly he asserts that these countries (Britain, France, Italy) are

figuratively speaking hostages to the U.S.S.R. and a guarantee against war." [128] If indeed this is the Soviet attitude, the numerical implications of intercontinental missile disarmament are much less important than they might otherwise be. Furthermore, the Soviet attitude may be one that puts less store on the numerical implications of military imbalances than do we.* And from the Soviet point of view, these strategic advantages, in which only a few of our military officers will put much faith, are of little importance. They are associated with limiting damage during a war that the Soviet Union does not intend to initiate or provoke.

Moreover, in the absence of a disarmament agreement, economic pressure on the Soviet Union will remain. The Secretary of Defense has suggested that

> . . . the Soviet leadership is confronted with a very severe resource allocation problem and must strike a balance among its various objectives: military; space; foreign aid; civilian housing; agriculture and improvement of the standard of living of the Soviet people; and so forth.[130]

By contrast the United States can more easily afford the expenses of the arms race. This was recognized by Khrushchev as, for example, when he told Walter Lippmann:

> If it comes to a war, we shall use only the biggest weapons. The smaller ones are very expensive, and they can decide nothing. The fact that they are expensive doesn't bother you because you don't care what you spend, and, what is more, many of your generals are connected with big business. But in the USSR we have to economize, and tactical weapons are a waste.[131]

In fact, it is not clear, especially to many Soviet writers, how the United States will fare economically under disarmament.

---

* For example, Tsarapkin, addressing this question in the Eighteen-Nation Disarmament Conference, said: ". . . it is one thing not to allow any State to obtain unilateral military advantages, and quite another thing to try to maintain the balance of forces with such scrupulous apothecary's precision as would not lend itself to definition in practice. After all, it is impossible to speak of disarmament measures under the pretext of maintaining the so-called military balance. Moreover, where are the yardsticks, where are the scales on which it would be possible to weigh the armaments of the two sides in order to be sure that the balance is being maintained?" [129]

And it is not only the U.S. economy but also the Western will to maintain the moral and material basis of the confrontation with the Soviet Union that may be at stake in disarmament. This is probably a common view in both major powers. Roswell Gilpatric discussed one application of this feeling when he said:

> Many of those who opposed the nuclear test ban did so not on grounds that there lay in the treaty a significant military risk to the West, but rather because they feared that any easing of tensions would soon find the Western democracies inviting disaster by letting down their guard long before a real resolution of differences between the two blocs was in sight.[132]

It seems that, from the point of view of a tough-minded Soviet "realist," the Soviet Union would do well to try to confront the West in a context of disarmament, rather than one of armament. This context might be *forced* upon the West by a determined disarmament offensive. In the course of this offensive, the Soviet Union would simply concede a series of fairly irrelevant strategic points. This is consistent at least with its declared point of view.*

Finally, many people believe that the world would, or might, be quite a different place after a significant disarmament measure had been agreed upon. The Soviet view, similar to that of some Americans, is that "as disarmament proceeds, the nature of inter-state relations will radically change, and today's tensions will give place to peaceful coexistence and broad cooperation. . . ."[134] Would it not be consistent with this view to attempt to pass quickly through a disarmament stage, in pursuit of this changed world? It seems that a wide spectrum of different Soviet views could find in missile disarmament the means to further Soviet interests.

---

* At Geneva the Soviets asserted that "in working out these measures, one should be guided not solely by the requirements of war departments or by the specific philosophy of generals concerning the maintenance of the military balance, but preference should be given to considerations for halting the armaments race, to the demands for a decisive reduction of the danger of a nuclear war, and to the interests of disarmament. In general, priority should be given to disarmament and not to any other considerations."[133]

21. *It could also be in the U.S. national interest to propose some form of the compromise agreement.* As noted in Conclusion 4, the official U.S. first-stage plan — comparable to the first stage of the proposed "compromise" agreement — would begin immediately to decrease the Soviet threat against U.S. cities. The compromise agreement could also, as noted in Conclusion 6, save billions of dollars committed to the future procurement of new weapons, and hundreds of millions of dollars for weapons dismantled. As noted in Conclusion 7, the reductions would increase little, if at all, the risks of a destabilizing technological breakthrough. And at this time, as indicated in Conclusion 10, almost any missile disarmament or missile freeze proposal would be more effective in maintaining U.S. superiority than a continuing arms race. Conclusion 12 suggests that the Soviet Union may not agree to inspection of launching sites or to a proposal that contains no significant disarmament. Finally, and most important, Conclusion 17 asserts that the relative and absolute strength of our forces, without unacceptable inspection clauses, would be likely to *increase* during the first stage of the compromise plan. Thus during the period of most concern, during which we would have least experience with disarmament, we would incur little risk. With the second stage, or thereafter, the United States would probably have to accept a situation in which both powers could effectively attack each other's cities but in which neither could effectively attack the other's forces. This situation is inherent in later stages of disarmament, and it is also inherent in later stages of the arms race. There is very little chance of avoiding it, whether by agreement or by unilateral action. What can be done is to drive the indicated bargain, in which there is initial strategic gain and little strategic risk. With this bargain, we would seek to lower the risks of national destruction if war occurred. At the same time we would try to lay the foundations for a world which would not require continuing struggles within an ever-dangerous major-power arms race.

A NEGOTIATOR'S PAUSE IN STRATEGIC WEAPON PROCUREMENT

Introduction

IN 1964 the discussions of disarmament at Geneva began to take a relatively realistic form. The United States proposed considering a freeze in the procurement of strategic weapons. This proposal envisaged freezing the numbers and characteristics of both offensive and defensive strategic weapons, including missiles of intermediate and intercontinental range, heavy bombers, and strategic antimissile missile systems.

The American representatives began by proposing that "The United States, the Soviet Union, and their respective Allies should agree to explore a verified freeze of the number and characteristics of strategic nuclear offensive and defensive vehicles."[1] They made the following points in support of the "proposal": (a) it should "include strategic missiles and aircraft" with the categories of weapons "defined along lines of range and weight"; (b) it should include antiballistic missile systems; (c) "the immediate objective of the freeze on numbers should be to maintain the quantities of strategic nuclear vehicles held by the East and the West at constant levels"; and (d) "the objective of the freeze on characteristics should be . . . to prevent the development and deployment of strategic vehicles of a significantly new type."[2] It was said that the verification system "could include the following": (1) continued inspection of declared facilities; (2) a specified number of inspections per year to check undeclared locations for possible prohibited activities; (3) the stationing of observers to verify all space launchings and all allowed missile firings; (4) observation of the destruction of — or, in case of accidents, other confirmation of — vehicles and launchers being replaced.[3]

That this proposal might conceivably be the basis for serious discussion is remarkable. But equally remarkable, despite all the discussion of arms control and disarmament over the last few years, little attention has been given to this type of proposal. It deserves more, partly because U.S. thinking about it sometimes seems to be based on a misconception about what it can be expected to achieve. Thus a discussion of the treaty's purpose is important. And since the conclusions reached are analogous to the conclusions that a similar discussion would have reached concerning the Test Ban, it may be useful to sketch that analogy first.

The Test Ban could have been an effort to halt a specific kind of research and development — testing. Many of the plans and preparations for the treaty were consistent with this purpose, if not motivated by it. When the treaty was finally negotiated, however, testing was not completely prohibited and the related research and development went forward underground. Why?

The purpose of the Test Ban, in terms of the political motivations that made it possible, was to halt pollution of the atmosphere and to achieve a "first step." Testing, in itself, meant virtually nothing. Underground testing was the most complicated part of the treaty by far; in terms of the coalition that backed the treaty, it was irrelevant. And in the end, in effect, the ban on underground tests was replaced by a willingness on both sides to continue to compete — so to speak — underground.

It is argued in this chapter that a similar evolution should take place in which the provisions of the freeze would become consistent with our real purpose. Further, it is suggested that the freeze be modified to a treaty of five years duration limiting only missile *numbers* and freezing, tacitly or formally, the procurement of missile defenses. In this no limitation would be placed on missile characteristics or on numbers of bombers. Such a freeze could be called a "negotiator's pause." During its five-year tenure, intensive negotiations with a view to achieving more substantial agreement would go forward. If further disarmament were not forthcoming, the "pause" could be renewed. In the absence of an agreement either to extend or to renew the pause treaty, the agreement would lapse and a return to unrestricted procurement would ensue.

The Purpose of the Freeze

This section discusses the *strategic* goals of the freeze, what it is supposed to achieve in terms of strategic weapons, their number, procurement, deployment, development, and control.

Many would consider this issue superfluous. Most people believe either that the freeze is a self-evidently good or a self-evidently bad idea. By contrast, at least some of those involved in deciding how great an effort the United States should make to negotiate a freeze probably have not yet made up their minds. This uncertainty is closely tied to the present ambiguity concerning its purpose.

Perhaps the best way of clarifying the strategic issues posed by the freeze is to put forth and discuss six different attitudes toward its role in controlling strategic weapons. In summary these attitudes are as follows.

First, the freeze can be viewed primarily as a step toward imminent substantial disarmament. But this view probably rests on misconceptions concerning the strategic and political feasibility of significant disarmament.

Second, the freeze can be taken at face value as an attempt to prevent further increases in levels of destructive capability. This is very much the point of view with which the notion was put forth at Geneva. This attitude toward the freeze is also misleading, partly because levels of destructive capability are so high already.

Third, a freeze treaty can be an attempt to maintain whatever U.S. strategic advantage now exists. It is this point of view that has made the freeze a relatively "realistic" proposal to the Department of Defense. However, the treaty most consistent with this approach has three disadvantages. It is complicated. It is relatively unlikely to be accepted by the Soviets. And it neither provides us with sufficiently large benefits nor resolves sufficiently pressing problems to motivate strenuous efforts in the face of the inevitable political obstacles.

Fourth, a freeze treaty can be pictured as an unnecessarily formal method of slowing aspects of the arms race — for example, growth in numbers of missiles and bombers — that can be halted by tacit agreement or that will come to a halt of their own accord. This approach seems to give insufficient attention to subtler benefits of the freeze and is too optimistic about, or too indifferent to, the perturbing impact of potential missile defenses in encouraging offensive weapon procurement.

Fifth, a freeze treaty may be justified because it is more likely to forestall future offensive weapon procurement than a tacit agreement, because it reduces incentives to procurement, and because it discourages proliferation. This point of view is, I believe, correct as far as it goes, but it may provide too diffuse a motivation to induce serious negotiation.

Finally, the freeze can be considered primarily as a method of grappling with the problems introduced by ballistic missile defenses. Indeed, it will be argued that, from the point of view of strategic weapon procurement, the freeze *must* be considered in this light; further, that this point of view leads to a resolution of the original question. In short, the chapter concludes that the strategic *purpose* of the freeze is to inhibit the procurement of ballistic missile defenses. From the point of view of narrow strategic weapon considerations, we should pursue the freeze intently if, but only if, it is our goal to avoid a round of arms race in which each major power procures expensive and unsettling missile defenses.

The Freeze as a First Step

The freeze can be pictured as a step toward substantial disarmament, and for many purposes this is a useful and proper perspective to take. Nevertheless, the mechanisms and motivations necessary to achieve disarmament are not yet apparent. Neither cost nor fear, neither social effects nor political effects of existing weapons seem sufficient to motivate the major-power political systems to grapple with the real and imagined problems of substantial reductions in weapons. In addition very substantial disarmament would be required to reduce the U.S. and Soviet capacity for destruction even to a few tens of millions of fatalities.

In any case, few people would assign a very significant probability to substantial reductions following a freeze. Rather, support for disarmament may be *diminished* following a freeze, much as the public interest in arms control diminished after the Test Ban. Still, viewing the freeze as a step toward disarmament has some validity. Disarmament without a prior freeze is especially unlikely. And even if the freeze were not likely to increase the probability of subsequent disarmament in the immediate future, it might still be proper and desirable for governments to portray the freeze as a "first step." This approach mobilizes support for arms control that might otherwise be lost because misdirected to less feasible arms control agreements.

In addition, the freeze as a step toward disarmament provides both major powers, but especially the Soviet Union, with an excuse for halting procurement. It plays the role that pollution of the atmosphere played in the Test Ban. Both the freeze and the Test Ban emphasize the long-run common interest rather than the short-run strategic interest. They provide a point around which public statements, if not private opinions, can rally without close examination of current and changing strategic realities. For the Soviet Union, which is presently behind in most aspects of strategic weapons, long-run disarmament is probably the only possible public explanation for a halt. In short, "a step toward disarmament" is a useful but somewhat misleading framework in which to place a freeze proposal. The primary immediate purpose for such an agreement must lie elsewhere.

The Freeze at Face Value

When the United States suggested that both major powers "agree to explore" the freeze, it made little reference to the prospect of later disarmament. It did describe the proposal as an "excellent point of departure for major arms reductions to follow," but it did not attempt to specify in concrete terms how these reductions might be realized. By contrast, great emphasis was placed on the rate at which the U.S. armory would continue to grow in the absence of a halt.

There are a variety of reasons for this approach. It was easy to be specific about the rate at which the destructive capability of the United States had been increasing. The Arms Control and Disarmament Agency could thus defend itself against criticism that the freeze was not "disarmament." It could assure observers, especially neutral observers, that the freeze would do something important that was comparable to disarmament.

On the other hand, the argument for the prevention of further increases in destructive capacity is not too compelling. To the Soviets, further increases in the U.S. capacity to attack their urban-industrial complex are redundant. In addition, procurement in the United States is coming to at least a temporary halt (in numbers of vehicles). In January 1965, for the first time, no new strategic missiles were programed, either land based or in submarines. Hence, interest in the freeze signifies more than our willingness to halt an increase in the numbers of offensive weapons. It reflects a prior decision to halt! Statistics quoted at Geneva to indicate how the freeze would halt increases in operational vehicles relied on a description of increases in the period 1962–1965. These figures are *not* appropriate for the coming time period.

It is true that the capacity of our force to attack Soviet land-based forces could increase significantly over the next few years. But this increase would result not from increases in numbers of operational vehicles but from changes in the characteristics of missiles as the existing force was modernized. And since these improvements are hard to control, it is not clear to what extent the treaty would restrain them.

The most important improvements are in increased yield, accuracy, and the capability to retarget. Thus, Minuteman II, destined eventually to replace Minuteman I, has been heralded as having eight times the capacity of its predecessor against hard targets; in addition it can be retargeted more easily. But its improvements in retargetability are not likely to be prohibitable, and increases in its accuracy are also difficult to prevent. Both involve internal mechanisms (or wiring) not likely to be open to inspection. Indeed, it might be that *all* of the improvements of the newer missile could be placed in its predecessor if provisions of the freeze required only that replacements be externally similar or of the same type.

Hence the force of the argument presented at Geneva — that the freeze would prevent the growth of our own strategic forces — might well be misleading on three grounds. First, the United States is not planning to increase numbers of operational vehicles. Second, it is nevertheless planning to strengthen its strategic forces considerably *without* increases in numbers of vehicles. Third, the proposed freeze on characteristics may not inhibit such increases.

In short, we may be proposing few changes in our plans for offensive weapons, but asking in return for a halt in the Soviet strategic buildup. This is not quite as bad as it sounds; our thinking might, in practice, reflect an opening bargaining position. In addition the Soviet buildup might also be due to end soon. Our estimates of it invariably turn out to be too high.

The Soviets, like ourselves, may soon be engaged primarily in qualitative rather than quantitative buildups, with the probable exception of Soviet submarine construction.

If the Soviets were not planning to halt missile construction rather quickly anyway, then the freeze would have a significant effect in limiting Soviet destructive capacity. But this effect can only be described as one that would enhance the prospects for U.S. national survival should war occur; numerical estimates of Western casualties are so dependent on the course of the war as to be misleading.

It is likely that the freeze on characteristics proposed by the United States would affect Soviet plans more adversely than would the freeze on numbers. For example, as noted earlier, such sources as the Institute for Strategic Studies portray the Soviet missile force as using liquid-fueled missiles. These are generally considered to be less efficient than our own solid-fuel rockets. If the Soviets ever changed from one type of fuel to the other, they would certainly have to change the "type" of rocket and would probably be prohibited from doing so by the present notion of a freeze.

Therefore, what can be said of the freeze taken at face value as an attempt to halt an increase in destructive capability? It may somewhat restrict the growth of Soviet destructive capacity by restricting numbers and changes in characteristics. Whether or not we could decrease the Soviet destructive capacity more substantially by avoiding the freeze and building ballistic missile defense systems is unclear — although the relative cost of achieving them in this fashion, both economically and in terms of the course of the arms race, may be considerable. As for the United States, in the form proposed the freeze would have little, if any, effect on our offensive weapon procurement. (Although the freeze in its present form seems fairly one-sided in our favor — in its restriction on offensive capacity — it may be equally one-sided in favor of the Soviets in its restriction on defensive capacity, which the United States has the economic resources to do more efficiently than the Soviets.)

Freezing Our Relative Advantage

The third approach embodies the congenial principle, "Quit while you're ahead." But freezing strategic advantages is not a simple thing to do and would require the difficult freezing of missile characteristics. In view of the complicated web of strategic and political problems, it is quite possible — maybe even likely — that no one could design a treaty that would achieve both a solid consensus in the United States and a semblance of acceptability to the Soviets. Such a treaty could be drafted to appear fair. But it would carefully have to permit those things that we wished to do and to prevent those things that we wished the Soviets not to do. The resultant treaty, complicated and tricky, would have no chance of being negotiated. And this in turn would discourage U.S. leaders from a serious effort to achieve it.

In addition, a treaty freezing Soviet modernization of their forces could not be completely successful in halting improvements. Hence it could be expected to provide a large and vulnerable target to its opponents; its proponents might be forced to admit that it could not very completely fulfill its proclaimed purpose.

More generally, the loss of our relative advantage does not provide the Defense Department with a pressing political problem comparable to that posed by the negotiation of a freeze. No one in Congress, or in the military, will object strenuously if the Secretary of Defense declines to make energetic efforts to restrain Soviet procurement through a freeze treaty.

A treaty designed merely to preserve our relative advantage is one that arouses only ambivalence and halfhearted support. Those most concerned with military advantages are least interested in treaties and most suspicious of them. Their support is characterized by a "Well, if we have to have a treaty, let's make it rough on the Soviets" attitude. Those most impressed by its rationale would be least interested in the treaty.

Those least impressed by its rationale would include important individuals in political circles, where it is often believed that we have no advantage of *strategic* significance worth preserving. In short, treating the freeze as if its purpose were to protect our strategic advantage has many problems. It can lead to failure when the freeze gets hopelessly complicated, when no one is found to support it, or when the Soviets refuse to sign. The real purpose of a freeze must lie elsewhere.

The Freeze as Unnecessarily Formal

The fourth point of view recognizes the problems and obstacles to a formal treaty of the kind just discussed and concludes that the present situation does not warrant a strong effort to achieve a freeze treaty.

Proponents of this approach realize that the strongest case for a freeze does not lie in its ability to diminish destructive capacity — to save lives in an unlikely and uncontrolled nuclear war. They put little faith in our strategic advantage over the coming years. Instead, they are concerned with managing the arms race, as part of our military-political policy, so as to produce the greatest benefits to the nation — primarily in terms of security, domestic tranquility, and solidarity with our allies. They are little concerned with the economic costs of the arms race.

According to this view, managing the arms race would now call for arranging some kind of halt, but this halt should not be purchased at too great a risk to political tranquility or future military flexibility. If a halt seems to be coming about "tacitly," without negotiation or formal treaty, and if the prospects for reaching an agreement on a formal treaty seem limited, this view would argue for not wasting the time and diplomatic effort necessary to pursue it. The temporary halt can be relied upon because the consequences of its disruption are not too serious. If each side wanted to, each could without much difficulty hold the numbers of missiles more or less fixed. Moreover, even in the context of a formal treaty, the control of many missile characteristics would require politically infeasible inspection provisions not likely to be accepted for some time by either side.

Is the freeze unnecessarily formal? There are two questions. First, would it be useful to have a treaty even if procurement of strategic weapons would halt in the major powers without it? Second, would the procurement of strategic weapons come to a halt without a treaty of some kind?

Even if we believed that strategic weapon procurement were drawing to a halt, a treaty would have three basic advantages. It would be more permanent and stable. It would affect *incentives* to procurement as well as *rights* to procurement. And it would discourage proliferation.

First, and most important, a halt in major-power procurement may be temporary in the absence of a treaty and more permanent in its presence. An unproclaimed and unnegotiated halt is not a conclusive, definitive, or solemn commitment. It is undertaken for no obvious considerations, and it is subject to pressures for further procurement of existing or novel weapons as technological, strategic, and political factors change. If our competition with the Soviets is a "long twilight struggle," then especially we must look to relatively permanent methods of containing the arms race rather than to more accidental conjunctions of intentions.

The stability of a formal treaty is enhanced by its precision. It spells out obligations, describes what is permitted as well as what is not, and reduces the likelihood that either side has misunderstood the other. Although abrogation or deception are still possible, the existence of the treaty and the solemnity with which it is negotiated tend to discourage such activities. In particular, the prospects for further comprehensive agreement would be at stake in any violation. Whatever limitations may be seen in relying upon a formal Soviet agreement, it is clear that no less deception can be practiced under a tacit agreement, and this deception need be no more than the result of a change in heart. Indeed a tacit agreement means relying upon winks rather than words and upon declarations rather than documents.

Not only is the formal treaty more stable, but it encourages future agreement to a far greater extent than does a tacit understanding. The latter has little effect in laying the groundwork for later formal agreements or even for its own continuation. A tacit agreement to show restraint is an agreement that no one, in Washington at least, will admit exists. This raises a series of problems, as gaps arise between the underlying attitudes of the highest officials and the reasons provided in public. If the effectiveness of the Nike-X ballistic missile defense improved, if the administration wished nevertheless to avoid procurement in an effort to avoid a new round of the arms race, and if it attempted to justify this restraint on the basis of cost effectiveness, these problems would certainly arise.

The formal treaty has the additional long-term benefits of building confidence that agreements can be negotiated and of building a consensus for trying to resolve strategic problems through treaties. If U.S. and Soviet force postures are to be linked by treaty during the coming years, then it would be useful to begin to accumulate the required experience in drafting, negotiating, and ratifying suitable instruments. The strategic dialogue might also be improved. At present, communications between the major powers seem too confused and ineffectual to control even minor aspects of procurement. Thus the treaty negotiations could be useful, whether or not they succeeded in producing a treaty. It is even possible that each government would give private consideration to tacit compliance with many of the restraints proposed by the other side; at least the rationalization of the restraints would be better understood. Serious negotiations could thus coordinate future actions, much as would the treaty they might produce. In addition, they could train experts on each side to understand the problems of the other.

Besides providing a more stable agreement, a formal treaty

will better diminish the *incentives* to strategic weapon procurement. Indeed, it is in recognition of this principle that opponents of arms control agreements, and cautious supporters, attempt to wrest from their governments during the ratification process commitments that "safeguard" measures will be taken. This attempt is never completely successful. It was possible to demand that the government commit itself to a vigorous program of underground tests as a price for support of the partial Test Ban Treaty. But it is not possible to prevent the Secretary of Defense and the Soviet Defense Minister from looking more favorably upon reductions in expenditures because the treaty ratification has changed the international atmosphere. Treaties will change government perspectives on the threats they face. This is one of the *opportunities* as well as one of the risks of agreements.

Finally, the formal treaty, but not the tacit agreement, will reduce the incentives to procure weapons that may exist or arise in nonnuclear countries. The prospects for major-power progress in disarmament have become highly relevant to the decision in India, for example, to build or refrain from building a nuclear weapon. These issues have become related in large part because the Indians and others in a nonnuclear role believe that they are. The impression is widespread that progress in major-power disarmament would make Indian weapons unnecessary and that an absence of progress would make Indian weapons inevitable. Whatever strategic merit this position may have, it must be treated with the respect due to a self-fulfilling prophecy; a treaty might therefore be useful in slowing the spread of nuclear weapons by enhancing the impression of imminent disarmament.

For the reasons just provided, the freeze treaty could be useful even if strategic weapon procurement were likely to come to a halt without it. Even on the basis of this assumption, however, these reasons do not provide a sufficiently strong motivation to catalyze a consensus for the treaty at the appropriate levels of government. That the treaty is more stable is interesting, but it does not resolve a pressing problem. That the treaty will affect incentives to procurement is also interesting, but controversial in its implications. Nonproliferation is a problem that might be resolved in other ways. And the prospect of spending a few to several billions of dollars in several years is not very frightening. In short, the arguments for a formal treaty do not present the freeze as a resolution to pressing problems involving large costs, and therefore they may not provide the necessary motivation for its negotiation.

In any case, offensive weapon procurement is *not* coming to a halt without a treaty. Over the next five or ten years it is certain that one side will make, or appear to make, enough progress in defensive weapons to encourage the other to procure additional offensive weapons. (This is certain because it is already happening.) The defenses of one side will encourage the other to procure bombers, nonballistic missiles, additional ballistic missiles, and new penetration aids. This is really the major objection to viewing the freeze treaty as "unnecessarily" formal. The tacit agreement will not work.

The last point of view puts the freeze in an appropriate perspective. Shall we have a freeze, or buy ABM systems? Shall we have a freeze, or a new round in the arms race? These are the pressing problems that underly the choice between a freeze and inaction.

The Freeze and Ballistic Missile Defense

Both major powers have based their hopes for a world without nuclear war on the efficacy of retaliatory weapons. In principle, these weapons could cease to be a reliable deterrent to attack if they could themselves be easily attacked or easily defended against. There is at present no real prospect of either of these destabilizing possibilities coming to pass. But one of them, ballistic missile defense, still retains the power to excite emotions and to galvanize the further procurement of strategic weapons. The prospect of an effective missile defense will be with us, I believe, throughout our lifetime. No one can be confident that such a defense will or will not be achieved over the coming decades.

It seems that the other possibility — that weapons might be effectively attacked — has been made sufficiently unlikely by the development of missile-firing submarines that it will soon cease to be a motive for procurement of additional strategic weapons. However, we have noted the possibility that land-based missiles might become suddenly and dramatically more vulnerable, and in the long run, sea-based weapons might also appear to be threatened.

At present, however, the key to a halt in strategic weapon procurement lies in the prospects for missile defense. It can probably be put quite unequivocally. If a defense against ballistic missiles were inconceivable, the procurement of ever greater numbers and ever more modern types of strategic weapons would gradually cease of its own accord. On the other hand, as ballistic missile defenses become more feasible or begin to be procured, then offensive strategic weapons will be bought to neutralize their political or strategic effect. In short, the negotiability of a freeze will depend, from a *strategic* point of view, very directly on the prospects for missile defenses, whether or not these prospects are reflected in treaty provisions.

Probably in both major powers it is also true that the prospects for a freeze depend, from a *political* point of view, on the prospects for missile defense. For example, assume that the United States considered it fairly likely that it would buy a ballistic missile defense during the late sixties. How would it treat the freeze proposal? First of all, if the freeze were to be taken seriously, the prohibition on defensive systems would have to be removed lest it compromise the later decision. But even so, if the agreement were ratified, the United States would be strongly pressured not to risk disrupting the treaty by introducing a defensive system. Just as we would consider a Soviet defense to be tacitly prohibited by a freeze on offensive weapons, the Soviets would claim that our defense violated the spirit of the agreement. This view would find support in the United States. In addition, the relaxation of tension associated with the treaty would further fragment the agreement to procure an expensive defense. In short, if we wanted a missile defense, the last thing we should wish to get involved with would be a partial or total freeze of strategic weapons.

What if we did not want to buy a defense? In this case, we should want to negotiate for a freeze — at least insofar as strategic factors are concerned; in the absence of a freeze we should eventually find ourselves buying the missile defense that we did not want. It only takes one "yes" to get the system started and, considering our general tendency to want to stay ahead in all aspects of the arms race, a Soviet decision to buy missile defenses would also spark our own. Hence one leadership group in either major power can start the process.

United States support for a defense can come from technical improvements, from unwillingness to rely upon our ability to deter potential Chinese missiles, from Soviet unwillingness to build offensive systems that would probably make our prospective defensive systems ineffective, and so on. Indeed, the government might simply yield to demands that it "do more" in national security and might find no other area in which to do it.

Soviet support for missile defense is also probably easy to anticipate: the Soviets always spend money on defenses. They may be unwilling to rely on their ability to deter Chinese missiles or those of France. They may fear our procurement and wish to be "first." And the Soviet government may also yield to internal pressures that it "do more" for defense.

Speaking generally, it is hard to believe that a tacit understanding not to procure defenses could so effectively withstand these shifting considerations that no decision to go ahead with procurement would be made in either major power for, say, ten more years.

Therefore the lines are very clearly drawn. If we want to try to fashion a defense against nuclear bombardment, we should avoid comprehensive freezes. If we do not want a defense, we need to strengthen the hands of those in both major powers who do not wish to spend the resources and disturb the present balance with all of its implications.

What, in brief, are the implications of the choice? The cost of procuring, improving, and maintaining a missile defense over ten or fifteen years could easily reach $50 to $75 billion. The cost of complementary improvements in air defenses — including a new interceptor — in antisubmarine defenses, and in fallout shelters (possibly with some blast shelters) could run into some additional tens of billions of dollars. Finally, the Soviets — who are rarely more than five years behind us — would produce a defense modeled after our own. This would necessitate continued improvements in our offensive weapons at a cost of some further additional tens of billions of dollars. The total cost during ten or fifteen years alone could easily be more than $100 billion. And during this time, we may, if we are unlucky, find ourselves emphasizing or worrying about relative advantages in defenses much as we previously competed in numbers of missiles. The defense gap could rival the missile gap, if things went badly.

If, on the other hand, we indulge in a freeze, we suffer none of these economic and political costs. Assuming that the defenses would work — something no one will really know until a war occurs — they might save some tens of millions of lives over and above those that would be saved without a defense. Because a general nuclear war is especially unlikely, we may not want to pay such costs for this potential but far from guaranteed protection.

Because this choice, these costs, and these risks completely overshadow the problems of maintaining a short-run relative advantage or of forestalling the procurement of only offensive weapons, the strategic *purpose* of the freeze can be said to be the avoidance of a new round in the arms race.

Why is it so important to try to determine a single "purpose" for the freeze? Because we must not make the mistake of committing ourselves or our efforts to the *wrong* kind of freeze. We must know what we are after if we are to maximize our chances of getting it. A freeze designed to prevent a new round in the arms race may be far more feasibly negotiated than one designed for another purpose. And it will be designed in quite a different way, as is discussed next.

Design of the Pause Treaty

This section discusses, in general terms, how a freeze treaty might be made consistent with the preceding conclusions. The discussion almost certainly leaves out certain considerations that are important, but it should nevertheless give an indication of the kind of treaty that might be suitable to the purpose. In addition, it should indicate the kind of reasoning that is appropriate in designing the treaty provisions. But it should also be mentioned that many crucial decisions about the contents of a freeze require political judgment. Here, especially, there is room for disagreement. And it should be understood that the design of a freeze is far more sensitive to small details, which may often depend upon secret information, than are other aspects of arms control and disarmament. The drafting of a suitable instrument must be done very carefully and with the best and most recent information.

The design of the pause treaty to follow is based on two important principles, simplicity and purpose. If the treaty has a very low probability of successful negotiation — which it certainly does — then we must not ask too much of it. If the treaty is to constitute an alliance between political leaders on both sides who wish to avoid expenditures, then it must be readily understood by them, and they must be able to argue for it against a hostile opposition — including at least some military leaders. If the treaty is to be unpopular with some of the military leadership, then it must not be *too* unpopular. Speaking very generally, if the military leadership in each major power would prefer to be unrestrained, even at the cost of having the adversary unrestrained, the treaty must not be too restrictive.

As a result, the treaty discussed below buys off its critics by permitting a continuation of the arms race through the modernization of forces, the procurement of bombers, and in other ways. But it insists upon (1) maximizing the chances for getting some kind of treaty; (2) seeming to have ended the arms race; and (3) preventing those costs and problems associated with the large-scale procurement of defenses.

The Negotiator's Pause

In the United States, discussion of the freeze has tended to assume that the treaty would be of indefinite duration. Although the treaty was to contain withdrawal clauses and the right of either party to call occasional or periodic meetings for renegotiation, it was not to be a treaty that lapsed automatically. (We shall refer to the government's proposal as "the Freeze.")

There seems to be merit, however, in designing a treaty so that it will indeed lapse in the absence of renewed agreement. Such an agreement might call for a treaty to last for a fixed period of years — for instance five or eight — during which intensive negotiations went forward with a view to achieving substantial disarmament. If these negotiations were unsuccessful, the treaty could be renewed — perhaps on different terms. If neither further agreement nor renewal were possible, the agreement would lapse, and a return to unrestricted procurement would ensue. This agreement could have a variety of political and strategic advantages over the Freeze.

First, the Pause treaty to a greater extent than the Freeze, would give the appearance, and have the appeal, of being a document oriented to disarmament. Since those most sympathetic to disarmament either have little influence in the U.S. government or would be satisfied to get any comprehensive arms control agreement — at least after a closer look at the obstacles — this advantage may be most important in providing the Soviets with an excuse for accepting a proposal that otherwise seems all "arms control" with no "disarmament."

Perhaps more important than its appeal to those sympathetic to disarmament is its ability to placate those who are hostile to disarmament. As a more limited commitment than an indefinite freeze, the Pause may be thought to be less drastic in its implications. For example, it might have less impact in inhibiting research and development. For the Soviets, the agreement might be portrayed internally as a potential "breathing spell" rather than as a decision to acquiesce permanently in an inferior posture.

Second, technical objections to an indefinite freeze will be vitiated by focusing the discusssion on a five-year period — the strategic implications of such a period are often fairly well understood — and many inspection requirements and related restraints might be thus simplified.

Third, because of its limited duration the Pause is less likely than the Freeze to end in an embarrassing abrogation; instead, parties anxious to terminate the treaty are likely to be willing to let it lapse automatically. While the specter of lapsing agreements is bound to be disturbing, it is hard to believe that the presuppositions of even a loose long-term freeze treaty would not change over a period of five to ten years. Hence the only question may be how changes are made in the treaty. It may be better to have modifications in the treaty go forward, under the threat of a lapsing agreement, than to have each power force the other to choose between outdated bargains and abrogation. Perhaps the fear of a return to the arms race, which the Pause treaty evokes, is the strongest, and politically the easiest, guarantee that we or the Soviets can give to negotiations in good faith.

Finally, specific political problems in one or both major powers, concerning the procurement of heavy bombers, for example, might be circumvented if it could be shown in advance, as it might, that the issues would not arise during the particular five-year period in question.

Numbers of Missiles

The treaty must control numbers of strategic missiles. Whether or not these numbers possess important strategic significance, the treaty can appear to have ended the arms race only if levels of missile inventories cease to grow or are precluded from growing past specified levels. For some years, the general perception of the arms race has been as a race in numbers of missiles; halting the race is therefore much the same as halting increases in numbers. In addition, the control provisions associated with limiting numbers of missiles are relatively simple, and it is hard to imagine restraints on other aspects of offensive capability in treaties that did not control numbers of missiles. It may be desirable to discuss limitations on numbers of missile launchers as well. It is possible that numbers of launchers could be inspected unilaterally if satellite observation were efficient enough.

The choice between freezing numbers of missiles and numbers of launchers has its parallel at sea where restraints could be based on submarine-launched missiles alone, or on missile-firing submarines *and* submarine-launched missiles. Again this could be subject to negotiation, and as before the important political issues would probably call for the freezing of missile numbers.

The restraints on missile-launcher ratios would be important if the purpose of the treaty were to freeze our advantage, but it has no particular importance for the three criteria mentioned earlier: getting a treaty, seeming to have ended the race, and preventing ballistic missile defenses. In justifying a loose treaty we need constantly to repeat: "What is it that the other side can do under this treaty that he could not do in its absence?"

Indeed, the looser treaty, focusing on missile numbers, would permit us many advantages. We could rearrange our land-based Minuteman force if deployment were not fixed. Thus we could substitute numbers of mobile missiles for the fixed-site Minuteman missiles. And we could also dilute the number of missiles per submarine to achieve greater numbers of missile-launching submarines.

Applying the principles of simplicity and purpose, we assume that the limitation would be only on missile numbers rather than on numbers and deployment. (Numbers would be frozen in the following separate categories: ICBM's, IRBM's, MRBM's, and submarine-launched missiles.) Obviously, however, a detailed study of the implications of this choice is necessary.

Similarly we leave unrestrained the characteristics of missiles that are very difficult to control without inspection that neither side would permit. Indeed, some of the characteristic improvements that might be made under our treaty would render defenses against missiles less feasible. Since a purpose of the treaty is to inhibit the procurement of defensive systems, there is some merit in permitting such missile improvement as would weaken the incentive to buy defenses.

Antiballistic Missile Systems

While the prohibition on increases in numbers of missiles would be the important part of the treaty from the public's point of view, the prohibition on missile defenses would be the crucial part of the treaty from an economic and strategic point of view. Despite its importance, there is some question about how it should be incorporated into the treaty.

At one extreme, it could be left out completely. The treaty could refer only to numbers of missiles, and both sides could perceive that the procurement of ABM defenses would so promptly destroy the presuppositions of the treaty that it would become a justification for withdrawal. (Alternatively the treaty could mention the fact that gross changes in strategic posture related to the treaty would justify withdrawal.) Probably if the understanding were to take this form, it should be framed not as a treaty but as a set of simultaneous announcements in which the Soviet Premier and the U.S. President stated their intention of holding down the numbers of weapons. As a treaty, an agreement on numbers alone might lack sufficient strategic substance. It might be *too* simple. Perhaps, if defensive systems were not to be mentioned, a somewhat more stringent control over offensive weapons, such as a freeze on deployment, would be appropriate.

If defensive systems were referred to in the treaty, either a freeze on ballistic missile defensive systems or a limitation on numbers of defensive launch sites might be appropriate. The latter would permit some deployment and relax the pressures associated with fear of Chinese threats to the larger cities of each major power.

The explanation for controlling defensive missile systems is the one given by the United States in including such restraints in its Freeze proposal — that a failure to restrict defensive systems would be "destabilizing." This term is, of course, more correctly applied to the stability of the treaty than to the tendency of the strategic situation to erupt into war.

Bombers and Bomber Defenses

Probably neither major power will procure heavy bombers in the future, and even if they do these bombers will have little important strategic effect. What effect they do have will tend to make missile defense systems less valuable if the bombers can elude the defenses. Hence there is merit in permitting the maintenance of bombers so as to support the central purpose of the treaty — to discourage the purchase of defenses. In addition, in this country, the political problems associated with preventing the procurement of new bombers are substantial. And any restraints on bombers would have to distinguish between our heavy bombers and our F-111 (TFX) aircraft, which it might be hard to do to the satisfaction of the Soviets. Finally, eliminating bomber restraints will simplify the treaty.

If bombers are not to be restrained, little need be said about bomber defenses. These are difficult to control, not likely to absorb much money in the absence of procurement of missile defenses, and unlikely to become a political issue.

Antisubmarine Defenses

U.S. and Soviet antisubmarine warfare capabilities do not lend themselves to control, for a variety of reasons. The defenses are composed of many different types of weapons and sensors. Some of these are highly secret, some are used for other purposes. Finally, to a great extent, the capabilities and methods of the two sides are not symmetrical. In addition, it seems likely that the failure to freeze antisubmarine warfare activities would not destroy the presuppositions of the rest of the treaty for the foreseeable future — certainly not until the period of the Pause lapsed. Thus the treaty can be simplified by permitting submarine defenses to be unrestrained.

Prospects in the Absence of a Pause

At the present time Soviet procurement may well be more significant in determining future weapon procurement in the United States than are U.S. policies in determining Soviet procurement. By our standards the Soviet Union ought to be less satisfied with its force posture and more likely, on military grounds, to indulge in adjustments of it that, in turn, could motivate corresponding changes in the U.S. force posture.*

Thus a large Soviet buildup in numbers would probably lead to large increases in the numbers of Minutemen or to the development of a new mobile missile in the United States. A new Soviet bomber could lead to changes in our air defense policies and to increased pressure for a new follow-on bomber of our own. An increased number of Soviet submarines would probably lead to greater ASW expenditures. Soviet antiballistic missile expenditures could lead to a decision in favor of our Nike-X or a nonballistic missile, and so on. In each of these cases, the U.S. decision is considerably less likely in the absence of Soviet encouragement. For example, *The New York Times* noted, after referring to the high cost and low efficiency of ABM: "A third factor [encouraging delay in decision mak-

* But U.S. standards are generally inappropriate to predict Soviet actions. In October 1964, R. Fryklund noted that missile predictions had been cut again for the year and remarked: "Since the wild days of the missile gap predictions, the Soviet Union never has built the force expected."[4]

ing] is the resistance in the Administration against undertaking a major strategic weapon development at a time when relations with the Soviet Union have reinforced hopes in ultimate disarmament agreements." [5]

Which Soviet decisions will be made is difficult to predict. Soviet decisions on strategic force procurement depend on a variety of factors: ideology, decisions already made, internal political considerations, costs, decisions concerning resource allocation, committed resources, personalities, Soviet vested interests, U.S. responses to Soviet actions, and so on. Even from our vantage point, our own procurement has little "inevitability" associated with it. The number of Minuteman procured, the emphasis on submarines, bombers, or defenses, are all the result of intense controversy and negotiation inside the Pentagon between those of differing views.* The outcome of similar Soviet discussions is even harder to predict than the outcome of our own discussions would be.

Indeed, there is wide disagreement as to the general Soviet attitudes underlying strategic force procurement. Soviet actions sometimes seem to be preparations to fight a sort of World War II with nuclear weapons — preparations that would presumably be the product of doctrinal lag or of vested interest. Alternatively, they may be acting as if security would be assured if only Europe were kept hostage to massive Soviet retaliation. Perhaps they believe that very few nuclear weapons, and fairly uncertain delivery capabilities, are sufficient to deter; perhaps they want badly to economize on offensive weapons; or, perhaps, they are simply confused.† Still further possibilities include an exaggeration — from the present standpoint — of the utility of secrecy, a desire to buy

* For example, the U.S. Air Force first proposed, in June of 1961, that 2,500 missiles be placed in silos and railroad cars over a five-year period from fiscal 1962 to fiscal 1967. This five-year plan was cut to 1,000 silo-based missiles in the fiscal 1963 budget, and Congress approved 800.[6]

† According to the Swedish spy, Colonel Stig. E. C. Wennerstrom, Russian leaders, "because of an inherent leaning toward landbased strategy," would not readily accept his report that American bombing of targets in the Soviet Union was unrelated to invasion.[7]

large numbers of weapons only when they are both cheap and reliable, or a desire to buy only those weapons that might "leapfrog" U.S. capabilities.

The most common fears of a Soviet military breakthrough in the absence of some kind of halt in procurement involve antiballistic missile systems; reports of Soviet ABM activity tend to support a common expectation that the Soviets will emphasize defense against missiles as they have emphasized defense against aircraft. Whether or not the next ten, fifteen, or twenty years could produce a new and effective Soviet defense, Soviet pretenses to a defense in the forthcoming years could have an extensive effect on U.S. procurement encouraging both the nonballistic missile and the follow-on bomber. Whether the Soviet Union will pretend to make substantial progress in this field is not completely clear.* But that an effective Soviet antiballistic missile system is not an immediate prospect seems quite clear. The Secretary of Defense has asserted that he sees "no possibility of any Soviet anti-ballistic missile system in any way eroding our present advantage" over the next five years at least.[9]

What are the Soviet choices in weapon procurement? The Secretary of Defense has made them apparent, in a statement quoted earlier. He noted that significant quantities of fully hardened land-based missile sites and submarines on station are required to neutralize U.S. capabilities for threatening a counterforce attack. The Soviet Union might elect to procure one or the other, both, or neither of these capabilities. Each possibility would lead to quite a different strategic context and to different responses by the United States. For instance, in early 1964, the Secretary reaffirmed previous comments and said: "As I pointed out last year, the Soviets are hardening

* Unquestionably, however, such pretensions give rise to concern in this country. Hanson Baldwin wrote in 1964 under the title, "New Soviet Anti-ICBM Site Seen as Increasing Pressure on Pentagon": "The apparent installation of a second Soviet anti-ballistic missile site near Moscow is expected to increase political pressure in the United States for the deployment of an American defensive system against ballistic missiles." [8]

some of their ICBM sites and are building missile-launching submarines." [10] But the following excerpt from a column by Richard Fryklund in the *Washington Star* shows our uncertainty:

> New intelligence figures indicate that the Soviet Union once again has failed to build the number of ICBM's predicted in the annual American estimates. As a consequence, officials say, American missile plans probably will be adjusted downwards. . . . The new long range predictions, which will be completed toward the end of this year, are expected to concede the Russians several hundred — but well under a thousand — ICBM's by 1970. [11]

The next general possibility for Soviet procurement would be one in which the Soviets elected to build high-quality Polaris-type submarines and to put them on station but not to make major changes in their land-based missile force. The Secretary of Defense has called the possibility of high-quality Soviet submarines "entirely probable" and one of the "major factors" in his conclusion that "given the size and kind of strategic offensive forces we project for the Soviet Union and for ourselves — great damage to both sides in an all-out nuclear exchange could not be avoided under any conceivable set of circumstances." [12] There are reports that Soviet submarines are, indeed, being procured at the rate of 7 to 10 a year, but there are also many indications that Soviet submarines are not now of high quality in their reliability, their range of firing, and their capacity to fire under water. It certainly seems possible from the available evidence that for a combination of political, technological, strategic, and cost-effectiveness reasons, the Soviets might not develop this capability for some time. The following are a few of the factors that might dissuade them: they might not possess the technology or resources necessary to provide easily handled missiles with light but high-yield warheads, with accurate submarine guidance capabilities, or with worldwide radio directional-signaling stations; they might be discouraged by U.S. antisubmarine warfare capabilities; they might fear defection or confrontation;

and the geography of Soviet submarine bases — in conjunction with a relatively small number of missiles per submarine — might make the cost per submarine on station seem prohibitively high. (Our submarines have 16 missiles per submarine and, from overseas bases, clearly travel much less distance to reach on-station positions.* A submarine base in Cuba, now somewhat improbable, would greatly improve the cost effectiveness for the Soviets of keeping submarines on station.)

If the Soviets were to procure high-quality submarines, the United States would logically increase its antisubmarine warfare capability but probably not its own Polaris fleet, unless and until the Soviet fleet challenged our own numerically. This last response is, of course, motivated by political rather than strategic concerns, since the two fleets of ballistic missile firing submarines do not interfere with each other's functions.

Secretary McNamara has noted the "highly tentative" nature of the U.S. ASW force structure, which depends upon a "number of uncertainties" concerning Soviet submarine capabilities.[14] Hence increases in ASW expenditures are a likely response to Soviet submarines.† But for the most part, the

---

* We probably should be cautious in evaluating estimates of the projected Soviet submarine threat, since two different influential sets of expectations would be realized if the threat materialized. First, the Navy might tend to believe in the likelihood of such a threat, because it would wish to be conservative in estimating an enemy threat and because our antisubmarine expenditures are in large part based on such estimates. Second, the widespread view that U.S. counterforce capabilities are waning and (hence) should be de-emphasized in favor of attempts to restrict the arms race is derived in no small measure from anticipated Soviet submarine forces. According to the *Washington Star*, the Soviet submarine-launched missile force is "lagging behind American intelligence estimates."[13]

† However, the extent of increases in antisubmarine warfare expenditures probably depends primarily on the effectiveness of the measure rather than upon the extent of the threat. For instance, in discussing the need to include antisubmarine warfare capabilities in any "damage-limiting" program, Secretary of the Navy Nitze remarked: "The nature of the threat would warrant spending additional billions. Yet, today, until we can provide improved ASW performance, I cannot in good conscience recommend large additional forces for this single purpose."[15]

procurement of ASW forces is one of the responses least likely to exacerbate the arms race or to interfere with the possibilities for a freeze. Much of the new activity would be secret or would be closely related to nonstrategic naval capabilities. Virtually none of it would be involved in hypothetical plans for a freeze because, for a variety of reasons, ASW does not lend itself to formal restraints. And if, as predicted, ASW continued to be relatively ineffective, our activity would not be especially likely to influence Soviet procurement. Finally, the response to Soviet submarines would be dampened by the relatively poor cost effectiveness of ASW.

Hence ASW preparations would not be likely to interfere with a Pause, which thus might be technically feasible immediately after the Soviet submarine buildup. In short, it would seem that the procurement of Soviet missile-firing submarines would have a relatively significant effect in decreasing Soviet vulnerability without a correspondingly significant effect on force procurement in the United States. It would be more likely to postpone than to prevent a tacit or negotiated halt.*

A third possibility for Soviet force procurement in the absence of a halt would be a few hundred land-based ICBM's. If immobile but fully hardened, they would, as noted, increase Soviet invulnerability. But, compared to Soviet submarines, they could encourage U.S. force procurement more substantially. In the first instance this would be because fixed-site ICBM's can be targeted, if they can be located, while submarines cannot. The Secretary of Defense testified in 1963: "The increasing strategic nuclear power in the hands of the Soviets has acted to increase our costs because it has been our

---

* This assumes that the appearance of missile-firing submarines off our shores would not have a more decisive impact on the U.S. tendency to buy an antiballistic missile system than did a few hundred Soviet ICBM's. Note also that the most immediate threat posed by the submarine-launched missiles, which is an almost warningless threat to air bases, has already been discounted in the anticipated nonprocurement of a follow-on bomber. (That is, if no new bomber is procured, the destabilizing impact of the submarine-launched missiles will be greatly diminished.) In any case, "pessimistic" Department of Defense estimates for the later sixties may already assume that no heavy bombers survive.

policy to endeavor to target those weapons for destruction to the extent they can be destroyed under assumed sets of circumstances." [16] Considering the existing numerical preponderance of the United States, it seems reasonable to assume that everything that can be located permanently has been targeted. The temptation to continue to target even fully hardened Soviet ICBM's should not be underrated. It would probably require a difficult-to-justify change of procedure to do otherwise. In the absence of a Soviet submarine buildup, the case for the inevitability of Soviet retaliation would be weakened and the argument for targeting land-based missiles would be strengthened.

But second, the Secretary noted earlier that it was "at this time" that we could not envisage the destruction of fully hardened land-based missiles. The argument that pay load, accuracy, and yield might eventually "beat" hardening would further encourage missile procurement by the United States.*

The justification for this procurement might be substantially reduced if the fully hardened missiles could be launched readily in salvos, as they presumably could be.† In this case the argument that targeting Soviet missiles would reduce damage if war occurred would be substantially undercut. Such a procedure would reduce damage only if the United States struck the first strategic blow, and this possibility would seem increasingly remote as the fears of an invasion on Western

---

* If an ICBM would be rendered unusable if its site were within two and a half times the radius of the apparent crater — the plastic zone — then accuracies for a 1-20 MT warhead would have to be between .25 and .75 miles.[17] Improvements in kill mechanisms or methods, increases in yield-to-weight ratios, pay load, etc., could also help change the balance.

† That Soviet missiles may not now be launched readily in salvos has been widely asserted in the press on more than one occasion. Most recently, for instance, an article in *Missiles and Rockets* under the title "USSR Can't Salvo ICBM's," suggested: "because of certain Soviet command and control arrangements, it is believed that a U.S. second strike could destroy a number of Soviet ICBM's before they got off the ground." The article speculated that these arrangements resulted from a deployment pattern of 6 to 8 missiles combined with a single launch-control center that could handle only 1 missile in the air at a time.

Europe dissipated. Nevertheless, the residual political pressures to maintain a sizable preponderance, the need to target the missiles on something, and the problem of determining where to draw the line in targeting targets that can be located, might well combine to produce a continuation of existing doctrines. Although from the U.S. point of view this would be considered politically desirable rather than strategically meaningful, the Soviets might not believe that they had achieved a high degree of security against a strategic attack. Hence the procurement "race" might not be a suitable stopping point.

If the Soviet Union then proceeded to build several hundred, rather than a few hundred, missiles, it is hard to believe that the United States would not return to procurement of at least a few hundred land-based missiles. These would be purchased in response to political pressure to stay further ahead and as a result of strategic concerns over the vulnerability, to a larger Soviet force, of Minuteman silos. If the Soviet pattern of development followed our own, the expensive liquid-fuel missiles, procured in relatively small numbers, would be followed by much larger numbers of solid-fuel missiles procured at a rate of one per day. (The gap between development and initial deployment of the Minuteman solid-fuel missiles was about five years.)[18] However, the Soviets have shown no signs of desiring to procure a large force of land-based missiles. The Secretary of Defense testified in 1963:

> It is clear that the Soviets do not have anything like the number of missiles necessary to knock out our Minuteman force, *nor do they appear to have any present plans to acquire such a capacity.* If they were to undertake the construction and deployment of a large number of very high-yield missiles, we would probably have knowledge of this and would have ample time to expand our Minuteman force, or to disperse it more widely.[19] (Italics added.)

A final possibility is that in the absence of a freeze, the Soviet Union would, indeed, buy many high-quality missile-launching submarines and a few hundred fully hardened launch sites. This combination would coincide with what seem to be present qualitative predictions and hence would tend to reinforce the conclusion drawn from these predictions that nothing can be done about a growing Soviet retaliatory capability. The impulse to target locatable ICBM's effectively would be diminished by the observation that submarines could not be targeted. In turn, the difficulty of targeting hardened ICBM's would diminish enthusiasm for strenuously tackling the difficult problem of antisubmarine warfare.

In summary, the Soviets can buy, or pretend to buy, an antiballistic missile system, make relatively slight changes in their missile force, procure a high-quality submarine force, or a relatively invulnerable land-based force, or both. The degree and extent of the response by the United States will be based primarily on three factors: the extent to which the Soviet action can be effectively neutralized; the extent to which it undercuts, or seems to undercut, the U.S. deterrent; and the extent to which it challenges the U.S. preponderance of forces. Applying these and other criteria to possible weapon systems that a forthcoming Soviet force might emphasize, a list of them, leading from most likely to gain a response to least likely, would read: (1) antiballistic missile systems, (2) large numbers of vulnerable, locatable, and slow-to-fire land-based missiles, (3) substantial numbers of fully hardened land-based missiles that can be salvoed, and (4) high-quality missile-firing submarines. The United States seems unlikely to permit Soviet ICBM's to exceed in numbers some fraction of our own missiles — much less to have a force exceeding our own in size. And in politically sensitive characteristics such as yield, the development of new types of nuclear explosives, new types of missile fuels, and so on, there would also be a tendency for the United States to try to maintain a competitive position.

Relation to Other Agreements

Nonaggression Pact

As always, the Soviets are likely to want to include a non-aggression pact, and as always the United States is not likely to wish to do so. The reasons go well beyond arms control, involve European politics, and occasionally verge on the scholastic.

Nonproliferation Treaty

It seems unlikely that the Pause could be negotiated in the absence of conditions suitable to a nonproliferation agreement. Hence nonproliferation might be part of the agreement.

Fissionable Material Cutoff

If the Soviets were willing to permit inspection of delivery-vehicle production centers as part of a Pause, they might be willing also to permit inspection of fissionable material production. Hence a formal agreement on a fissionable material cutoff might be conjoined with the Pause treaty.

Relation to an Underground Test Ban

For much the same reasons, the Soviets might be willing to permit a few on-site inspections for tests if inspection of production centers was also going on. Hence a complete Test Ban Treaty might be achieved in conjunction with a five-year Pause. Whether or not this attempt should be made is not clear. A prohibition of underground testing is, in and of itself, not very important, and the five-year Pause is a much bigger "first" step. On the other hand, the Test Ban has achieved a certain priority.

Nuclear Test Ban Treaty and the Pause

Presumably the abrogation or violation of either one of these agreements would provide justification for the other party to withdraw from both commitments. Nevertheless, it might be well to reaffirm and seek Soviet reaffirmation of the Test Ban Treaty if the Pause were to break down after ratification.

Other Parties

Chinese Procurement

While a major-power renewal of procurement does not effectively threaten the Chinese — they are so far behind anyway — the existence of the Pause treaty would increase the possibility of joint U.S.-Soviet action against them. The Pause in procurement would not affect the offensive weapons likely to be involved in Chinese conflicts. The major powers would retain many weapons, and the Chinese would presumably be most interested in relatively short-range missiles and rockets suitable for deterring the Soviets and for threatening nearby Asian countries.

Negotiation with the Chinese poses still further problems. It is not clear what the United States could offer that would be acceptable to the Chinese as an inducement to halt Chinese procurement. Moreover, the Soviet Union and the United States can neither negotiate separately nor jointly with China. To negotiate together poses complicated problems so long as the Soviets and the Chinese are formally bound by ideology against the United States. But to negotiate separately poses military problems. Neither major power separately can hope to undermine the Chinese military incentives for procurement, because the Chinese perceive potential military threats from *both* major powers.

French Procurement

The military problems associated with French strategic weapons arises from their tendency to induce Soviet defensive procurement. French procurement might be slowed through political mechanisms with the emergence of a Pause treaty; but it is hard, as it is with the Chinese, to see military mechanisms through which it could be discouraged. During the transition from aircraft to land-based and sea-based missiles, French procurement may, on military grounds, be especially difficult to interrupt.

Multilateral Force

The multilateral fleet is a more serious obstacle to a Pause agreement than either French or Chinese procurement. As far as the Pause agreement is concerned, it would be useful if the multilateral fleet were not established at all or, if established, were composed of as few ships as possible — and these built or converted as quickly as possible. And if the proposal should no longer be actively pushed, it would be useful if it were, in one sense or another, formally withdrawn.

Current Prospects

In early 1964, when the United States first proposed the indefinite freeze of strategic weapon procurement it seemed to do so with very little previous thought. Indeed, the United States did not really propose an agreement but only its consideration.

Quite obviously we learn more and more concerning the nature, purpose, and design of a freeze over time. To this extent, the prospects for a freeze improve. However, the technical problems associated with certain freezes may, in combination with political problems, make them obviously nonnegotiable. In addition, there are a wide variety of world events, political attitudes, or attitudes of particular decision makers that would prevent the negotiation of the treaty. A formal freeze treaty is, by its nature, of low probability.

On the other hand, it is also unlikely that the procurement of weapons on each side will continue at the same pace as it has in the past, and it is possible that this slowing down will eventually be supported by some kind of understanding. This understanding could be expressed in simultaneous announcements from the U.S. President and the Soviet Premier, in an exchange of speeches in which each tries to deter the other from expanding the arms race, or in a very loose executive agreement. Certainly, some kind of freeze is far more likely than any agreement on reductions.

It is hard to expect a much better team for effective negotiation of a freeze treaty than that of President Johnson and Secretary McNamara. They combine relatively firm control over both the military and political aspects of the problem with a relatively high degree of sympathy for the objectives of arms control, including especially economy.

The Soviet leadership may find a freeze more desirable as time goes on if its economic problems become more difficult, if its failure to reach a rapprochement with the Chinese becomes more obvious, if it establishes itself more firmly, and, most important, if it begins to perceive the necessity of an agreement to forestall further U.S. expenditures that will stir up the arms race.

Whether or not these conditions are sufficient to induce a formal treaty, it is clear that the period between 1966 and 1968 may be relatively opportune, politically and strategically, for a freeze, if the war in Vietnam is resolved. Assuming, as is likely, that the Soviet Union would not have agreed to a freeze before developing its own nuclear weapons, and that to forestall the development and procurement of intercontinental missiles would have been impossible, this may be the first period since World War II in which a freeze agreement could be plausibly conceived.

How long it will remain feasible is unclear. Once the purchase of antimissile systems is begun, a freeze must either interrupt plans for procurement of defenses or acquiesce in them. This is likely to be difficult on many political, technical, and strategic grounds. Once contracts are let and work begun, it is no simple task to halt the process. Probably neither side would find it politically feasible suddenly to decide to defend only one-half as many cities as it had planned, after the deployment of a few batteries had begun. By this time, the procurement of the later batteries would be well under way.

It is not so obvious, but may also be true, that a freeze would be very difficult to design once missile defenses had been deployed around the major metropolitan areas. Treaty designers could not freeze effectively the penetration capability of missiles, because neither side would be willing to permit the necessary inspection. Hence, they could not justify freezing either the numbers of missile interceptors or their efficiency. In turn, if the capability of the defense could not be controlled, then even the numbers of offensive weapons might not be suitable for restraint in a feasible treaty. In short, it might not be possible to freeze the missile defense contest while it was being played out through the procurement of weapons. Any restraints that were imposed might upset the balance or appear likely to do so. These restraints might decide the contests rather than freeze them.

If an offense-defense race could not be frozen in its course, the prospects for a freeze after the United States had begun to procure Nike-X would be poor for a long time. Soviet procurement would follow our own, and for an indefinite period the defenses of one or both sides would be of some effectiveness. We would then have to wait until the offense-defense contest was decided or superseded in both major powers before we could reach agreement. It is as if we had determined in the early fifties that a freeze was impossible so long as bombers and bomber defenses were in delicate balance: we should then have had to wait until the missile age made the bomber versus bomber-defense contest irrelevant. At the present time it is unclear what new weapon system might eventually make irrelevant the contest between ballistic missiles and ballistic missile defenses. Whatever it turned out to be — perhaps nonballistic missiles — it might take ten years or more before it came upon the scene. And, at that time, the situation might or might not lend itself to a freeze. It should also be mentioned that, once the initial down payment has been committed for missiles defenses, much of the motivation for avoiding a new round may be diminished. Finally, the impetus for a freeze is presently encouraged by the general belief in both major powers that it would be helpful in coping with nonproliferation problems.

For these reasons it may not be an exaggeration to speculate that the present strategic situation is more likely to produce a freeze agreement than at any other period between 1945 and 1980 at least; by the latter date the missile-ABM race might cease to occupy the center of the strategic stage.

Those most responsible in the governments of both major powers would undoubtedly like to avoid the expenses and headaches associated with a new round of procurement. Each would also, undoubtedly, like to avoid the painful process of trying to negotiate a comprehensive arms control treaty with the other. But it seems that both sets of problems cannot be avoided. How much will each major power spend, and what will each undergo, in an effort to avoid a formal agreement? This seems to be the question posed jointly by the freeze and the ballistic missile defenses.

DEVISING FURTHER ARMS CONTROL PROPOSALS

WHILE MANY would argue that the plans put forward are too conservative, they are unlikely to be negotiable in their present form — almost all arms control proposals are; the ideas they present need to be further watered down. To those who do not find this obvious from the exposition of the plans and the arguments made for them, it may be useful to point out that the benefits of arms control or disarmament are equivocal. For every advantage perceived by some, disadvantages will be seen by others. If resources are saved by both sides, some will complain that we are not exploiting our economic advantage in the arms race. If weapons are to be destroyed in agreement with the Soviets, many will think the bargain — whatever it is — a poor one, and many others will believe that no bargain can be a good one. Reductions in weapons, even obsolete weapons, are not supported by everyone, even in principle. The "Hot Line" has, or had, many who opposed it for one reason or another; and a less controversial arms control agreement would be hard to find.

For these reasons, and for other institutional and bureaucratic ones, it is most unlikely that we shall be able to trade very substantial losses for very substantial gains even when that trade may seem highly favorable to one, or a few, or even a great many of us. From the perspective of an arms controller, the government seems a conglomeration of vetoes, a process fraught with inertia. And vetoes can arise from allied foreign governments as well, and from our perception of their concerns.

Especially important, we get little or no help from the Soviets. Their plans and proposals generally reflect even less wisdom and preparation than our own. Their initial responses to our suggestions are almost invariably negative and discouraging — at least until they think the matter over. And while we may put too much emphasis on technical matters, their emphasis on political issues has become an obstacle to technical discussions of details. This has contributed to a continuing Soviet ignorance both of strategic "realities" (as we see them) and of our point of view — perhaps these are the same. And their use of arms control proposals for political purposes is far more marked than our own. None of this helps, and it contributes to a general confidence, in those Western circles unfriendly to arms control, that the Soviets can be depended upon to save us from the consequences of our own suggestions. In this regard, the Soviet willingness to sign the Test Ban was a shock to many in the West.

There are many other obstacles. Recurrent elections in the West make planning difficult. Every Soviet governmental transition induces a slowing down. Vietnam is a dramatic example, but not a unique one, of the perturbing impact of events outside the area of direct confrontation. Even plans like that for the multilateral force can prevent arms control proposals from being considered; more startling is our inability to pronounce them obsolete after they are virtually dead. Changing technology and new strategic concepts also have a conflicting effect. It is very difficult for the Secretary of Defense to predict his position on issues even a few years hence, and most far-reaching disarmament proposals require him to take such a position. The net effect of these, and many other restraints, is to place most current proposals for formal arms control well below the threshold at which the government can be forced to consider them seriously.

But if we consider all of the restraints in order to avoid cutting across them, if we mold plans as closely as possible to the shape of things, and if we seek the support of many influential groups, the proposals we produce are very much less significant than we could wish. Perhaps it would be better to hammer away at the "system" independently of the chances for success. The hammering process might be useful in itself and, perhaps, some President will change all of these "realities" through the force of his dedication and the power of his office. This is the approach of many concerned with arms control; it is reflected to some extent in the proposals just supplied, but I am not sympathetic to it and grow less so with time.

There is a long history of arms control efforts; it provides little that is hopeful and positive and much that is neither. In the light of that history, it is better to settle for the possible than to seek the improbable. This is not a bad rule simply because it is being applied to an area in which much that is desirable is most unlikely. It is no solution to insurmountable difficulties to ignore them.

Fortunately, the possible may be more powerful than at first it appears. A little arms control can go a long way if it exploits the attention focused on the subject and the symbolic significance that now attaches to every agreement. Within limits, arms control agreements can be made to mean or signal whatever both sides want them to. Nonaggression pacts can preclude military maneuvers; destruction of obsolete bombers can undermine the prospects for new weapon systems; and a ban on war propaganda can substitute the arms race for the adversary as the villain of the mass media. Therefore, there is merit in trying to seek agreements in the substance of which we are little interested. The form of an agreement and the fact of its ratification may go further than its substance. It may become more than the sum of its intended parts. It may interact with unanticipated political factors to provide new opportunities or new successes. The very meaning of the agreement may change. With time, its sanctity, its importance as a precedent, and the field of application of its provisions may grow.

If so, perhaps we should not try to do too much. Perhaps our proposals should seek to achieve goals in subtle ways or to seek goals that are themselves rather subtle; perhaps they should seek ends not clearly related to their substance; perhaps they should anticipate favorable effects that are not easily opposed because they are not clearly indicated. This is not to suggest that we and the Soviets should attempt to deceive each other, or ourselves, with proposals that have "small type" or deceptive clauses. It does mean that we should attempt to use agreements less to dictate, and enforce, desirable changes, and more to encourage them gently and to increase their probability. Our proposals should be part of a process rather than a series of ends in themselves. This process should be easier to achieve because it is designed to be encouraged rather than to be suddenly ratified. Perhaps we want to shape an atmosphere rather than destroy a weapon system; perhaps we want to show and encourage rapprochement or a common understanding.

In a sense, we want to expand the notion of a withdrawal clause. If none of our agreements are *really* binding, perhaps they should be much looser so as to be more susceptible to whatever kind of ratification they require, while still signifying whatever they wish. In the last analysis, it is often much easier to agree that certain acts should, and therefore will, signify progress than it is to achieve a comparable formal advance. A formal agreement is better in a world under law but not clearly necessary in a world without it.

We may be approaching a rather important opportunity to apply these considerations. Perhaps it would be well to conclude a book of specific proposals with a concrete approach to the design of their successors. If so, attention might be directed to the question, "After Vietnam what?" As this is being written the war in Vietnam approaches a crisis; but eventually it must end or cease to be such an obstacle to U.S.-Soviet arms control activities. As the war subsides U.S. and Soviet officials may be anxious to make progress, perhaps quick progress.

Impatient with the delay in improving U.S.-Soviet relations, eager to improve the damage now being done to those relations, conscious of many events that could abruptly arise to forestall progress, freshly reminded of the dangers of U.S.-Soviet opposition, and released from the pressures of the crisis, both sides may engage in a coordinated search for something that will signal a change in heart, a new attitude, a fresh start, a beginning, or an end. There is more than a slim chance here. Perhaps in arms control, it will be darkest before the dawn. What should we make of this possibility?

Perhaps we should prepare an act, or pair of acts, that to most (uninformed) persons would signal the end of the arms race itself. In mechanical terms it may be easy to do this. Perhaps all that are required are the right *statements* on both sides made in an appropriately dramatic setting. The pronouncements could be embedded in a communiqué after a Presidential visit to Moscow, in a set of parallel coordinated announcements by governments, in a couple of good speeches exchanged on television, or even in a new disarmament effort with new faces and new terms of reference. These statements would not signify that the cold war was over, but only that the procurement contest in strategic weapons, the numbers game with missiles, and the efforts to achieve a strategic advantage were all past. Maybe we want to say that we both have enough missiles; that there is no merit in pushing onward in this direction; that we both recognize this fact; that some kind of halt, freeze, or pause is inevitable; that the world is faced with overkill; that the President of the United States and Premier of the Soviet Union should instruct their negotiators to clean this mess up and to stamp "finis" on something already expiring.

It may be that this sort of thing would achieve much that we desire. There is, after all, very little that we can realistically hope to achieve that will not follow quickly and easily from a *détente* and a general realization that the arms race has run its course. Perhaps we should forget arms control that emphasizes and presupposes a military relationship with an adversary. Instead, measures that signal, and hence effect, a political change in the relationship itself may produce more arms control than either side could ever ratify in any fixed atmosphere of suspicion. It may be easier to thin out troops in Europe, to dampen the incentive to embark on new and expensive weapons, to avoid constructing additional missiles, and to cut military budgets, if we simply work for a set of acts that will tell people the present contest is over. And these acts might have a much easier time passing through the bureaucracy than would a comparable set that, in itself, *legislated* an end to the arms race through comprehensive and detailed agreement.

Furthermore, the acts may benefit from timing. Opponents of arms control and *détente* could not oppose the Test Ban on the grounds that the Soviets and the Chinese had just had a particularly angry exchange; nevertheless the extent to which such a proposal may have relaxed U.S.-Soviet tension was certainly influenced by its temporal proximity to signs of feuding. Thus, if political events throughout the world lent themselves to a convincing Presidential declaration that the acts to be undertaken reflected a (post-Vietnam) "new start," the agreement would be enormously enhanced but no more easy to oppose.

In devising further proposals we want to consider these kinds of possibilities carefully. Whatever we do, arms purchases will continue in one form or another — we shall be replacing old tanks with new ones for at least a few hundred more years. No formal agreement, no matter how comprehensive, can stop everything. Nor need it. If, after Vietnam, we announce that the arms race is over, we shall have begun where eventually the competition must end — in the minds of men.

POSTSCRIPT

AS THIS VOLUME goes to press, in February 1966, Secretary McNamara's statement in support of the fiscal '67 budget has not been issued; the first hearings have not yet been held. On January 25th, however, he testified before a Bomber Subcommittee of the House Armed Services Committee, which was exercised about his decision to phase down the bomber force and his failure to order a new strategic bomber. His statement could not be restricted to bombers alone since decisions concerning them must be related to the other strategic forces. As a result, judging by its form and content, his prepared remarks were the larger part of his annual statement on strategic forces yet unreleased to the full committee. It permits us to bring this book precisely up to date.

The main surprise in the budget is not a surprise to the reader. The decision to scale down the heavy bomber forces, while a variant of TFX is phased in, has now been made. Potentially more important is the evidence that ballistic missile defenses are becoming even more effective. And underlying the significance of these changes are signs of a continuing failure or inability of the Soviet Union to achieve forces that are highly secure against attack — a failure that may have far-reaching consequences in time.

The defense statement actually listed the following as a major issue: "Should a manned bomber force be maintained in the 1970's; if so, what aircraft should be selected for the force?" Its answer, for now, was to propose to discard 345 of the 600 B-52's left (Models C through F) and to replace them over the 1967–1971 period with 210 FB-111A's (a bomber

version of TFX). Newspaper reports say that the FB-111A will
have a speed range from 100 miles per hour to 1,700, will
weigh 10–20,000 pounds more than the fighter (which weighs
60–70,000 pounds), have a range of 4,000 miles empty, and
the ability to carry fifty 750-pound bombs as does the B-52
operating in Vietnam. The budget contains provisions for the
modification of the other 255 operational B-52G-H's to keep
them in a "satisfactory operational status" at least through
fiscal year 1975. This switch from B-52's to FB-111A's was not
hard; there was nothing else ready and the cost of substitution was somewhat smaller than the cost of modifying the
older B-52's. The Air Force was persuaded to propose the replacement and the Chiefs to support it. We noted in early
1964 (see the top of page 77) that the distinction between
fighter bombers would be clouded by TFX. Now two years
later, a version of it is programed to substitute for a heavy
bomber, and it is referred to as a "truly effective strategic
bomber" for the next five-year period. With this substitution,
the distinctions — real or apparent — which encouraged considerations of *heavy* bomber disarmament are further weakened.

Missile Defense

The missile defense questions are much more important,
and they are becoming more urgent. The testimony speaks of
a new kind of missile defense that seems to have been a
breakthrough of 1965. It uses missile interceptors, variously
referred to as "long-range," "new extended-range," and "exoatmospheric." Such defense would permit an "area" rather
than a "point" defense. One supposes that enough batteries
of such weapons might cover the United States as a whole
rather than only a few tens of metropolitan centers. This
breakthrough, combined with on-going progress, has produced
a number of surprisingly optimistic statements. For example,
"An ABM system employing long-range exoatmospheric interceptors in addition to lower altitude interceptors could com-

plicate even a sophisticated attacker's ballistic missile penetration problem." Or, "it now appears to be technically feasible
to design a defense system which would have a reasonably
high probability of precluding major damage to the United
States from an *N*th country nuclear threat, e.g. Communist
China in the 1970's." And this optimism is reflected also in a
related concern: "We now propose to carry [our work on
penetration aids] forward on an accelerated basis, particularly
with regard to the development of new penetration aids, which
would be needed to defeat an area ABM defense employing
exoatmospheric missiles."

While it is admitted that there are still "many unresolved
questions" about the design and performance of such a system, the development of long-range methods of destroying
incoming missiles may eventually turn out to be the breakthrough — or a prelude to the breakthrough — that so many
feared might sharply modify the balance between offense and
defense. Certainly a few more years of progress like this could
be unsettling. One numerical signpost, important mainly in
reflecting a change in attitude, is revealed in the following
comparison between McNamara's statements.

In early 1965:

> There is no defense program within this general range of expendi-
> tures which would reduce fatalities to a level much below 80
> million unless the enemy delayed his attack on our cities. . . .

In early 1966:

> Against likely Soviet postures for the 1970's [even at] substantial
> additional cost to the U.S., . . . against a massive and sophisti-
> cated Soviet surprise attack on civil targets, there would be little
> hope of reducing fatalities below 50 or more million.

If the debate remains focused on a "light" ABM system for
Chinese missiles, and if the debate really reflected the Pentagon interest in a ballistic missile defense, the decision to go
ahead could wait five to ten years. This report says the Chinese
could "possibly" deploy a small force of ICBM's by the "mid
to latter part of the 1970's." By this measure a four-year-lead-
time ballistic missile defense would have to be started only

between 1971 and 1976. Unfortunately, the Defense Department has its own unique brand of political science — which is really applied war-gaming — and it shows a naïve tendency to believe that missile defenses might deter the construction of Chinese missiles. (The statement asserts that the "prospect" of an effective U.S. defense might possibly weaken the incentives to produce and deploy such weapons altogether.) But in the end, many in the United States will ignore the distinction between "prospect" and "existence," and make a still-anticipated Chinese missile an excuse for action. (In fact, atomic-submarine warfare capabilities in the Pacific may be the real answer to a more plausible Chinese threat.)

The fact that the exoatmospheric missile defense system is an "area" defense can hardly be overestimated in importance. The statements assert that it would, "for the first time, give hope of achieving a high confidence defense against a light ICBM attack not just for a few selected cities but for the entire nation." One particular consequence of importance is that it weakens the link between missile defense and fallout shelters. This statement suggests that "against small unsophisticated attacks," something less than a "full fallout shelter program" might be appropriate. If, eventually, fallout shelters are to cease to be a presupposition of missile defense, the prospects for missile defense will improve. More generally, an area defense element in the posture weakens — without completely eliminating — a great many points against missile defense, some unreal but all complicating the debate. The capacity of the Russian attacker to strike undefended cities disappears, the calculated attempt to create fallout outside defended areas is less plausible still, and the political question as to "whom to defend" is removed from the debate.

What does all this cost? The light system will cost $2 billion a year for the first five years. The system designed overtly against Soviet forces would cost $5 to $6 billion a year over the early 1970's and $4 to $5 billion thereafter. The smaller system could be augmented to increase its effectiveness. For this reason, it is still likely to be the first step — a step not yet taken. (In December, *The New York Times* reported that the long lead-time items for a missile defense system would be bought, but this quiet and ambiguous beginning seems to have become a victim of the Vietnamese war expenditures.)

That ballistic missile defenses are evidently showing more promise will not have a dramatic effect on the standard war-outcome computations so long as U.S. and Soviet missiles are hard to attack on the ground; an ABM defense against an undamaged enemy missile force is not likely to seem promising even on paper. Unfortunately it is getting easier to destroy hardened missile silos with incoming missiles. In 1964, the Secretary's statement said:

> Neither could we count, with any reasonable degree of assurance, on destroying all or almost all of the Soviet's hardened missile sites, even if we were to double or triple our forces.

Two years later, it reads:

> Feasible improvements in missile accuracy and re-entry vehicles could greatly increase the efficiency of our offensive forces against Soviet hard targets. However the effectiveness of offensive forces in the damage-limiting role, is sensitive to the timing of a nuclear exchange.

In other words, the safety of Soviet forces may eventually depend a good deal more than we had expected on who strikes first.

We discussed in Chapter Four the very sizable improvement that Minuteman II will be over Minuteman I as we phase it in over the next few years. The Secretary now announces that he will begin in fiscal 1967 to buy a model of Minuteman so much improved that it warrants being called Minuteman III. According to the *Washington Star* (January 24, 1966), it has improved guidance devices and multiple warheads; the latter improve the prospects for destroying targets. Since the Soviet submarine-launched missile force is not growing especially rapidly, and since the Soviet Union has only just begun to show the new missiles that are capable of greater protection in deep underground silos, we may speculate that we are in a period in which our capacity to strike Soviet forces is growing more rapidly — perhaps much more rapidly — than their capacity to defend them.

Speculating freely now, we may be faced with the following possibilities for the medium run. It may be that Soviet land-based forces cannot, without great effort, be protected beyond the capacity of our forces to find and destroy them with high certainty. Our missiles, in numbers and accuracy, may have made it pointless, or useless, for the Soviets to follow our pattern of replacing the early and unprotected liquid-fuel missiles with the newer, solid-fuel ones in fixed silos. And it may be that, for any number of reasons such as costs, technology, geography, traditions, and bureaucracy, the Soviet forces will never include large numbers of submarine-launched missiles on station. Then, especially, we should retain for a long time an incentive to use ICBM's first if war broke out in Europe.

These incentives pose two kinds of problems. There is first the problem that a missile war might indeed seem imminent, that a President might in fact be persuaded during a local conflict to try to disarm the Soviet Union for the safety of Europe and ourselves. True, the probability of U.S.-Soviet war seems so low, and so nicely declining, that these fears seem to be nightmares only. But partly because this is true, the Soviet Union may devote its resources to other problems. And a great imbalance may last for a long, and hence risky, period. Our own dynamic for retaliatory weapon production is now so well established as to be almost independent of the real likelihood of war; it will not falter. Hence the differences in U.S. and Soviet capabilities could conceivably get even larger as we continued to exploit one breakthrough after another. And if we achieve successes in one area of weaponry, we may be tempted to devote other resources to complementary weapons. A great success in the capacity to destroy land-based missiles would induce us to spend additional funds on antisubmarine warfare. So also would a lag in the Soviet development of submarines. We have a compulsive urge to achieve whatever strategic superiority is possible, and only resistance on the part of technology or of the Soviet government can prevent us from achieving it.

On the other hand, Soviet resistance also tends to encourage our efforts. The numerical growth of their missile force would encourage ours, and the development of a Soviet ballistic missile defense would encourage us to build one also. It is hard to know which one prefers: sufficient Soviet efforts to achieve a secure deterrent force, or a continued Soviet apathy. When we thought there was a simple solution to the problem of building invulnerable weapons — land-based missiles and submarines — such secure forces on both sides seemed to be the thing to wish for. Neither side's effort to achieve secure forces of this type would have encouraged the other to buy more: more would not help an attack, and would not be necessary to prevent an attack on one's own. But if there is no simple Soviet counter to our efforts, we might learn to hope that they would acquiesce, as they have so far, in a degree of U.S. superiority that is, after all, not very relevant to real issues. We might hope that the Soviet leadership would not lose its nerve; that it would continue to ignore irrelevant computations; and that it would muzzle those of its military officers who might complain. We might hope that the Soviet government would prefer to forget about the race than attempt to shift the balance more nearly toward parity — a parity that may be further from achievement than it was two years ago.

But if parity is desired, the best Soviet strategy is ever more clearly defined by McNamara's statement. The Soviet government should first quietly persuade the United States government to continue to put off ballistic missile defenses in return for comparable Soviet restraint. It should then set about building submarine-launched missiles. The first is absolutely critical; if the Soviet Union fails to dissuade us from ballistic missile defenses, the case for improved U.S. strategic forces will be improved across the board. Every single new weapon system will be encouraged, some of them very substantially, by our effort to achieve a "balanced" defense, and by our encourage-

ment in the notion that the effects of nuclear war can be minimized. To our Defense Department these days the whole is
more than the sum of its parts. Each individual part of a
defense against Soviet strategic forces is, in effect, too inadequate to be worth buying; but the total is thought to be meaningful, and ballistic missile defense batteries are most of the
total. They will lead promptly to the purchase of the rest.

The case for Soviet submarines is equally clear. No land-
based system can complicate the problems of defense and
surprise attack with as high a level of confidence as can sea-
based forces. If Minuteman II is eight times as effective as
Minuteman I; if Minuteman III is comparably improved; if
reconnaissance has improved at a rate to challenge science fiction; if the United States is going to retain a 3 or 4 to 1 preponderance in missile numbers; and if the capacity of these
missiles to be retargeted will make it unnecessary to fire several at once at each target, then Soviet land-based missiles
may become vulnerable as fast as they are built. The Secretary's statement practically shouts this assertion and it is impossible to believe that elements in the Department are not
just as happy to let the Russians know — most of them in the
interests of slowing the arms race, perhaps some in the interests of persuading the Russians to lie back and relax.

The submarines are not the only answer, only the best one.
No one knows what we will be able to do in detecting and
destroying submarines ten years from now. But submarine
warfare will never lend itself to the nice computations associated with land-based missiles, just as "bomber wars" have
not. There are uncertainties associated with submarine warfare that are very unlikely to be eliminated. No one can now
imagine how even a few Soviet submarines could be destroyed simultaneously and by prearranged plan. And in the
long run, when submarines have global missiles that can hit
any target from any point, the problem of surprise attack
will be reduced to the ultimate problem of trailing submarines
through the waters of the globe.

If this is what the Soviet *should* do — if they want to buy weapons at all — what they *will* do is another matter. As likely as not, the Russians will buy a small ballistic missile defense (the main effect of which will be to induce our own) and then fail to buy secure retaliation forces — lacking either the resources or the conception of how to go about it. Such a blunder would be most un-Bolshevik — a pointless provocation leading to unnecessary weakness. Nevertheless, their bureaucracy may be capable of it. And the mistake would be easy to make both because defensive systems seem harmless and also because in the fifties, secretaries of defense, arms controllers, and the budget-minded, all *slowed* U.S. procurement by arguing that high estimates of Soviet procurement of offensive weapons were *not* accurate. Now the argument *against* U.S. weapons purchases is based on expectations that they would be wasted if the Soviets *did* fulfill high estimates. This is why the Secretary of Defense continually emphasizes the potential growth of Soviet forces in a future that sometimes fades further and further away. And this is why arms controllers have emphasized the real possibility of a dramatic Soviet response to U.S. construction of a ballistic missile defense. Whether this peculiar reversal of attitudes will be made clear to the Soviet Union before it plays into the hands of those most hostile to it, and fearful of it, is unclear.

In general, the Defense Department statements are getting blunter in talking about some strategic computations that do in fact influence our military decisions to some extent. One column of a table of U.S.-Soviet war outcomes is even entitled "U.S. first strike." (It assumes "that events leading up to the nuclear exchange develop in such a way that the United States is able to strike at the Soviet offensive forces before they can be launched at our urban targets.") Part of this frankness is simply the culmination of an evolution permitted by a presumed decline in Soviet sensitivity and an increasing familiarity with the real issues on all sides. Part of it is a desire to be frank where frankness will disarm Soviet fears: the column entitled "U.S. first strike" claims that, even in this case, we would suffer very large numbers of U.S. casualties.

But part of the greater frankness is an attempt to discourage China. The statement actually refers to the possibility that our missiles might engage in "pre-emptive countermilitary strikes" upon them; the phrase would have been eschewed in earlier years. It is presumably related to the President's assertion, after the first Chinese detonation, that this nuclear device could "only increase the sense of insecurity of the Chinese people." All this represents a strain of government thought that is devoted to the veiled threat. It is not necessary to inform the Chinese that their forces might be attacked in a pre-emptive strike: this is what they expect of us. Such references reshape only our expectations about ourselves. And when statements read like this, they encourage those elements among us, and in us, that are superficial, impulsive, and obsessed with unreal military solutions to unreal military threats.

This budget is McNamara's sixth. He has at most six more to present, at least as part of a Johnson administration, and since no ballistic missile system has yet been begun, any created will be only barely completed by about 1972. Thus we are now talking about systems for Johnson's successor, or successors, and about periods during which others will have to make the decision to push ahead with them or halt. And we are talking in terms that may seem as foolish in 1972 as terms of six years ago, such as "Sino-Soviet bloc" and "Cold War," have begun to sound today. The phases of our political competitions now occur as rapidly as we can build new weapon systems. We must therefore try to avoid fighting today's political problems with tomorrow's weapon systems. We ought to try to avoid estimating unconsciously the worth of weapons systems in terms of today's enmities. And we ought, out of respect for the opinions of Presidents and secretaries of defense to come, to try not to saddle them with the dead weight of avoidable programs — programs that it will be their job to finance or quietly dismantle. Whether considerations such as these will receive appropriate weight in today's atmosphere is not clear.

BIBLIOGRAPHICAL NOTES

INTRODUCTION

1. Ware Adams, "On Regulation by Law or Agreements" (Typescript, 1964).
2. Donald G. Brennan and M. H. Halperin, "Policy Considerations of a Nuclear Test Ban," in *Arms Control, Disarmament, and National Security,* Donald G. Brennan, ed. (New York: George Braziller, 1961).
3. McGeorge Bundy, "The Presidency and the Peace," *Foreign Affairs,* Vol. 42 (April 1964), p. 362.
4. Allen Dulles, *The Craft of Intelligence* (New York: Harper & Row, 1963). See also "Swedish Spy Details Soviet ICBM Gamble," *Aviation Week and Space Technology* (December 14, 1964).
5. Dulles, *The Craft of Intelligence.*

CHAPTER 1

1. For this quotation and an interesting discussion by Congressman Gerald Ford and Secretary McNamara, see U.S. Congress, House, Subcommittee of the Committee on Appropriations, *Department of Defense Appropriations for 1964* (88th Cong., 1st sess., 1963), Part 2, pp. 312 ff. Cited hereafter as *House Hearings on Defense,* by year.
2. V. D. Sokolovskii (ed.), *Soviet Military Strategy,* trans. RAND Corporation (Englewood Cliffs, N.J.: Prentice-Hall, 1963), p. 316.
3. U.S. Congress, House, Committee on Armed Services, *Hearings on Military Posture and H.R. 2440* (88th Cong., 1st sess., 1963), p. 613.
4. Maxwell Taylor, *The Uncertain Trumpet* (New York: Harper and Brothers, 1959), p. 68.
5. *House Hearings on Defense, 1964,* Part 1, p. 434.
6. *Ibid.,* p. 435.
7. U.S. Congress, Senate, Committee on Armed Services, *Military Procurement Authorization Fiscal Year 1964* (88th Cong., 1st sess., 1963), p. 150. Cited hereafter as *Senate Hearings on Military Procurement,* by year.
8. U.S. Congress, House, Committee on Armed Services, *Hearings on*

Military Posture and H.R. 9637 (88th Cong., 2nd sess., 1964), p. 7016.

9. U.S. Congress, Senate, Subcommittee of the Committee on Appropriations, *Department of Defense Appropriations for 1964* (88th Cong., 1st sess., 1963), p. 133. Cited hereafter as *Senate Hearings on Defense,* by year.

10. J. S. Butz, Jr., "'Super' Guns for Missile Defense," *Air Force and Space Digest,* Vol. 47 (November 1963), p. 51.

11. *House Hearings on Defense, 1964,* Part 1, p. 439.

12. U.S. Congress, Senate, Committee on Foreign Relations, *Nuclear Test Ban Treaty* (88th Cong., 1st sess., 1963), p. 163. Cited hereafter as *Nuclear Test Ban Treaty.*

13. "Remarks of Secretary of Defense Robert S. McNamara before the Economics Club of New York; November 18, 1963," Department of Defense Press Release No. 1486-63 (November 13, 1963).

14. *The New York Times,* February 6, 1963.

15. *Senate Hearings on Military Procurement, 1964,* p. 60.

16. *Nuclear Test Ban Treaty,* p. 531.

17. See *House Hearings on Defense, 1964,* Part 1, p. 115; and *Senate Hearings on Military Procurement, 1964,* p. 45.

18. *Senate Hearings on Military Procurement, 1964,* pp. 67–68.

19. *House Hearings on Defense, 1964,* Part 1, pp. 433–437.

20. *House Hearings on Defense, 1965* (88th Cong., 2nd sess., 1964), Part 4, pp. 187, 351.

21. *Senate Hearings on Military Procurement, 1965* (88th Cong., 2nd sess., 1964), p. 44.

22. *House Hearings on Defense, 1965,* Part 4, pp. 187–188.

23. *The New York Times,* January 19, 1965.

24. *Nuclear Test Ban Treaty,* p. 543.

25. Sokolovskii (ed.), *Soviet Military Strategy,* p. 315.

26. *The New York Times,* April 18, 1963. See also *Nuclear Test Ban Treaty,* p. 778.

27. *Senate Hearings on Defense, 1964,* pp. 132–133.

28. *Senate Hearings on Military Procurement, 1964,* p. 149.

29. *John F. Kennedy, January 1 to December 31, 1962,* Public Papers of the Presidents of the United States (Washington, D.C.: GPO, 1963), p. 188. Cited hereafter as *Kennedy Papers.*

30. Nelson A. Rockefeller, "Background Memorandum — Nuclear Test Ban Treaty" (Press Release, August 12, 1963). The second sentence may be found in *The New York Times,* August 12, 1963.

31. *Nuclear Test Ban Treaty,* p. 30.

32. *House Hearings on Military Posture and H.R. 2440* (88th Cong., 1st sess., 1963), pp. 308–309.

33. *Senate Hearings on Military Procurement, 1964,* pp. 89–90.

34. *The New York Times,* June 24, 1963.

35. *Senate Hearings on Military Procurement, 1964,* p. 89.

36. *Ibid.,* pp. 103–104.

37. See, for instance, McNamara, "Remarks before the Economics Club of New York."

38. *Nuclear Test Ban Treaty*, p. 163.
39. *House Hearings on Defense, 1964*, Part 2, pp. 32, 131, 314, 586; *House Hearings on Military Posture and H.R. 2440*, p. 1234.
40. Taylor, *The Uncertain Trumpet*, p. 68.
41. See *The New York Times*, November 8, 1963.
42. *House Hearings on Military Posture and H.R. 2440*, p. 1192.
43. Matthew Meselson, "Possible Efforts towards Missile Defense and Their Effect on International Relations" (Typescript, 1964).
44. *Nuclear Test Ban Treaty*, pp. 784, 788.
45. Sokolovskii (ed.), *Soviet Military Strategy*, p. 345.
46. Speech of October 22 on Soviet arms buildup in Cuba, in *Kennedy Papers*, p. 807.
47. U.S. Congress, House, Subcommittee of the Committee on Government Operations, *Civil Defense, 1961* (87th Cong., 1st sess., 1961), p. 216.
48. *Senate Hearings on Military Procurement, 1964*, pp. 40–41.
49. *Nuclear Test Ban Treaty*, p. 104.
50. U.S. Congress, Joint Economic Committee, *Dimensions of Soviet Economic Power* (87th Cong., 2nd sess., 1962), Annex, p. 21.
51. *House Hearings on Defense, 1964*, Part 1, p. 112.
52. *Nuclear Test Ban Treaty*, p. 568.
53. *American Foreign Policy, 1950–1955*, General Foreign Policy Series 117; Basic Documents, Vol. I, Department of State Publication 6446 (Washington, D.C.: GPO, 1957), p. 82.
54. Stewart Alsop, "Kennedy's Grand Strategy," *Saturday Evening Post* (March 31, 1962), p. 14.
55. *The New York Times*, October 23, 1962.
56. *Ibid.*, March 28, 1962.
57. Press conference, Washington, D.C., September 28, 1962, cited in *The New York Times*, September 29, 1962.
58. *The New York Times*, November 9, 1963.
59. See Sidney G. Winter, Jr., *The Sources of Economic Collapse*, RM-8662 (U.S. Air Force PROJECT RAND, 1961), p. 169.
60. *Nuclear Test Ban Treaty*, p. 30.
61. *Ibid.*, p. 117.
62. *Ibid.*, p. 859.
63. *Senate Hearings on Defense, 1964*, p. 196. See also U.S. Congress, House, Committee on Armed Services, *Hearings on Military Posture and H.R. 9751* (87th Cong., 2nd sess., 1962), p. 3217.
64. *House Hearings on Military Posture and H.R. 2440*, p. 544.
65. *Senate Hearings on Military Procurement, 1964*, p. 80.
66. See "Gun Launches Show A-ICBM Potential," *Missiles and Rockets*, Vol. 13, No. 1 (July 1, 1963); Butz, Jr., " 'Super' Guns for Missile Defense"; and Butz, Jr., "Soviets May Have Ultimate ABM," *Missiles and Rockets*, Vol. 13, No. 12 (September 16, 1963).
67. Sokolovskii (ed.), *Soviet Military Strategy*, p. 419.
68. *Nuclear Test Ban Treaty*, p. 531.
69. *Ibid.*, pp. 588, 377.
70. *Philadelphia Inquirer*, February 1, 1965.

71. *Statement of Secretary of Defense Robert S. McNamara before the House Armed Services Committee on the Fiscal Year 1966–70 Defense Program and 1966 Defense Budget* (Washington, D.C.: House Armed Services Committee Secretary, 1965), p. 46. The table of estimated casualties was taken from this source.
72. *Ibid.,* pp. 62–63.
73. *Ibid.,* p. 49.
74. *The New York Times,* February 18, 1965.
75. *Ibid.,* February 28, 1965.

CHAPTER 2

1. *The New York Times,* January 29, 1964.
2. *Ibid.,* January 29, April 3, and June 20, 1964.
3. U.S. Congress, Senate, Subcommittee of the Committee on Appropriations, *Department of Defense Appropriations for 1964* (88th Cong., 1st sess., 1963), pp. 191–193. Cited hereafter as *Senate Hearings on Defense,* by year.
4. *Senate Hearings on Defense, 1963* (87th Cong., 2nd sess., 1962), p. 977.
5. U.S. Congress, Senate, Committee on Armed Services, *Military Procurement Authorization Fiscal Year 1964* (88th Cong., 1st sess., 1963), p. 475. Cited hereafter as *Senate Hearings on Military Procurement,* by year.
6. This information is taken from Institute for Strategic Studies, *The Military Balance, 1963–1964* (London, 1963); International Aerospace Specification Tables, issued by *Aviation Week and Space Technology;* Hanson W. Baldwin, "Strategic Air Outlook," *The New York Times,* November 21, 1963; and *Senate Hearings on Defense, 1962* (87th Cong., 1st sess., 1961), pp. 862–863.
7. U.S. Congress, House, Subcommittee on Committee on Appropriations, *Department of Defense Appropriations for 1960* (86th Cong., 1st sess., 1959), Part 1, p. 800. Cited hereafter as *House Hearings on Defense,* by year.
8. *Senate Hearings on Military Procurement, 1964* (88th Cong., 1st sess., 1963), p. 47.
9. *Senate Hearings on Defense, 1964,* p. 356.
10. U.S. Congress, Senate, Subcommittee on the Air Force of the Committee on Armed Services, *Air Power* (84th Cong., 2nd sess., 1956), Part 2, p. 83. Cited hereafter as *Air Power.*
11. See *Senate Hearings on Military Procurement, 1964,* p. 96; and *House Hearings on Defense, 1962* (87th Cong., 1st sess., 1961), Part 5, pp. 467–469.
12. *House Hearings on Defense, 1962,* Part 5, p. 465; Part 6, p. 192.
13. *House Hearings on Defense, 1960,* Part 1, pp. 330–331.
14. *House Hearings on Defense, 1964* (88th Cong., 1st sess., 1963), Part 2, pp. 530–531.
15. Herman Kahn, *On Thermonuclear War* (Princeton, N.J.: Princeton University Press, 1960), p. 373.

16. *Statement of Secretary of Defense Robert S. McNamara before the House Armed Services Committee on the Fiscal Year 1965–69 Defense Program and 1965 Defense Budget* (Washington, D.C.: House Armed Services Committee Secretary, 1964), p. 50. Cited hereafter as *McNamara Statement*. See also *Senate Hearings on Military Procurement, 1963*, p. 67.
17. *Senate Hearings on Defense, 1964*, p. 191.
18. *McNamara Statement*, p. 33; *House Hearings on Defense, 1961* (86th Cong., 2nd sess., 1960), Part 7, p. 100.
19. *Air Power*, Part 2, p. 146.
20. *McNamara Statement*, p. 37.
21. *House Hearings on Defense, 1964*, Part 1, p. 318.
22. *McNamara Statement*, pp. 37–38.
23. *House Hearings on Defense, 1960*, Part 1, p. 836.
24. *Senate Hearings on Military Procurement, 1964*, p. 93.
25. *House Hearings on Defense, 1964*, Part 1, p. 114.
26. *Ibid., 1963* (87th Cong., 2nd sess., 1962), Part 2, p. 15.
27. *Ibid., 1960*, Part 2, p. 378.
28. *Senate Hearings on Defense, 1964*, p. 192.
29. J. S. Butz, Jr., "The Future of Manned Bombers," *Air Force and Space Digest*, Vol. 46 (March 1963), p. 29.
30. *Senate Hearings on Military Procurement, 1964*, p. 932.
31. *Ibid.*, p. 85.
32. N. S. Khrushchev, "The Present International Situation and the Foreign Policy of the Soviet Union," report at session of U.S.S.R. Supreme Soviet, December 12, 1962, cited in *Current Digest of the Soviet Press*, Vol. 14 (January 16, 1963), p. 5.
33. *The New York Times*, May 17, 1960.
34. Hans Speier, *Divided Berlin* (New York: Praeger, 1961), p. 109.
35. *House Hearings on Defense, 1964*, Part 2, p. 527.
36. *McNamara Statement*, pp. 31–32.
37. Stewart Alsop, "Our New Strategy: The Alternative to Total War," *Saturday Evening Post* (December 1, 1962), p. 18.
38. Quotations from *House Hearings on Defense, 1964*, Part 1, p. 317; *Senate Hearings on Military Procurement, 1964*, p. 77.
39. Baldwin, "Strategic Air Outlook."
40. Figures may be found in Baldwin, "Strategic Air Outlook"; *House Hearings on Defense, 1964*, Part 1, p. 114; and *Senate Hearings on Military Procurement, 1963*, p. 17.
41. See *House Hearings on Defense, 1964*, Part 2, p. 530; and Baldwin, "Strategic Air Outlook."
42. *The New York Times*, February 7, 1964.
43. Butz, Jr., "The Future of Manned Bombers," pp. 31–32.
44. Hanson Baldwin, "France's A-Bomb Deterrent Power," *The New York Times*, January 25, 1963; *Air Power*, Part 3, p. 269.
45. This information is taken from Institute for Strategic Studies, *The Military Balance, 1963–1964*; and the International Aerospace Specification Tables, issued by *Aviation Week and Space Technology*.

46. *Senate Hearings on Defense, 1964,* p. 192.
47. "Statement on U.S. Military Strength," Department of Defense Press Release No. 308-64 (April 14, 1964).
48. The information in this paragraph comes from comments of H. S. Dinerstein, L. Gouré, and T. W. Wolfe in their annotation of V. D. Sokolovskii (ed.), *Soviet Military Strategy,* trans. RAND Corporation (Englewood Cliffs, N.J.: Prentice-Hall, 1963), pp. 351–352.
49. *Ibid.,* pp. 346–347.
50. *House Hearings on Defense, 1964,* Part 2, pp. 529–530.
51. U.S. Congress, House, Committee on Armed Services, *Hearings on Military Posture and H.R. 2440* (87th Cong., 2nd sess., 1963), p. 1192.
52. See Stuart Symington, "Where the Missile Gap Went," *Reporter,* Vol. 26 (February 15, 1962).
53. "Remarks of Secretary of Defense Robert S. McNamara before the Economics Club of New York; November 18, 1963," Department of Defense Press Release No. 1486-63 (November 13, 1963).
54. Institute for Strategic Studies, *The Military Balance, 1963–1964.*
55. *Air Power,* Part 3, p. 255.
56. *Ibid.,* p. 294.
57. *House Hearings on Defense, 1963,* Part 2, p. 250.
58. Kahn, *On Thermonuclear War,* p. 345.
59. *Air Power,* Part 2, pp. 332–333.
60. For McNamara, see *Senate Hearings on Military Procurement, 1964,* p. 63; for Brown, see *Senate Hearings on Defense, 1964,* p. 1243.
61. *McNamara Statement,* pp. 44–45.
62. Institute for Strategic Studies, *The Military Balance, 1963–1964.*
63. See *Aviation Week and Space Technology* (January 14, 1963), p. 30; W. Root, "France Explodes A-Bomb Readiness against an Enemy by the End of the Year," *Washington Post* (January 23, 1963).
64. Baldwin, "France's A-Bomb Deterrent Power."
65. *Documents on Disarmament, 1945–1959,* Department of State Publication No. 7008 (Washington, D.C., 1960), Vol. II, pp. 1230–1243.
66. P. M. S. Blackett, "Steps Toward Disarmament," *Scientific American,* Vol. 206 (April 1962).
67. *The New York Times,* August 21, 1963.
68. U.S. Congress, Senate, Committee on Foreign Relations, *Nuclear Test Ban Treaty* (88th Cong., 1st sess., 1963), p. 978.
69. *House Hearings on Defense, 1964,* Part 1, p. 115.
70. *McNamara Statement,* pp. 33, 36.
71. *Aviation Week and Space Technology,* Vol. 79, No. 13 (September 23, 1963), p. 39.
72. *Senate Hearings on Military Procurement, 1965,* p. 33.
73. See *The New York Times,* August 18, 1964 (picture).
74. McNamara, "Remarks before the Economics Club of New York"; *Senate Hearings on Military Procurement, 1964,* pp. 125, 147.

75. *McNamara Statement,* p. 35.
76. *Documents on Disarmament,* Vol. II, p. 990.
77. *Senate Hearings on Military Procurement, 1964,* p. 47.

CHAPTER 3

1. U.S. Congress, House, Subcommittee of the Committee on Appropriations, *Department of Defense Appropriations for 1965* (88th Cong., 2nd sess., 1964), Part 5, p. 50. Cited hereafter as *House Hearings on Defense,* by year.
2. Richard Fryklund, "Manned Bomber Plan Offered by Air Force," *Washington Star,* August 24, 1964.
3. U.S. Congress, Senate, Subcommittee of the Committee on Appropriations, *Department of Defense Appropriations for 1965* (88th Cong., 2nd sess., 1964), Part 2, p. 452.
4. Address by Secretary of Defense Robert S. McNamara before the American Legion, Dallas, Texas, September 22, 1964; cited in *The New York Times,* September 23, 1964.
5. *House Hearings on Defense, 1965,* Part 5, p. 50.
6. U.S. Congress, Senate, Committee on Armed Services, *Military Procurement Authorization Fiscal Year 1962* (87th Cong., 1st sess., 1961), p. 336. Cited hereafter as *Senate Hearings on Military Procurement,* by year.
7. *Washington Star,* October 9, 1964.
8. *Senate Hearings on Military Procurement, 1965,* p. 714.
9. U.S. Congress, House, *Additional Views on H.R. 9637 of Messrs. Stratton, Cohelan, Pike, and Nedzi, To Accompany H.R. 9637* (*Authorizing Defense Procurement and Research and Development*) (88th Cong., 2nd sess., 1964), Union Calendar 471, Report 1138, Part 2.
10. Roswell Gilpatric, "Our Defense Needs: The Long View," *Foreign Affairs* (April 1964), p. 373.
11. J. Atwater, "Last Stand of the Big Bomber: Debate Between McNamara and LeMay," *Saturday Evening Post* (June 20, 1964).
12. *Senate Hearings on Military Procurement, 1965,* p. 47.
13. *Washington Star,* October 9, 1964.
14. *House Hearings on Defense, 1962* (87th Cong., 1st sess., 1961), Part 3, p. 11.
15. *The Christian Science Monitor,* November 30, 1963.
16. See *Washington Post,* November 18, 1963; *New York Herald Tribune,* November 17, 1963.
17. *The New York Times,* August 21, 1964.
18. *Senate Hearings on Military Procurement, 1965,* p. 65.
19. *Ibid.,* p. 715.
20. *Washington Star,* October 9, 1964.
21. Fred C. Iklé, *How Nations Negotiate* (New York: Harper & Row, 1964), p. 21.
22. U.S. Congress, House, Committee on Armed Services, *Hearings on*

Military Posture and H.R. 9637 (88th Cong., 2nd sess., 1964), p. 6986; *New York Herald Tribune,* March 16, 1964.

23. United Nations, *Verbatim Records of the Conference of the Eighteen-Nation Committee on Disarmament* (U.N. Secretariat, 1964), Document ENDC/PV. 163, February 4, 1964, p. 19.
24. *Senate Hearings on Military Procurement, 1965,* p. 52.
25. *Ibid., 1964* (88th Cong., 1st sess., 1963), p. 77.

CHAPTER 4

1. Vannevar Bush, *Modern Arms and Free Men* (New York: Simon & Schuster, 1949), p. 128.
2. U.S. Congress, Senate, Subcommittee on the Air Force of the Committee on Armed Services, *Hearings on Study of Airpower* (84th Cong., 2nd sess., 1956), Part 1, p. 38. Cited hereafter as *Senate Hearings on Airpower.*
3. Quotations from, respectively, "Remarks of Secretary of Defense Robert S. McNamara before the Economics Club of New York," Department of Defense Press Release, No. 1486-63 (November 18, 1963), p. 7; and U.S. Congress, Senate, Committee on Armed Services, *Hearings on Military Procurement Authorization, Fiscal Year 1965* (88th Cong., 2nd sess., 1964), pp. 30–31. Cited hereafter as *Senate Hearings on Military Procurement,* by year.
4. Quoted from Herbert Ritvo, "Internal Division on Disarmament in the USSR," in *Disarmament, Its Politics and Economics,* Seymour Melman, ed. (Boston: American Academy of Arts and Sciences, 1962), p. 212.
5. U.S. Congress, House, Subcommittee of the Committee on Appropriations, *Hearings on Department of Defense Appropriations for 1960* (86th Cong., 1st sess., 1959), Part 5, pp. 636–637. Cited hereafter as *House Hearings on Defense,* by year.
6. U.S. Congress, Senate Subcommittee of the Committee on Appropriations, *Hearings on Department of Defense Appropriations for 1964* (88th Cong., 1st sess., 1963), p. 1241. Cited hereafter as *Senate Hearings on Defense,* by year.
7. U.S. Congress, House, Committee on Armed Services, *Hearings on Military Posture, Fiscal Year 1965* (88th Cong., 2nd sess., 1964), p. 7414. Cited hereafter as *House Hearings on Military Posture,* by year.
8. *Senate Hearings on Military Procurement, 1962* (87th Cong., 1st sess., 1961), p. 386.
9. U.S. Congress, Senate, Preparedness Investigating Subcommittee of the Committee on Armed Services, *Hearings on Inquiry into Satellite and Missile Programs* (85th Cong., 1st and 2nd sess., 1958), Part 1, p. 826. Cited hereafter as *Satellite and Missile Inquiry.*
10. *Documents on Disarmament 1945–1959,* Department of State Publication 7008 (Washington, D.C., 1960), Vol. II, p. 920.
11. *Satellite and Missile Inquiry,* pp. 822–823.

12. *Ibid.*, p. 6.
13. *Ibid.*, p. 58.
14. *House Hearings on Defense, 1960,* Part 1.
15. *Ibid., 1958* (85th Cong., 2nd sess., 1957), Part 2, p. 371.
16. The information in this table is well known and comes from the following sources: *House Hearings on Military Posture, 1963* (87th Cong., 2nd sess., 1962), p. 3960; *ibid., 1965,* p. 6949; *House Hearings on Defense, 1962* (87th Cong., 1st sess., 1961), Part 1, p. 372; *Senate Hearings on Military Procurement, 1962,* p. 45; *ibid., 1964* (88th Cong., 1st sess., 1963), pp. 962–963; *ibid., 1965* (88th Cong., 2nd sess., 1964), pp. 34, 71; *Senate Hearings on Defense, 1960* (86th Cong., 2nd sess., 1959), p. 738; Institute for Strategic Studies, *The Military Balance, 1963–1964* (London, 1963), p. 35.
17. *Senate Hearings on Military Procurement, 1965,* p. 54.
18. U.S. Congress, Senate, Committee on Foreign Relations, *Hearings on Nuclear Test Ban Treaty* (88th Cong., 1st sess., 1963), p. 102. Cited hereafter as *Nuclear Test Ban Treaty.*
19. *Ibid.*, pp. 529–530.
20. *Senate Hearings on Military Procurement, 1965,* p. 754.
21. *Nuclear Test Ban Treaty,* p. 102.
22. Quotations from *Senate Hearings on Military Procurement, 1964,* p. 151; and *Senate Hearings on Military Procurement, 1965,* p. 53.
23. *The New York Times,* August 18, 1964.
24. *House Hearings on Defense, 1958* (85th Cong., 1st sess., 1957), Part 1, p. 1033.
25. *Senate Hearings on Military Procurement, 1964,* p. 96.
26. *House Hearings on Defense, 1961* (86th Cong., 2nd sess., 1960), Part 6, p. 420; "State of the Union Address," *The New York Times,* January 8, 1960.
27. *Senate Hearings on Military Procurement, 1964,* p. 52.
28. McNamara statement from *House Hearings on Military Posture, 1965,* p. 6941; Zuckert testimony from *Senate Hearings on Military Procurement, 1965,* p. 724.
29. Hanson W. Baldwin, "Russian Missiles Guarded by Concrete Installations," *The New York Times,* July 26, 1962; Stewart Alsop, "Our New Strategy: The Alternatives to Total War," *Saturday Evening Post* (December 1, 1962); Baldwin, "Strategic Air Outlook," *The New York Times,* November 21, 1963; Baldwin, "Soviet Bomber Threat," *The New York Times,* February 14, 1964.
30. Institute for Strategic Studies, *The Military Balance, 1963–1964,* p. 35.
31. Baldwin, "Russian Missiles Guarded by Concrete Installations."
32. *Ibid.*
33. McNamara statements from *Senate Hearings on Military Procurement, 1965,* pp. 31, 30.
34. *House Hearings on Military Posture, 1962* (87th Cong., 1st sess., 1961), p. 398.
35. Institute for Strategic Studies, *The Military Balance, 1963–1964,* p. 3.

36. "Preventive War, Nuclear Suicide," *International Affairs*, No. 9 (1962), p. 18.
37. *House Hearings on Defense, 1961*, Part 2, pp. 388 (White), 277 (Power).
38. *Senate Hearings on Military Procurement, 1965*, p. 721.
39. *Address by N. S. Khrushchev at World Congress for General Disarmament and Peace, July 10, 1963* (New York: Crosscurrents Press, Inc., 1963).
40. *Satellite and Missile Inquiry*, p. 378.
41. *Nuclear Test Ban Treaty*, p. 102.
42. *Aviation Week and Space Technology*, Vol. 76, No. 3 (May 14, 1962), p. 26.
43. Herman Kahn, *On Thermonuclear War* (Princeton, N.J.: Princeton University Press, 1960), pp. 468–469.
44. Glenn A. Kent, *On the Interaction of Opposing Forces under Possible Arms Agreements*, "Occasional Papers in International Affairs," No. 5 (Cambridge, Mass.: Harvard University Center for International Affairs, 1963), p. 36.
45. *House Hearings on Defense, 1965* (88th Cong., 2nd sess., 1964), Part 4, p. 537.
46. Information in this paragraph from *House Hearings on Defense, 1962*, Part 3, p. 8, and Part 5, p. 302; *Senate Hearings on Military Procurement, 1964*, p. 45.
47. See *House Hearings on Defense, 1964*, Part 1, p. 115; *Senate Hearings on Military Procurement, 1965*, p. 34; *House Hearings on Defense, 1963* (87th Cong., 2nd sess., 1962), Part 2, p. 15.
48. *House Hearings on Defense, 1962*, Part 3, p. 8.
49. Information in this paragraph from *Senate Hearings on Military Procurement, 1963*, p. 20; *ibid., 1964*, p. 53; *ibid., 1965*, p. 35; *House Hearings on Defense, 1960*, Part 5, p. 306; *House Hearings on Military Posture, 1964*, p. 1078.
50. *House Hearings on Defense, 1962*, Part 3, p. 325.
51. *Senate Hearings on Military Procurement, 1964*, pp. 71–72.
52. *House Hearings on Defense, 1962*, Part 3, p. 326.
53. *The New York Times*, February 16, 1964.
54. *House Hearings on Defense, 1962*, Part 1, p. 452.
55. *Ibid., 1963*, Part 5, p. 238.
56. *Ibid.*, Part 4, p. 152.
57. *Nuclear Test Ban Treaty*, p. 380.
58. *House Hearings on Military Posture, 1964*, p. 1081.
59. *House Hearings on Defense, 1965*, Part 4, pp. 660, 676.
60. *House Hearings on Military Posture, 1964*, p. 1081.
61. *Senate Hearings on Military Procurement, 1962*, p. 81; *House Hearings on Defense, 1965*, Part 2, p. 398.
62. *House Hearings on Defense, 1965*, Part 4, p. 704.
63. Information in this paragraph is from *Senate Hearings on Military Procurement, 1965*, p. 35; *House Hearings on Military Posture, 1965*, p. 6955; *House Hearings on Defense, 1965*, Part 2, p. 392; *Missiles and Rockets*, Vol. 14, No. 1 (January 13, 1964), p. 18.

64. Quotations in this paragraph are from *House Hearings on Defense, 1960*, Part 5, p. 280; *Senate Hearings on Defense, 1962* (87th Cong., 1st sess., 1961), p. 932; *House Hearings on Defense, 1965*, Part 2, p. 400. See also *House Hearings on Defense, 1965*, Part 2, p. 416.
65. *House Hearings on Military Posture, 1964*, p. 612.
66. Institute for Strategic Studies, *The Military Balance, 1963–1964*, p. 35.
67. *House Hearings on Military Posture, 1965*, p. 7569 (Brown); *Senate Hearings on Defense, 1964*, p. 544 (Anderson).
68. *The New York Times*, March 3, 1964.
69. The proposals named in this paragraph have been garnered from *Aviation Week and Space Technology*, Vol. 77, No. 2 (October 15, 1962); *Missiles and Rockets*, Vol. 12, No. 2 (April 29, 1963), p. 9.
70. Institute for Strategic Studies, *The Military Balance, 1963–1964*, p. 6.
71. U.S. Congress, House, Committee on Armed Services, *The Fiscal Year 1965–69 Defense Program and 1965 Defense Budget* (88th Cong., 2nd sess., 1964), p. 74.
72. Information in this paragraph is from "Statement on U.S. Military Strength," Department of Defense Press Release No. 308-64 (April 14, 1964); *Aviation Week and Space Technology* (May 6, 1963), p. 36; Baldwin, "Soviet Missiles."
73. V. D. Sokolovskii (ed.), *Soviet Military Strategy*, trans. RAND Corporation (Englewood Cliffs, N.J.: Prentice-Hall, 1963), p. 348.
74. See, for example, U.S. Department of Commerce, *Military Strategy USSR: A Comparison of the 1962 and 1963 Editions* (Washington, D.C.: Office of Technical Services, 1963).
75. *House Hearings on Defense, 1964* (88th Cong., 1st sess., 1963), Part 1, p. 342.
76. *Ibid.*
77. Hanson W. Baldwin, "Soviet Submarine Lag," *The New York Times*, April 18, 1963; *Senate Hearings on Military Procurement, 1964*, p. 665.
78. *Satellite and Missile Inquiry*, Part 2, p. 1979.
79. *Senate Hearings on Defense, 1962*, p. 936.
80. *Satellite and Missile Inquiry*, Part 1, p. 651.
81. *House Hearings on Defense, 1958*, Supplemental Appropriations, p. 243, and Part 2, p. 241.
82. *Ibid., 1961*, Part 2, p. 37.
83. *Senate Hearings on Defense, 1964*, p. 1285; *House Hearings on Defense, 1962*, Part 4, pp. 320–321.
84. *House Hearings on Defense, 1962*, Part 3, pp. 257–258.
85. *Ibid., 1960*, Part 1, p. 746.
86. *Ibid., 1961*, Part 6, p. 15.
87. *House Hearings on Defense, 1960*, Part 2, p. 318.
88. *House Hearings on Defense, 1962*, Part 4, pp. 320–321; *Aviation*

Week and Space Technology, Vol. 78, No. 3 (May 27, 1963), p. 19.
89. *House Hearings on Defense, 1962,* Part 3, p. 258, and Part 4, pp. 320–321.
90. *Ibid.,* Part 4, p. 321.
91. *Senate Hearings on Military Procurement, 1962,* p. 73.
92. *Aviation Week and Space Technology,* Vol. 76, No. 3 (May 14, 1962), pp. 292–293.
93. *House Hearings on Defense, 1965,* Part 4, p. 693.
94. *Senate Hearings on Military Procurement, 1962,* p. 74.
95. *Ibid.,* p. 73.
96. *House Hearings on Defense, 1961,* Part 2, p. 23.
97. *Ibid., 1963,* Part 2, p. 539.
98. *House Hearings on Military Posture, 1965,* pp. 7569–7570.
99. *Aviation Week and Space Technology,* Vol. 79, No. 13 (September 23, 1963).
100. *Senate Hearings on Military Procurement, 1964,* p. 147.
101. *Nuclear Test Ban Treaty,* p. 102.
102. U.S. Congress, House, *Report No. 1561 To Accompany H.R. 11998* (86th Cong., 2nd sess., 1960), p. 32.
103. Roswell Gilpatric, "Our Defense Needs," *Foreign Affairs* (April 1964), p. 373.
104. *Documents on Disarmament, 1962,* U.S. Arms Control Agency Publication No. 19 (Washington, D.C., 1963), Vol. I, p. 353.
105. United Nations, *Verbatim Records of the Conference of the Eighteen-Nation Committee on Disarmament* (U.N. Secretariat, 1964), Document ENDC/PV. 163, February 4, 1964, p. 32.
106. *The New York Times,* December 3, 1963. See also C. L. Sulzberger, *The New York Times,* March 4, 1964.
107. *House Hearings on Military Posture, 1964,* p. 571.
108. ENDC/PV. 163, pp. 33–35.
109. *House Hearings on Military Posture, 1964,* p. 409.
110. *Senate Hearings on Military Procurement, 1965,* p. 44; *Nuclear Test Ban Treaty,* p. 163.
111. ENDC/PV. 163, p. 37.
112. Quotations from Department of Commerce, *Military Strategy USSR,* p. 6; and ENDC/PV. 163, p. 22.
113. *Documents on Disarmament, 1945–1959,* Vol. II, p. 1283.
114. *Senate Hearings on Defense, 1963;* Department of Commerce, *Military Strategy USSR,* p. 92.
115. Sokolovskii (ed.), *Soviet Military Strategy,* pp. 384, 398.
116. *Documents on Disarmament, 1962,* Vol. I, p. 136.
117. *Ibid.,* p. 501.
118. *Ibid.* (Statement by Foreign Minister Gromyko, March 15, 1962), p. 94; Department of Defense, *Statement on U.S. Military Strength.*
119. ENDC/PV. 165, February 11, 1964, p. 41.
120. *Ibid.*
121. *Nuclear Test Ban Treaty,* p. 856.
122. Figures obtained from Nuclear Bomb Effects Computer, a cal-

culating device issued in conjunction with Department of Defense, *The Effects of Nuclear Weapons,* Samuel Glasstone, ed. (Washington, D.C.: Atomic Energy Commission, 1962).

123. *Senate Hearings on Military Procurement, 1965,* pp. 34, 38.
124. *Ibid.,* p. 316; *House Hearings on Defense, 1965,* Part 2, p. 392.
125. *Senate Hearings on Military Procurement, 1964,* p. 52.
126. *Ibid., 1965,* p. 34.
127. Institute for Strategic Studies, *The Military Balance, 1963–1964,* p. 35.
128. *Izvestia,* September 9, 1961.
129. ENDC/PV. 163, pp. 21–22.
130. *House Hearings on Defense, 1964,* Part 1, p. 105.
131. *House Hearings on Military Posture, 1962,* p. 511.
132. Gilpatric, "Our Defense Needs."
133. ENDC/PV. 163, p. 22.
134. *International Affairs,* No. 3 (March 1964).

CHAPTER 5

1. United Nations, *Verbatim Records of the Conference of the Eighteen-Nation Committee on Disarmament* (New York: U.N. Secretariat, 1964), Document ENDC/PV. 157, January 21, 1964, p. 11.
2. *Ibid.*
3. Adrian S. Fisher, in a statement made at the Conference of the Eighteen-Nation Committee on Disarmament, April 16, 1964.
4. Richard Fryklund, "Missile Output of Reds Falls under Estimate," *Washington Star,* October 1, 1964.
5. *The New York Times,* June 13, 1964.
6. *Aviation Week and Space Technology* (November 26, 1962), p. 27.
7. *Aviation Week and Space Technology* (December 14, 1964).
8. *The New York Times,* July 24, 1964.
9. *Ibid.,* May 7, 1964.
10. U.S. Congress, House, Subcommittee of the Committee on Appropriations, *Department of Defense Appropriations for 1965* (88th Cong., 2nd sess., 1964), Part 4, p. 27. Cited hereafter as *House Hearings on Defense,* by year.
11. Fryklund, "Missile Output of Reds."
12. *House Hearings on Defense, 1965,* Part 4, p. 57.
13. Fryklund, "Missile Output of Reds."
14. U.S. Congress, Senate, Preparedness Investigating Subcommittee of the Committee on Armed Services, *Hearings on Military Procurement Authorization Fiscal Year 1964* (88th Cong., 1st sess., 1963), p. 665.
15. Speech at Forty-sixth Annual Dinner of the American Ordinance Association, Chicago, May 19, 1964; quoted in *The New York Times,* May 31, 1964.
16. *House Hearings on Defense, 1964* (88th Cong., 1st sess., 1963), Part 1, p. 328.

17. Roswell Gilpatric, "Our Defense Needs," *Foreign Affairs* (April 1964).
18. U.S. Congress, Senate, Subcommittee of the Committee on Appropriations, *Hearings on Department of Defense Appropriations for 1963* (87th Cong., 2nd sess., 1962), p. 194.
19. U.S. Congress, Senate, Committee on Foreign Relations, *Hearings on the Nuclear Test Ban Treaty* (88th Cong., 1st sess., 1963), p. 102.

INDEX

PUBLICATIONS WRITTEN UNDER THE AUSPICES OF THE CENTER FOR INTERNATIONAL AFFAIRS HARVARD UNIVERSITY

Created in 1958, the Center for International Affairs fosters advanced study of basic world problems by scholars from various disciplines and senior officials from many countries. The research at the Center focuses on economic and social development, the management of force in the modern world, and the evolving roles of Western Europe and the Communist bloc. The published results appear here in the order in which they have been issued. The research programs are supervised by Professors Robert R. Bowie (Director of the Center), Hollis B. Chenery, Rupert Emerson, Samuel P. Huntington, Alex Inkeles, Henry A. Kissinger, Edward S. Mason, Thomas C. Schelling, and Raymond Vernon.

Books:

The Soviet Bloc, by Zbigniew K. Brzezinski (jointly with the Russian Research Center), 1960. Cambridge, Mass.: Harvard University Press.

The Necessity for Choice, by Henry A. Kissinger, 1961. New York: Harper & Brothers.

Strategy and Arms Control, by Thomas C. Schelling and Morton H. Halperin, 1961. New York: The Twentieth Century Fund.

Rift and Revolt in Hungary, by Ferenc A. Váli, 1961. Cambridge, Mass.: Harvard University Press.

United States Manufacturing Investment in Brazil, by Lincoln Gordon and Engelbert L. Grommers, 1962. Boston, Mass.: Harvard Business School.

The Economy of Cyprus, by A. J. Meyer, with Simos Vassiliou (jointly with the Center for Middle Eastern Studies), 1962. Cambridge, Mass.: Harvard University Press.

Entrepreneurs of Lebanon, by Yusif A. Sayigh (jointly with the Center for Middle Eastern Studies), 1962. Cambridge, Mass.: Harvard University Press.

Communist China 1955–1959: Policy Documents with Analysis, with a Foreword by Robert R. Bowie and John K. Fairbank (jointly with the East Asian Research Center), 1962. Cambridge, Mass.: Harvard University Press.

In Search of France, by Stanley Hoffmann, Charles P. Kindleberger, Laurence Wylie, Jesse R. Pitts, Jean-Baptiste Duroselle, and François Goguel, 1963. Cambridge, Mass.: Harvard University Press.

Somali Nationalism, by Saadia Touval, 1963. Cambridge, Mass.: Harvard University Press.

The Dilemma of Mexico's Development, by Raymond Vernon, 1963. Cambridge, Mass.: Harvard University Press.

Limited War in the Nuclear Age, by Morton H. Halperin, 1963. New York: John Wiley & Sons, Inc.

The Arms Debate, by Robert A. Levine, 1963. Cambridge, Mass.: Harvard University Press.

Africans on the Land, by Montague Yudelman, 1964. Cambridge, Mass.: Harvard University Press.

Counterinsurgency Warfare, by David Galula, 1964. New York: Frederick A. Praeger, Inc.

People and Policy in the Middle East, by Max Weston Thornburg, 1964. New York: W. W. Norton & Company, Inc.

Shaping the Future, by Robert R. Bowie, 1964. New York: Columbia University Press.

Foreign Aid and Foreign Policy, by Edward S. Mason (jointly with the Council on Foreign Relations), 1964. New York: Harper & Row, Publishers.

Public Policy and Private Enterprise in Mexico, by M. S. Wionczek, D. H. Shelton, C. P. Blair, and R. Izquierdo, ed. Raymond Vernon, 1964. Cambridge, Mass.: Harvard University Press.

How Nations Negotiate, by Fred C. Iklé, 1964. New York: Harper & Row, Publishers.

China and the Bomb, by Morton H. Halperin (jointly with the East Asian Research Center), 1965. New York: Frederick A. Praeger, Inc.

Democracy in Germany, by Fritz Erler (Jodidi Lectures), 1965. Cambridge, Mass.: Harvard University Press.

The Troubled Partnership, by Henry A. Kissinger (jointly with the Council on Foreign Relations), 1965. New York: McGraw-Hill Book Company.

The Rise of Nationalism in Central Africa, by Robert I. Rotberg, 1965. Cambridge, Mass.: Harvard University Press.

Communist China and Arms Control, by Morton H. Halperin and Dwight H. Perkins (jointly with the East Asian Research Center), 1965. New York: Frederick A. Praeger, Inc.

Pan-Africanism and East African Integration, by Joseph S. Nye, Jr.,
1965. Cambridge, Mass.: Harvard University Press.
Problems of National Strategy, ed. Henry A. Kissinger, 1965. New
York: Frederick A. Praeger, Inc.
*Deterrence before Hiroshima: The Airpower Background of Modern
Strategy,* by George H. Quester, 1966. New York: John Wiley
& Sons, Inc.
Containing the Arms Race, by Jeremy J. Stone, 1966. Cambridge,
Mass.: The M.I.T. Press.

Occasional Papers, Published by the Center
for International Affairs:

1. *A Plan for Planning: The Need for a Better Method of Assist-
ing Underdeveloped Countries on Their Economic Policies,* by
Gustav F. Papanek, 1961.
2. *The Flow of Resources from Rich to Poor,* by Alan D. Neale,
1961.
3. *Limited War: An Essay on the Development of the Theory and
an Annotated Bibliography,* by Morton H. Halperin, 1962.
4. *Reflections on the Failure of the First West Indian Federation,*
by Hugh W. Springer, 1962.
5. *On the Interaction of Opposing Forces under Possible Arms
Agreements,* by Glenn A. Kent, 1963.
6. *Europe's Northern Cap and the Soviet Union,* by Nils Örvik,
1963.
7. *Civil Administration in the Punjab: An Analysis of a State
Government in India,* by E. N. Mangat Rai, 1963.
8. *On the Appropriate Size of a Development Program,* by
Edward S. Mason, 1964.
9. *Self-Determination Revisited in the Era of Decolonization,* by
Rupert Emerson, 1964.
10. *The Planning and Execution of Economic Development in
Southeast Asia,* by Clair Wilcox, 1965.
11. *Pan-Africanism in Action,* by Albert Tevoedjre, 1965.
12. *Is China Turning In?* by Morton H. Halperin, 1965.